# Gospel and Culture in Vanuatu 5

## About the Editor

The Rev Randall Prior is Professor of Ministry Studies and Missiology for the United Faculty of Theology and the Director of the Uniting Church Theological College in Melbourne. He served in the Presbyterian Church of Vanuatu for five years from 1983 to 1987, in the early years following the independence of Vanuatu in 1980. He was part-time minister in the local parish of Vila and part-time resource person in education and administration for the national church.

While in Vanuatu, Randall became immersed in the challenges of the relationship between the gospel and the local cultures of the people. After his departure in 1987, Randall completed a Diploma of Mission Studies at Selly Oak Colleges in Birmingham, England, and on his return to Australia undertook a Masters Thesis on 'Gospel and Culture in Vanuatu', with a particular focus on the work of the first missionary, the Rev John Geddie. Randall is also a graduate of the World Council of Churches' School of Ecumenical Studies at Bossey, Switzerland.

Randall has been very active in the field of gospel and culture in Australia, being instrumental in the foundation of the Commission on the Gospel and Cultures of the Victorian Council of Churches, which he chaired for its first six years. He also compiled its publication *The Gospel and Cultures: Initial Explorations in the Australian Context* (Victorian Council of Churches, 1997).

He is also the author of the first four volumes in the 'Gospel and Culture in Vanuatu' series: *Gospel and Culture in Vanuatu: The Founding Missionary and a Missionary for Today* (Gospel Vanuatu Books, 1998), *Gospel and Culture in Vanuatu 2: Contemporary Local Perspectives* (Gospel Vanuatu Books, 2001), *Gospel and Culture in Vanuatu 3: The Voice of the Local Church* (Gospel Vanuatu Books, 2003) and *Gospel and Culture in Vanuatu 4: Local voices on Jesus Christ and Mission* (ATF Press and Gospel Vanuatu Books, 2006)

Over more than twenty years now, Randall has retained a close association with Vanuatu and remains actively involved in issues of gospel and culture, both in the South Pacific and in Australia.

# The Gospel and Culture in Vanuatu Series

Also available
*Gospel and Culture in Vanuatu:*
*The Founding Missionary and a Missionary for Today*
By Randall Prior

*Gospel and Culture in Vanuatu 2:*
*Contemporary Local Perspectives*
edited by Randall Prior

*Gospel and Culture in Vanuatu 3:*
*The Voice of the Local Church*
edited by Randall Prior

# GOSPEL AND CULTURE IN VANUATU 5

# WOMEN IN CULTURE AND CHURCH

# AND OTHER ISSUES

edited by

## Randall Prior

**ATF Press**
&
**Gospel Vanuatu Books**

First published in 2006
by Gospel Vanuatu Books
6 Fowler Street
Wattle Park 3128
Australia
Telephone + 61 3 98887508
Email: priority49@optushome.com.au

And

ATF Press
PO Box 504
Hindmarsh SA 5007
Australia
www.atfpress.com

The National Library of Australia
Cataloguing-in-Publication Data:


Prior, Randall.
Gospel and culture in Vanuatu : women in culture and church and other issues

ISBN 1 920691 70 7

1. Christianity and culture – Vanuatu. 2. Women – Vanuatu.
3. Women – Religious life – Vanuatu. 4. Presbyterian Church –
Missions – Vanuatu. 5. Vanuatu – Church history.
I. Title. (Series : Gospel and culture in Vanuatu).


261.099595

Brilliant Printers Pvt. Ltd., Bangalore - 94

# Contents

Introduction to the Series     vii

Introduction to this volume     x

## Part One: Women in Culture and Church

1. Sitting on the Mat in Vanuatu (Hpuku Ita Potu):
   The Mutual Relationship Between Man and Woman     1
   *Fiama Rakau*

2. The Roles of Men Versus Women in the Ministry of     14
   Church Leadership
   *Selerik Michel*

3. The Ordination of Women in the Church of Melanesia     27
   *Sharyn Wobur*

4. Cultural Barriers and Women's Ministry in the
   Presbyterian Church of Vanuatu     38
   *Mary Luan*

## Part Two: Other Issues of Gospel and Culture

5. Marriage in Toga Island     57
   *Winston Elton*

6. The Importance of Youth Ministry     73
   Edward Meswia

7. Migration on the Island of Tanna Today     100
   *Simon Vani*

8. Division in Vanuatu Communities     118
   *Morrison Marcel*

9. The Traditional Concept of Peace in North Pentecost     127
   *Benjamin Tosiro*

10. Respect for the Nakamal as a Model for the Church
    Within the Culture of the Bathot People     153
    *Amanrantes John Fred*

# Contents

11. Sacrifice in the North Pentecost: Relating the Gospel
To Traditional Melanesian Belief     168
*Emmanuel Tanihi*

12. Human Sacrifice in North Pentecost     196
*Colin Steve Sosori*

13. The Ownership of Land in East Santo: A Biblical
Reflection     202
*Gideon Paul*

14. Kava Consumption as an Issue of Gospel and Culture     217
*Christopher Iawak*

15. A Comparative Study of Heaven and Hell With
Reference to Vanua-Lava in the Banks Islands     233
*Keith Kalapitas*

Conclusion     242

Contributors     246

# Introduction to the Gospel and Culture in Vanuatu Series

Since the arrival of John Geddie on the southern island of Aneityum in 1848, and the establishment of the first Christian church there, Christians have had the task of sharing the message of the gospel within the unique context of Vanuatu cultures. In the early days of Christian mission, it was generally assumed that in order to become a Christian certain basic elements of traditional culture, if not the whole culture, must be set aside and the culture of the missionaries be adopted.

In 1948, one hundred years after the arrival of John Geddie, the Presbyterian Church in these islands became an independent church—the Presbyterian Church of the New Hebrides, and this became a catalyst for the development of indigenous leadership within the local church. It was no accident that it was local church leaders who pioneered the movement which led finally to the achievement of political independence from the joint colonisers, Britain and France, in 1980. The achievement of Independence and the establishment of a locally elected indigenous parliament became a powerful impetus for the renaissance of traditional Vanuatu cultures and for the rejection of colonial cultures. This led in turn to sharper challenges for the church in matters of gospel and culture. The question facing the church became: 'How can a person be faithful to the Christian gospel within their own culture?'

This basic question is accompanied by other related questions:

- If I accept the Gospel, do I need to leave behind some or all of my culture and its practices and beliefs?
- How can the local church respond faithfully to the challenges from traditional cultural beliefs and practices?
- What does the Gospel say about particular cultural issues facing my community?
- How can the church in Vanuatu continue to give leadership at national level in the face of significant cultural changes?

Since 1980 there has been a great deal of passion given to these questions and issues; they are energetic priorities for all Christians and their church communities. However, because the cultures of Vanuatu are essentially oral cultures, there is very little that has ever been written down and made available as a resource for the local or wider public. The 'Gospel and Culture in Vanuatu' series seeks to redress that fact. It is offered so that local people can put their ideas into print and thereby generate further local discussion, as well as giving the Vanuatu church a voice in the international missionary debate regarding gospel and culture.

This volume follows on from four earlier publications, *Gospel and Culture in Vanuatu: The Founding Missionary and a Missionary for Today* (1998), *Gospel and Culture in Vanuatu 2: Contemporary Local Perspectives* (2001), *Gospel and Culture in Vanuatu 3: The Voice of the Local Church* (2003) and *Gospel and Culture in Vanuatu 4: Local Voices on Jesus Christ and Mission.* The first volume comprised two parts: the first part examined the earliest missionary impact of the Christian gospel on the cultures of Vanuatu; the second was the pictorial representation of the Christian faith made by a talented young ni-Vanuatu man. The second volume, a collection of interviews and workshop reports from the staff and students of the local Talua Ministry Training Centre, had the purpose of recording insights of ni-Vanuatu people about contemporary issues regarding the relationship between the Christian gospel and their own cultures, and to do so in such a way that it was the local people who were the book's authors. The third volume was the product of a series of workshops which I was invited to run at the national assembly of the Presbyterian Church on the island of Makira in 2002. Published in time to be launched at the 2003 assembly (which marked the 50th anniversary of Church's Secondary School at Onesua), the third volume comprises workshop reports from a much wider range of Presbyterian Church leaders, ordained and lay, men and women, elderly and young, across the whole island group. It also includes the transcript of interviews conducted with various individuals—church leaders and chiefs. One aim of the interviews is to record the experience and wisdom of the older generation of traditional leaders, church and cultural, while it is still possible to do so.

Having duly launched the third volume in 2003, the assembly made a decision that a fourth volume be done, and gave the task of compiling the material to their own staff at the Talua Ministry Training Centre, with a proposal that this volume focus on 'Christology' (that is, 'how we under-stand the person and message of Jesus Christ within the context of Vanuatu cultures'). So successful has the response been to this initiative that enough material was collected for the publication of two volumes (four and five). Volume four was published recently under the subtitle: *Local Voices on Jesus Christ and Mission*, satisfying the church assembly's decision to have a volume on Christology. This companion volume gathers the remaining articles together, some of which focus on the theme of *Women in the Culture and the Church*, hence the subtitle of this volume.

Each of the volumes in this series has marked a forward step in the process of the local church in Vanuatu taking ownership of the books, their purpose and their contents. The first book included material of my own together with the artistic representations of the Christian gospel by talented young Christian artist Graeme Louhman; the second book recorded the insights of staff and students at the Talua Ministry Training Centre gathered from a series of workshops; the third book was an extension of the second, with material gathered from a series of workshops and interviews held at the Presbyterian Church assembly at Makira Island; the fourth and fifth volumes have been written, compiled and gathered by the local staff at Talua.

It remains my privilege to be a participant in the growing team of those who are engaged by the issues of gospel and culture in Vanuatu, and to facilitate the recording of the insights and ideas of the people.

Randall Prior
Series Editor

# Introduction to this Volume

## Prologue to the introduction

This publication is really a companion volume to the previous and recent publication *Gospel and Culture in Vanuatu 4: Local Voices on Jesus Christ and Mission* (ATF and Gospel Vanuatu Books, 2006). In order to appreciate this volume the earlier volume with its introduction ought to be read before or alongside this volume. Because both volumes form part of a single publication project it makes sense to repeat here much of what was said in the general part of the introduction to volume four.

## Introduction

The publication of this volume constitutes a breakthrough in the progress of this series, indicating as it does that the local church 'owns' the project and wants to set its agenda. For this volume it has been the local people who have shouldered the responsibility of preparing and gathering the material. A working committee was established from staff members at the Talua Ministry Training Centre under the chairmanship of Father Stanley Ure from the Church of Melanesia, and it has been his committee which has done the groundwork in compiling the material.

## One or two volumes?

So successful has the project been that the amount of material gathered is more than twice the material included in volume three. This posed three main problems. If we were to publish all the material into one book, the cost of purchase would be out of the reach of many people. Further, the character of the book would be very different from the previous three volumes. Finally, it became clear that the larger book would take longer to publish and so not be ready within the agreed time. For these reasons a decision was made to publish two volumes from this material, the first in time for the 2005 Presbyterian Church assembly and the second just a few months later.

## An ecumenical venture

It is another significant development that these two volumes, more obviously than the previous volumes, represent perspectives and input across different traditions of the church in Vanuatu. Talua is now home to staff and students from both the Presbyterian Church and the Church of Melanesia (that is, the Anglican Church) traditions, and these are well represented in the two volumes. There are one other 'first' worthy of note. In volume four there is a significant contribution from a student of the Protestant Evangelical Church in Vanuatu (the Eglise Evangelique) and one article from the Roman Catholic Church (by Noclam Olivier, a Tannese man who has recently graduated with a Masters Degree in Melbourne and now taken up priesthood with the Catholic Church). It is hoped that this forecasts a widening of the scope of future publications in this series to represent all the traditions of the church in Vanuatu.

## Editing Process

Because most of the material has come to me already in writing and already in English, I have had to consider carefully the task of editing. In addition to obvious corrections in spelling and in grammar, what I have done is to make only those changes which I thought were necessary in order to make the material easily understood, while at the same time preserving the content and style of the article. It has not been a simple process—some articles required significant if not complete rewriting. However I hope I have done justice to each article and to each author. In some cases, where there were pictures or art included in the articles submitted, it has not been possible to reproduce this in the publication.

## Volume five

In sorting out which material would be used for volume four and which material would be used for volume five, it became clear that priority for the fourth volume would need to be given to those articles which were clearly focused on the topic decided by the assembly in 2003, namely, the person and message of Jesus Christ in the context of Vanuatu today (Christology). To this theme were added also those papers which addressed the accompanying theme of Mission and finally a selection of four papers on major issues of Gospel and Culture.

Volume Five is unique because it features four important articles on the role of women in the culture and in the church. This is the first time that this theme has appeared in the Gospel and Culture publications, thus the subtitle chosen for this volume. Two of the articles are by women. One, Mary Luan is now an ordained minister of the Presbyterian Church and serves in a parish in partnership with her ordained husband. She challenges the cultural barriers which form an obstacle to the leadership role of women. The other, Sharyn Wobur is the first ni-Vanuatu woman from the Church of Melanesia ever to have completed the ordination course; she now waits hopefully for her church to change its policy so that women in the Church of Melanesia will be able to serve as ordained Priests. Sharyn challenges those views based on Scripture which would see women play a role inferior to men. Both women argue articulately in support of the leadership of women in both culture and church and in particular for the ordination of women as Ministers and Priests. The remaining two articles on this same theme are by pastors of the Presbyterian Church, who are now serving as teachers at the ecumenical Talua Ministry Training Centre, Fiama Rakau who has just commenced as the new Principal and has long been active in teaching Gospel and Culture, and Selerik Michel who has just returned from three years further studies in the Philippines. Rakau takes a theological view founded upon the creation of both man and woman in the image of God while Michel speaks of man and woman as being equal in importance but having different roles. They take quite different approaches to the topic and reach differing conclusions, which itself will ensure that, in the cultural setting of Vanuatu where women and men have traditionally had clearly defined and distinct roles, this issue will remain a topical if not controversial one.

The second part of this volume gathers together eleven articles which, with one exception, were prepared as research articles by students in their final year of ordination training. (Four others appeared in the previous volume.) They all address focal issues of Gospel and Culture in the contemporary context of Vanuatu. In his paper on Marriage, Winston Elton takes a detailed look at the three forms of marriage current in Vanuatu: cultural, civil and church and appeals for retention of important aspects of traditional cultural marriage. Edward Meswia tackles in detail the vexed issues around youth ministry in a climate where there are rapid changes taking place in the culture of young people; he sets out the way in which youth ministry must respond to the challenges. Simon Vani speaks about the migration of people away from their local villages. Interestingly he explains that migration has always been part of his own traditional island life, and he goes on also to explore the relevance of the fact that the people of God, in both Old and New Testaments, have always been a migrating people. Morrison Marcel addresses one of the most vexing issues of life in Vanuatu—the problem of divisions in local communities. He asserts that it is now a much greater problem than it has ever been and that it plagues all aspects of local life, including the life of the churches. He concludes with some lessons that can be learned from traditional culture and from biblical stories. Benjamin Tosiro gives us a detailed description of the ways of peace on northern Pentecost and with some fascinating comments about the relationship between Gospel and Culture he links together the profound nature of traditional cultural peace and the nature of peace in the Gospel of Jesus Christ. Amanrantes focuses on the favoured theme of the traditional village meeting centre, the *nakamal*. He offers informative detail about the function of the *nakamal* in his culture on Malekula and reflects insightfully on ways in which Jesus Christ and the church can be better understood in terms of the traditional *nakamal*. Two articles follow on the theme of sacrifice, both of them written by men from North Pentecost, but both of them cover quite different material. Emmanuel Tanihi gives a detailed description of the range of forms of sacrifice in his cultural tradition and offers practical suggestions about how the Gospel may engage with these traditions. Colin Sosori focuses on the unusual practice in his own tradition of human sacrifice as a means of reconciliation between warring tribes, and then goes on to consider the significance of the death of Jesus Christ in relation to this. Gideon Paul tackles one of the primary causes of conflict in Vanuatu today—land disputes. He sets out the ways in which land was traditionally understood and used and offers a biblical reflection on land, primarily focused on the Old Testament, and sets out some proposals to resolve disputes over land. Kava is another favoured topic when discussing Gospel and Culture in Vanuatu; Christopher Iawak from Tanna Island, where kava has a profound cultural role, deals with this topic by exploring its original significance and then lamenting the serious social consequences of the huge change in the way kava is now used. He offers a thoughtful theological approach to the problem, drawing much from the writings of Paul on the theme of freedom. The final article from Keith Kalapitas explores the understanding of heaven and hell in his culture of Vanua-lava, the way in which these relate to the traditional god Qet, and the implications of the message of the Christian gospel.

## A change in publisher

The ATF Press (imprint name of the Australasian Theological Forum Ltd) has recently agreed to co-publish (with the established publisher of this series, Gospel Vanuatu Books) further volumes of this series. It is part of their genuine commitment to support and encourage theological publications in Asia and the Pacific. They have graciously understood that in order to make this commitment, they need to take a slightly different approach to their normal requirements for publication because the character and method of theology in these cultures is very different from the normally accepted character and method of theology in the western world. Especially in the South Pacific, theology is essentially oral and communal and does not feature the elements of modernist critical thought and rationality. At the same time, it is no less a passionate and genuine theology. Any changes which may result in the form of publication are reflected in this volume; overall there is little visible difference. I am most appreciative to Hilary Reagan and the Board of the ATF for this new cooperation and trust that it will serve both parties, the ATF and the church in Vanuatu, well.

## Thank you

Father Stanley Ure and his working committee, together with Talua's immediate past Principal Pastor Masia Nato have been key resources in putting volumes four and five together. They have given direction and encouragement for people to put their ideas onto paper. In a culture which communicates orally, this is no simple task. An unofficial part of this local Talua team has been Linda Vutilolo, secretary-typist, who has done a conscientious job in gathering and typing articles and has forwarded them to me.

A sincere word of gratitude to the Theological College of the Uniting Church in Victoria which has contributed towards the funding of this publication. The College is my new place of ministry and my colleagues there have offered generous encouragement for me to continue to pursue my keen interests in the field of Gospel and Culture in Vanuatu. It was during a period of study leave in New Haven that the final editorial work was done for this fifth volume.

Upon my arrival in Vanuatu in 1983, I developed a passionate interest in the local cultures of these people and in the engagement between the Christian Gospel and Culture. This has continued throughout the period of over twenty years and has had a profound influence upon my life and upon my work. I must say that at every step of the way, the people of Vanuatu have been gracious, generous and encouraging. I am particularly thankful to Fiama Rakau, Masia Nato, Kalsakau Zecharie Urtalo and Dorothy Regenvanu, local church leaders who have been colleagues and fellow-travellers in this enterprise. Already plans are under way for further projects which expect to lead to publication of more material in this series.

**And especially**

A particular thank you is offered to Kevin Mark who has handled the technical editing and prepared the material for publication of each of the volumes so far. Kevin has been a friend and adviser in publication from the very beginning of the series and his own interest in the project has been instrumental in enabling the publications to be produced. Without Kevin there may never have been a word of Vanuatu theology in print in this way. With the change of arrangement for publishing, it is not yet clear whether or how Kevin will continue to have a role. Whether or not he does, I want to make it clear that I have been very grateful, not only for his conscientious approach but for his encouraging interest in my work.

# Part One


# Women in the Culture and the Church

# Sitting on the Mat in Vanuatu (*Hpuku Ita Potu*): The Mutual Relationship Between Man and Woman

## Fiama Rakau

### Introduction

> Then God said, 'Let us make man in our image, in our likeness; and let them rule over the fish of the sea, and the birds of the air, over the livestock, over all the earth, and over all the creatures that move along the ground.'(Genesis 1:26)

The basis of mutual dominion is set out here. 'Let them—man and woman—have dominion'. God gave the right to both man and woman to exercise dominion or to rule together. Woman was never created inferior to man, nor was she created to be dominated by man. Woman was created in the image of God just the same as man was created in the image of God. They were both blessed by God to be fruitful.

The idea that man is superior to woman is alien to God's image, and God's idea of mutual dominion over the work of God's hands. God's idea was mutual dominion. However, through disobedience Adam and Eve brought upon themselves and humanity alienation and broken relationship. Their disobedience affected their relationship to God, to each other and to creation. This affected the whole human race. Instead of ruling together and exercising mutual dominion there is superiority of one over the other. Therefore, there is the presence of discrimination, violence and oppression of women by men in society.

God did not give up his idea of man and woman ruling together. Therefore, in Jesus Christ the broken relationship and alienation was restored. Jesus laid down his life so that those under oppression and in captivity could be set free. This calls into question the continuing presence of discrimination and oppression of women in the world today, particularly in the Republic of Vanuatu, which is the concern of this study. This is the issue at stake which I aim to address. My thesis is that the new relationship between man and woman is to be based on the servanthood model of Christ. It is not for us to lord it over others in a

1

position of superiority, but to lay down one's life in a position of humility to liberate the oppressed and provide service to them as set forth in Jesus Christ.

In order to discuss this thesis, the paper is divided into three parts. The first part looks at the hierarchical view of man-woman relationships. The second is a discussion of three doctrinal principles to guide our theological reflection on the relationship between man and woman [namely, human persons are created in the image of God; human persons are sinners-fallen; human persons are recipients of divine grace in Christ). The third section considers the realities of today's situation, and looks at what Christian communities are doing about it. This third section is an attempt to recover local values that have been replaced by colonial values. I intend to explore these traditional local values in the light of the servanthood model of Christ within the Vanuatu context.

## The hierarchical view of the man/woman relationship

The hierarchical view of the relationship of man and woman cannot remain unchallenged in a time of inclusive and mutual emphasis. It is a time to build society and the church by people who see themselves as equals and not as superiors and subordinates. People are equally endowed by God with abilities and are equally resourceful in fulfilling their calling by God in family, church and society.

Karl Barth came close to removing the hierarchical view when he pointed to the 'full equality of man and woman', but he couldn't because he maintained 'female subordination and order'. Even Karl Barth, whose thinking in this area pointed in the direction of the full equality of man and woman in the fellowship of life, argues for female subordination' (Jewett, 1975; 69). The hierarchical view is in question because it was and is a system of inequality. It provides room for inferiority and oppression. Jewett identified both a weakness and a problem in female subordination: 'Its obvious weakness is the occasion which women's dependency affords the man to suppress her rights as a person.' ( Jewett, 1975; 129) The problem he identified is that 'it breaks the analogy of faith'. Jewett gave the following explanation of this:

> The basic creation narratives imply the equality of male
> and female as a human fellowship reflecting the fellow-
> ship in the Godhead; and Jesus, as the perfect man who
> is truly in the image of God, taught such equality in his

2

fellowship with women so that one may say—must say—that in Christ there is no male and female. Any view which subordinates the woman to the man is not analogous but incongruous with this fundamental teaching of both the Old and the New Testament. To affirm that woman, by definition, is subordinate to man does not correspond to the fundamental radicals of revelation, rather it breaks the analogy of faith (Jewett, 1975; 134).

The rejection of the hierarchical view between man and woman, and the critique of the concept of female subordination, invite an alternative approach to the relationship of man and woman. There are three doctrinal principles to guide our theological reflection on the relationship between man and woman, as an alternative view.

## An alternative view in place of the hierarchical man/woman

*Humans are created in the image of God*
Then God said, 'Let us make humankind in our image, according to our likeness; and let them have dominion . . .' (Gen 1:26).

Man and woman were created; they did not evolve. Christ confirmed this declaration (Matt 19:4; Mk 10:6). They were both created in the image and likeness of God. They were equally given abilities such as spiritual, moral, rational, creative and social. 'Let them have dominion' is in the plural form, indicative of mutual dominion. The idea for the man to rule by himself and above the woman contradicts God's idea of mutual dominion. It is the 'them' that 'have' dominion, not the 'him' alone. They share alike what their Creator has endowed upon them.

It is evident from Scripture that both the male and the female share alike the distinctive endowments whereby man differs from the animals; that is to say, men and women both participate in the divine image. Therefore, in understanding man, there should be no striving to transcend the distinction between male and female, no appeal made to the masculine principle, in contrast to the feminine, as the primary and proper paradigm of humanity (Jewett, 1975; 23).

3

The understanding that both man and woman participate in the divine image provides a basis for equality. However, the appeal to the masculine principle in the past brought unbalanced understanding. The question of whether there is a female part of God's image must be addressed. 'The female part of God's image has been suppressed and then forgotten by society, and even by Christian theology' (Song, 116). This is a dilemma, because without the woman man is not complete. It is not good. In arguing for the female dimension of God in the understanding of 'image' CS Song said:

> Adam is not Adam if it is male only. Humankind is not
> humankind if it is male alone. For Adam to be Adam
> there must be female as well as male. It is male and
> female together that makes Adam into Adam, and it is
> they together that make humankind to be humankind.
> This is common sense (Song,118).

The point is clear here that man and woman are created in the image of God and both are to exercise mutual dominion.

*Human persons are fallen and are sinners*
The fall of human persons was occasioned by the temptation of the serpent which sowed in Adam and Eve's mind the seeds of distrust and unbelief. In consequence they disobeyed God by eating the forbidden fruit and brought upon themselves separation and death. In their hiding God walked into the garden and questioned Adam, 'Where are you? Who told you that you were naked? Have you eaten from the tree that I commanded you not to eat?' (Gen 3:3–11). In response to God the man said, 'The woman you put here with me gave me some fruit from the tree, and I ate it' (Gen.3:12). This biblical account revealed two negative forces that destroy human relationships—pride and blame. Had they humbled themselves, they would have admitted that they had done wrong, but instead the man blamed the woman and the woman blamed the serpent. From there on, the concept of 'blame' found common ground in the human relationships. It has affected the status of woman in relationship to man. The man blamed the woman, and this has continued on even into theological thinking. One such theologian who blamed the woman for the fall was Louis Berkhof. In his *Manual of Christian Doctrine,* he said:

4

It was undoubtedly the intention of the tempter to cause Adam, the head of the covenant, to fall, yet he addressed himself to Eve, probably because she (a) was not the covenant head and therefore would not have the same sense of responsibility; (b) had not received the command of God directly but only indirectly, and would consequently be more susceptible to argumentation and doubt; and (c) would undoubtedly prove to be the most effective agent in reaching the heart of Adam (Berkhof, 1933; 136).

This seems to suggest that the woman is the most effective agent in reaching the heart of man. However, the real issue here is not the question of who ate the fruit first and who ate it last. God's question of 'Where are you?' was addressed to the man, but he irresponsibly blamed the woman. Had he acted responsibly by saying, 'we are down here, we are fallen, and we are sorry for what we have done,' history would have taken a different course. The heart of the issue was that they had both fallen. The idea of 'blame' is itself a fallen concept. In other words man was not acting normally when he blamed the woman. Calvin rejected the idea of blaming the woman as an indication of being dull of understanding. In his commentary on 1 Timothy 2:14 which said: 'Adam was not deceived, but the woman, being deceived, was found in transgression,' Calvin gave the following understanding. 'By these words Paul does not mean that Adam was not involved in the same diabolical deception, but only that the cause and source of his deception came from Eve. In other words, Eve was deceived directly by the tempter, and then Adam's turn came; he too was deceived by the evil one' (Jewett, 67).

There are two important points to underline here. First, both man and woman had equally fallen. Both were entitled to the name 'sinner'. They had both fallen short of the glory of God. The man had no excuse to blame the woman because he too was fallen. The man was not in a better position than the woman. He was not superior to the woman, for they were both subject to disobedience. The second important point to underline is the fact that they both made excuses. They had fallen but were not ready to admit it. They had other reasons to point to as the cause of their failure. By doing so they brought upon themselves further problems in life: pain in child bearing, and sweat to produce food. For these reasons the theological argument based on hierarchical relationship

5

of the man creates a problem because man is no better than the woman. They were equals in God's image and were equals in their assigned responsibility over creation. However, in disobedience, they were also equals as sinners in need of a Saviour.

*Human persons are the recipients of divine grace in Christ*

> But the gift is not like the trespass. For if the many died by the trespass of the one man, how much more did God's grace and the gift that came by the grace of the one man, Jesus Christ, overflow for the many. For just as through the disobedience of the one man the many were made sinners, so also through the obedience of the one man the many will be made righteous (Romans 15:15,19).

Humanity is redeemed and brought under grace. It is a place of better things. There is something new that has taken place. In his dying on the cross and resurrection from the dead, Jesus placed humanity under a new order. Man and woman are no longer under the old order. Jesus the new Adam established a new order in which he alone has supremacy over humanity and creation. The relationship between man and woman finds its fulfilment in Christ, because in him, all things have their proper place. 'He (Jesus) is before all things, and in him all things hold together' (Col 1:17). Under the new order of things, humanity is enabled by the Holy Spirit to live a life of responsibility to love God and neighbour. There is renewal in the divine image. As redeemed humanity man and woman are able to recover their God-given endowments. They are to live in a life of fellowship and humble service to God, neighbour and each other. They are subject under Christ who is head of the church. Jewett said that,

> The Church is the sphere in which such redeeming grace is principally operative, the place of woman and her rights must be a prime concern of the theologians as teachers in the Church (Jewett, 1975; 22).

The Apostle Paul with his Jewish background thought of the woman as subordinate. 'Neither was man created for woman, but woman for man' (1 Cor 11: 19). In terms of the revelation in Christ, Paul thought of

6

the woman as equal to man. 'There is neither Jew nor Greek, slave nor free, male nor female, for you are all one in Christ Jesus' (Gal 3: 28). This was not just an idea, but in Paul's ministry, he recognised women in the church. In his letter to the Romans he commended Phoebe as a servant of the church, and he requested the church in Rome to greet all women who served in the church (Romans 16:1–16). In Christ the man and the woman are redeemed from stereotypes which inhibit their relationship. In Christ they become what God meant them to be when God created them. Christ restored their mutual dominion over creation.

### Today's realities and Christ's servant model for Vanuatu

There are two parts in this third and final section: first, today's realities concerning the relationship between man and woman; secondly, Christ's Servant model as an appropriate model by which the relationship between man and woman is fashioned.

*Today's realities*
There still exists in today's situation in human societies, strife, conflict and oppression. There are patterns of social oppression, sins in economic structures and sins in political structures. People have not changed much in their attitudes towards women. Men still oppress women, and women are speaking out against these situations of women's violence and oppression. This is a global issue of concern. The *United Nations Report on Human Rights* reported that, 'domestic violence exists as a powerful tool of oppression' (UN Report, 5). The report went on to describe the existing violence and oppression that are manifest in different ways.

> Under domestic violence are: 'discriminatory practices of sex-selective abortion and female infanticide, enforced malnutrition, unequal access to medical care, physical and emotional abuse, incest, female genital mutilation, early childhood marriage, sale of children for prostitution'. Violence associated with courtship includes: 'woman battering, marital rape, dowry violence, domestic murder, forced pregnancy, abortion and sterilization, abuse of widows' (UN Report, 10).

The list is extensive, and these confirm the reality of today's situation of the existing presence of violence and oppression against women.

7

Moelle wrote a paper on the role of Christianity in the oppression of Women and claims that,

> For almost two thousand years, there has been one single institution which has had a significantly powerful realm of control and oppression over the everyday lives of the majority of individuals, especially women, in Western Europe and subsequently North America. This insidious institution is the Roman Catholic Church, or in fact, Christianity in general (Moelle, l).

In the Pacific, the *Fiji Women's Crises Centre Regional Newsletter* reported that:

> Women are bringing issues of concern to women, particularly violence against women, into the public. They claim that women work in adverse, and sometimes life threatening conditions and face considerable criticism, hostility and resistance within their communities because they are challenging the forces of patriarchy, including religious and cultural practices that oppress women (FWCC Regional Newsletter, l).

The issue of oppression and violence against women is real. There is evidence of this reality in many parts of the world where women are experiencing oppression. In Vanuatu we have inherited hierarchical structures, which are also dominant. We have been led to believe that these structures were for the good of the church. However, we observe that the decision-making bodies of the church are male-oriented. Some churches ordain women and others don't. Yet women make up more than half the members of the local congregation. The oppression is real, and women are speaking up loud and clear. What should the church do about it?

*The servant model of Christ*
The question of what the church should be doing is an important question. I am proposing the Servant Model of Christ as a partial solution to the question and the issue addressed here, that is, the issue of the

8

hierarchical view of seeing man in a superior position, and woman in an inferior position. That view has given man the chance to take advantage of the subordination of woman and to oppress her. The hierarchical view that subordinates women, from the apostle Saint Paul's view, was intended to be subordination under the supremacy of Christ. Within the marriage relationship Paul gave these instructions:

> Wives, submit to your husbands as to the Lord. For the husband is the head of the wife as Christ is the head of the church, his body, of which he is the Saviour (Eph 5:22 NIV).

The idea of man as 'head of the woman' is to be in the same way as Christ is 'head of the Church'. Therefore the right relationship between man and woman is a living parable to reflect the relationship between Christ and the Church. The model that Christ laid down was not hierarchical but humble service. Jesus is the Saviour of his Body the Church. He laid down his life to save the Church. The same Paul, who wrote about subordination, wrote to the Philippians and said,

> Your attitude should be the same as that of Christ Jesus who, being in very nature God, did not consider equally with God something to be grasped, but made himself nothing, taking the very nature of a servant, being made in human likeness ( Phil 2:5–6 NIV).

The phrases 'taking the very nature of a servant, being made in human likeness', imply that 'being made in human likeness is taking the very nature of a servant'. To be human is to be a servant. Jesus' disciples had a conflict over position of power and authority, so Jesus said to them:

> You know that the rulers of the Gentiles lord it over them, and their high officials exercise authority over them. Not so with you. Instead, whoever wants to become great among you must be your servant, and whoever wants to be first must be your slave—just as the Son of Man did not come to be served, but to serve,

and to give his life as a ransom for many (Matt 20:25–28).

The idea of the servant model of Christ is clearly set out here and elsewhere in the Bible. 'I am among you as one who serves' (Luke 22: 27, NIV). Followers of Christ are to walk in the same footsteps. Paul was a slave of Christ Jesus (Rom 1: 1). Jesus said, 'Whoever serves me must follow me; and where I am, my servant also will be. My Father will honour the one who serves me' (John 12:26). The servant model of Christ is what men should follow. The man is head as Christ is head. As Christ gave his life for the church, so man has this example to follow.

The servant model is not a strange concept in the Melanesian context. The following indicates traditional values that reflect the servant model of Christ and the equality between man and woman.

**Traditional leadership**

There were many forms of community leadership. The concept 'chief' as a hierarchical model is not an indigenous category. Bolton did a study of chiefly leadership in Vanuatu, and he said that, 'The term "chief" and the developing formulation of leadership which that term invokes today is something which was introduced in the colonial process' (Bolton, 1998, 180). The concept 'chief' is foreign and it invoked a different understanding of leadership. The concept used in the island of Futuna for a chief is *Teriki or Ariki*. It means the one who leads as a servant of the people, the one who provides and protects the people. He/she represents the people, by speaking on their behalf, or taking action to protect and provide for the people. Through the years of his ministry, Rev John Geddie, an early missionary to Vanuatu, made a personal contact with Nohoat who was a traditional leader, and he wrote this about him.

> After some years, Nohoat abandoned heathenism. He took the side of Christianity at the very time when the mission was in the midst of its great trials . . . no man did more for Christianity on this island than Nohoat (R Prior, 10).

The missionaries did not eradicate the traditional leadership but used it for the cause of the gospel. Nohoat was a traditional leader who did more for his island as a servant. He did this by serving the people and

10

becoming a servant of the missionary. When the missionaries arrived in Vanuatu, it was the traditional leaders who welcomed them and provided them with land to build mission stations. They became the servants of the missionaries by travelling around with them carrying the missionary's handbag. Many of those who were first ordained elders were leaders in their communities. That contributed to the advance of the spreading of the gospel in the islands.

## The community and village life

The traditional leader was a servant of the community. The leader lived in the same village as everybody else. They shared similar types of houses. It was a life of sharing. In birth and in death, in sorrow and in festivity, the one that people looked to as leader interacted between families and communities to ensure that needs were met. There was a sense of equality. No one was higher than the other. All needs were met because the leader served them well. The services provided by the leader of the community were freely given to the people by the one who lived and shared their lives as a servant. The modern urban settings are now a great challenge to this traditional value of servant leadership as it originally took place in a village setting.

## The value of the traditional thatch house, and sitting on the mat

The missionaries brought chairs and stools and separated men and women in the church building. Men were to sit on one side of the church and the women were to sit on the other side. Men sat on chairs, and women sat on mats. This is in contrast to the traditional practice of sitting on a mat. In our traditional homes, everybody sits and sleeps on mats on the floor. There were no rooms that separated people in the house. In sitting down to eat we all sat on mats, sharing the same food. The sense of equality and caring was strongly felt in such a setting. There was openness to each other, which was vividly laid out in the structure of the local thatch house. There was no hierarchical structure to follow in entering a house. Families would come and go any time during the day or night. Even knocking and making appointments were not necessary. Whenever food was prepared at home, the mother and father had to make sure that there was extra cooked food. Extended family members could come at any time. The mat was always on the floor always ready for the family and the community to gather and sit.

11

This idea of a mat was also reflected in the community. In my home island of Futuna it was a custom in all villages that whenever a family member or visitor arrived, he/she would be given a green coconut, a young edible growing coconut (nafara), sugarcane or some cooked food. This tradition is known in Futunese as *ari kavakava, which* means 'cool your sweat after the journey'. The leader (*Ariki*) as a servant had to make sure that relatives and visitors who arrived were properly cared for. The *Ariki* in the Futunese concept is one who sweats in order to provide for the people. In feasting and in rituals the *Ariki* is busy running around or busy cooking, sharing and distributing food among the people. The leader in traditional society is one who serves the people.

## Conclusion

In reflecting on these ideas in the light of the servant model of Christ, I come to the following conclusion: that the man is not higher than the woman, nor is he superior in any way to the woman. The man is head as Christ is head; therefore the man has a role of giving his life to the woman to serve her, as Christ gave his life for the Church to save her. That life of service does not demand lording over others but it demands sacrifice in the service of others in the spirit of love and humility.

> The most important one of you should be like the least important, and your leader should be like a servant (Luke 22:26, NIV).

Sitting on the mat reflects service in humility. It reflects equality and the recognition of the worth of every individual person. Nobody is higher and there is no hierarchy in sitting on the mat, because the mat is flat. It is cleverly woven by the wisdom of motherhood in a position of humility. She wove it while sitting down, for the purpose of sitting down. The mat is the place of humility. Wisdom says the way to go up is to sit on the mat. The way up is down in service. This is the meaning of the cross of Christ.

I believe that Christ did not come from heaven with a chair or sitting cushions. He even came without a mat, but choosing between a chair and a mat he would prefer to sit on the mat. Jesus came through the humility gate in the stable in Bethlehem, and he returned via the same route of the humility gate at Calvary. As his followers we have no other gate to enter but the same humility gate. We are to take up our cross and follow the

12

same footsteps. Therefore, the issues at stake in which men are dominating and oppressing women have no theological and biblical foundations. Men are to serve as Christ came to serve. For us in Vanuatu, Christ has left us with water in a dish and a towel to remind us of our humble duty to serve one another in love and lay down our life for the sake of the gospel. That gospel is to liberate those who are under oppression.

## Bibliography

Berkhof, Louis. *Manual of Christian Doctrine* (Grand Rapids: Eerdmans Publishing Company, 1933.

Bolton, Lissant. *The Journal of Pacific History,* Vol 33, No 2 Suva, 1998.

Song, Choan-Seng. *Third-Eye Theology* (New York: Orbis Books, 1979).

Jewett, Paul K. *Man as Male and Female* (Grand Rapids: Eerdmans Company, 1975).

Prior, Randall. Gospel and Culture in Vanuatu: The Founding Missionary and a Missionary for Today (Melbourne: Gospel Vanuatu Books, 1998).

*Fiji Women' Crises Center-Regional Newsletter,* Volume 5, Issue 1 July 1999.

UN Commission on Human Rights Thematic Reports-Violence against Women. February, 1996.

Moelle, *The Role of Christianity in the Oppression of Women,* 1999.

*The Journal of Pacific History,* Vol 33, No 2, Suva, 1998.

# The Roles of Men Versus Women
# in the Ministry of Church Leadership

## Selerik Michel

### Introduction

Women's ministry in churches today is still a strongly debated issue especially with the long held predominance of male leaders in the traditional churches. This creates tension with those churches and organizations who feel that women should be fully involved in leadership and ministry. In these latter groups women have been allowed to lead in various ways in their church's activities and to take positions of high rank in their organisations. This very sensitive and unsettled issue will continue to be debated in different fields.

Although this paper attempts to summarize these views with high respect given to our traditional cultural values, it depicts and values the Scriptures as our unique source to direct the flow of our discussions. It may be too broad and general to speak of 'cultural values'; our discussions will be more specifically in the area of leadership with sensitivity to the differences in handling the case.

This calls for careful exegetical and theological analysis as a means of helping the readers discover which areas of women's leadership roles are God-given that need preservation and encouragement, and which roles are prohibited and need to be avoided. To do this will help strengthen our working relationship in the church, building one another up, instead of treating women's status as an island floating in isolation from other entire islands dominated by males at the top of hierarchy. It is by way of clear biblical interpretation of texts that we can come to a helpful conclusion on this issue, and uproot the distorted meaning of various Scripture texts often quoted as a basis for arguments.

Furthermore it is crucial to come back to the Scripture to make our arguments because it is a legacy of our cultural belief in Vanuatu that decision-making to a great degree is a role which belongs to men and excludes women. This in one sense is well supported by most Scripture passages, but how do we reconcile this with churches that base their arguments also upon some Scripture passages in support of women's ordination for ministry? While the difference exists and divides, continuous argument over this issue is inevitable. For some people, the more they debate about it, the more indignant they become. But instead, this writer encourages the readers to recognise that the more we go in depth into the

14

Scripture, the more we will appreciate the differences it conveys. This will be discussed in the next section. Craig S Keener (egalitarian), and Thomas R Schreiner (complementarian) will be used beside Wane Grudem and other writers to represent the different views and positions concerning the issue. Jean-Marc Philibert will also be used in a specific situation in Vanuatu to counterbalance the other influences in one of the local communities as an example.

## Argument on different views in answering the problem of leadership

While there are differences of opinion in the church about how to resolve the status of men and women, and how to understand the principles of equality, there is a need to seek for God's direction in order to arrive at acceptable conclusions. There are various opinions and categories of leadership of women which the writer believes would fall in line with the sort of evidence upon which some would base their arguments. These arguments may come in negative or positive forms either to support or demolish their cultures or the Scripture. These cultural and scriptural views clearly depict how difficult it is to deal with the issue, especially when some Scripture texts prohibit the leadership roles of women while some endorse them in various ways, both in the Old and New Testaments. However, we have to pay special attention to the different approaches of the biblical writers and from what cultural background they have come. This will assist us in recapturing a better understanding of the topic and shedding some light on the whole discussion in areas where there is more likelihood of there being conflicts.

Having read through some of the Old Testament texts and quotations used by Keener as supportive of the equality of men and women, I wanted to select two of them which to some extent need to be clarified further, namely 2 Kings 22: 14–20 and Judges 4:6–10. These two texts need special exegetical and theological treatment for clarification. From these texts the writer learns that although women were playing some crucial roles at that time, there is limited information about the nature of these roles. It looks as if the Old Testament writers culturally restricted the roles that women played in public. This clearly teaches us that when women were involved in the leadership roles as such, we need to specify the reasons and purposes of God's intention of their involvements. To some extent in support of the egalitarian writers such as Keener, this writer would further argue that women and men should be given fair treatment in dealing with their respective roles despite their cultural differences. This respect should also be given in areas of prohibition. In this case the church should stand in a neutral position and find ways to reconcile both sides while at the same time appreciate the underlying differences. This means that even if women were prohibited in the leadership roles of the church, they should be encouraged to lead within their own realms. For example, Deborah, though she was given a leadership role as prophetess, judge, military leader and a song writer to inspire people, this did not really make her prominent in public. In fact, we are not given the full details of her role, but it is evident that women would have felt more comfortable working with and under her than they would the male dominant roles.

Although women and men were both created in the divine image of God, this insight should not influence the case for the church to identify obstacles or hindrances which would lead to the separation of both genders in various church roles where appropriate. For example in 1 Timothy 2:12, Paul strictly prohibits a woman from having authority over a man. With this view, the writer would agree, but I would also want to argue that Paul did not strictly prohibit women's rule over women as they would always appreciate the actual lower and caring roles they actively played in their respective levels. For example, in Exodus we learn of Miriam who played a distinctive role in leading other women in celebrating the victory of God, but under the authority of men. Deborah was a prophetess and judge of Israel who resolved disputes privately with God's wisdom (Judges 4:4). If that is the case then the writer would argue that women can play leadership roles up to a certain stage but not equivalent to men's authority. There are distinctive roles which are biblically based and ordained by God and should be appreciated in a way that God's name will be glorified.

The differences of our roles should not be seen as a dividing line between both genders, but as God's divine character. 'They are equal in importance, but they have different roles.'[1] The Scripture clearly shows us the different roles played between members of the Trinity. As Grudem further states, 'Although all three members of the Trinity are equal in power and in all other attributes, the Father has a greater authority. He has a leadership role among all the members of the Trinity that the Son and Holy Spirit do not have.'[2]

In the Vanuatu context, there are various aspects of church roles that need to be clarified so as not to create confusion. For example, in the Presbyterian Church, the two primary causes of conflict between men and women concerning their distinctive roles are summed up in the questions: 1) what is meant by church authority and who has it? 2) what are the caring

---

1. Wayne Grudem, *Systematic Theology: An Introduction to Biblical Doctrine* (Grand Rapids: Zondervan, 1984), 460.
2. *Ibid*, 459

16

roles of men and women. I shall now briefly comment on these two questions.

1) What is meant by church authority and who has it?
In relation to authority, there are differences drawn between men and women. This difference is not necessarily bad, however. In fact, the Bible teaches that some differences are natural and beneficial. Since God has created us as unique individuals, as women and men, we have different opinions, desires, perspectives and priorities that we can share together. In relation to church authority we need patiently to see what the Bible has to say. In Judges 4:5, Deborah did not go out and publicly proclaim the word of the Lord, but individuals came to her in private under the palm tree. Women with the authoritative gift of prophecy in the Old Testament did not exercise it in public as male prophets did and, therefore, their authority did not contradict male headship but rather endorsed it.

2) What are the caring roles of men and women in the church?
The actual practice of women as recorded in the Scriptures, and in almost every culture and in every society, was never meant to indicate that they had authority over someone in a hierarchical manner. Their leadership roles were not publicly expressed; they were mainly to do with exercising social responsibility for people in desperate need. Therefore, the writer believes that women would naturally accept this as their rightful position rather than the roles that are beyond their strengths. As Schreiner states in agreement with the views of the egalitarians, 'I believe egalitarians are correct in saying that some of the commands and norms in Scripture are the result of cultural accommodation'.[3] For example, culturally related problems are evident in 1 Timothy 2:11–14; they would need further consideration and clear interpretation in handling the ministry roles of the church. In fact the apostle Paul was more concerned about order in the church with respect to the standards of leadership. Therefore, he wrote to advise Timothy to avoid the dangers that might possibly occur especially on such matters as worship procedures and the control of unruly women. Paul is advising Timothy to take extra precautionary steps in trying to bring order back to the church in Ephesus. As for Paul's perception of roles and responsibilities in this particular situation, this may easily cause some Christians to be sidetracked with false doctrines and be misled. Furthermore, we should also be aware of the particular cultural setting that Paul is dealing with, which will not be the

---

3. Thomas R Schreiner, 'Women in Ministry', in Two Views on Women in Ministry, edited by, James R Beck and Craig L Blomberg (Grand Rapids: Zondervan, 2001), 216.

same in every culture. 'They were written to specific situations and to cultures that differed from our own.'.[4] We need to understand what it means to honour the Scriptures as uniquely important within our culture. Again as Schreiner states, 'The Bible, not our culture, must reign supreme'.[5] Therefore, in such a situation, and as scholars, we need to have a deeper sense on how our interpretations can become remedial instruments to heal wounds of the differences between men and women in the church of Jesus Christ, who loves all, died for all to save all for the extension of his kingdom. To mention 'all' means men and women together in the ministry, but with high regard given to their God-given designated roles.

To go further on this, the writer feels that there is a need for people who are deeply sensitive to this issue to be trained and be equipped to help the church with better interpretations of this unsettled issue. As Blomberg states, 'We need the very best scholarship executed by the finest of trained men and women to pursue this subject'.[6] With this process it would help the church to embrace its stance in support of women in ministry roles with a clear understanding as to where the limitations are.

## Biblical support texts versus prohibited texts

In 2 Timothy 4:19 Paul is affirming Priscilla and Aquila who had been a faithful couple in supporting him to make sure that the ministry of the gospel, previously planted by him, continued to flourish. The reason Paul mentioned Priscilla first was because of her dedication and commitment fully rendered to the ministry work. As Ralph Earle states, 'Evidently she was the stronger character of the two. It may well be that their moves were due as much to her missionary concern as to her husband's trade'.[7] However, Paul's various writings and especially his first letter to Timothy seem to lead us to different views. It may be true that Priscilla exercised an active role at the end of her life, but we are not given enough information for that claim. As Keener states, 'If some texts seem to point in one direction and others in a different direction, this leaves us several options . . .'[8] He says this to mean that Paul sometimes shares negative ideas about the roles of women in the church not because of their inability to occupy the office of

---

4.   *Ibid*, 219.
5.   *Ibid*, 219
6.   James R. Beck and Craig L Blomberg, editors. *Two Views on Women in Ministry* (Grand Rapids: Zondervan, 2001), 325.
7.   Ralph Earle, '2 *Timothy,'* Barker, Kenneth L, and John R Kohlenberger III, editors The *Zondervan NIV BibleCommentary* (Grand Rapids, MI: Zondervan Publishing House, 1992).
8.   Craig S Keener, 28.

leader, but in response to the different cultural context that he was facing. Because of this Paul knew that, "in breaking new ground for God's kingdom, women would have faced special obstacles in that culture, as they would in many cultures even today.[9] Keener tries to pull together all the different views and compare one with another to see what would be an appropriate and acceptable view most closely consistent with the teaching of the Scriptures. In most cases like Keener, Schreiner accommodates a complementary view which states that women should be encouraged in their ministry except in the role of the ordained pastoral office. As he states, 'My thesis in this essay is that women were not appointed to the pastoral office'.[10] The writer would feel comfortable to accept this view because he feels that although women may not be ordained as pastors, they are able to serve faithfully within their domain in dealing with specific needs for the benefit of all. This would really have great importance in their ministry among women where a male pastor would more likely be ineffective. In the writer's previous ministry, he noted with special attention the roles of women as crucial. When it comes to a. certain point in dealing with women's needs and problems, he would delegate this responsibility either to his wife, or to a capable woman leader in whom he had full confidence. Women are capable of dealing with their own problems and difficulties and finding solutions to them. They would always take extra care in dealing with those matters that they know would open them to criticism by males if things were to go wrong. Therefore, the writer believes that Scripture texts such as that in 1 Timothy 2 will always be highly respected by women in designating their proper roles instead of pushing themselves up to prohibited positions. This reserves a place for women to be successful through good deeds and respectful dressing, and in this way offer their unique worship to God (cf 1 Tim 2:9–10). This approach will ultimately cause no hindrance to the hierarchical position of male headships, but will maintain their status within their own realm. The text tends to portray women in a very traditional role but one which the writer believes should be maintained today, and cannot be changed by any interpretations of theologians.

However, the only solution to the dilemma about roles is to focus our attention on the teachings of Christ. For example, if the coming of Christ was meant to fulfil the Old Testament and bring the transformation of all cultures, then women, though in a lower class status, should be highly respected by men in various ways. This is the approach taken by Jesus in his ministry.

---

9.    *Ibid*, 34.
10.   Thomas R Schreiner, 183.

Almost everything we read and learn about women nowadays in our societies has been interpreted, explained and written from different cultural perspectives. This has created several problems in our knowledge and understanding of women's roles and their status in our societies. The next section of this paper will provide us with some biblical evidence for the prohibition of women in certain ministry roles, and indicate how the Scriptures challenge and correct the types of mentality that is always negative about the roles of women in ministry.

There are some Scripture passages that were quoted by the two authors which would need careful consideration. For example, according to Keener, the passages in 1 Timothy 2 were written for specific cultural purposes and so they should not be interpreted loosely. He stated, '. . . we must interpret the Scriptures in their historical and cultural context'.[11] From the writer's point of view, let us not force the Scriptures into the flow of our own minds and what we think women should be doing in relation to our cultures. But instead, let the Scriptures speak for themselves about what God intends would be an appropriate role for women to play in the ministry today. This personal distorting of the texts is exactly what happens with the interpretation of Paul's letter to Timothy. It is currently a problematic text for theologians who strictly hold on to their cultural behaviour when interpreting it instead of basing their interpretation purely on the Scriptures. In fact, the text itself is a straightforward Scriptural teaching appropriate to correct a particular cultural setting. For example as Schreiner further states, 'I would suggest that the verse seems difficult because it runs counter to our own cultural institutions. But the Scriptures exist to challenge our worldview . . .'[12]

As stated in the above section, if women were prohibited from holding an ordained pastoral office or hierarchical position in societies, there are simple areas of responsibility that they are able to handle. The writer feels that Paul's words are written explicitly for women who were teaching false doctrine as he states in 2 Tim 2:23–26. However, in today's churches women are still respecting this not only in teaching responsibilities, but in other high ranking positions. Therefore, this needs a clear definition of how they would be involved in their appropriate position in churches without causing much interference to male dominant roles in leadership. In fact, what Paul experienced and advised Timothy to be aware of might not be the same in other places. But as a young church worker this information was appropriate during his time.

---

11.  *Ibid*, 219.
12.  *Ibid*, 224.

## How do we respond to the situation while maintaining biblical teachings?

In today's situation in various presbyteries within the Presbyterian church of Vanuatu, women have been ordained and inducted as pastors and elders. This is identical with the view of other churches in the Pacific and in other parts of the world. For the Presbyterian church of Vanuatu, the direction in these matters deviated very recently from what it used to be. The majority of leaders within the church seemed to accept this new direction of the church in support for women's ordination without raising important questions. For some the ordaining of women is still held as a deviation from the standards of belief and there is a need for further study. Few with conservative views made a determined attempt to persuade the majority to uphold the previous position but with no success; they were dragged on by the majority vote. Some leaders were caught in the middle between different views without stating their position, and felt that a vote had to be dragged out forcefully from them by the church. Some were filled with remorse after having taken a decision and then regretted being forced by others to vote in favour of the motion.

Because of all the above reasons, the writer feels that the church needs to caution its leaders to be critical in their biblical interpretations on this issue. When this caution is overlooked, possible mistakes will result as people will easily be led astray towards heretical teachings. In fact, this is actually what is happening in the Vanuatu Presbyterian church context where a division has developed between male and female leaders for lack of proper biblical interpretations. This should not be the case since the writer feels that both male and female are important in God's eyes. The difference exists in the roles of both sexes. Areas of difference should be appreciated and should not be used as a means of creating hindrances between men and women.

The diversion of the church and its tradition on this issue is caused by various factors, namely practices incorporated with culture and shallow biblical interpretations. This leaves the church in an unstable and tense situation. What the writer means by this is that after having trained the first few women in the church, leading on to their ordination and induction, some of these women are still waiting to be called to serve. The church is brought to a halt as it tries to ask why local parishes refuse to call these women pastors. The underlying root cause of the problem is not with local parishes but with leaders who introduced change with unclear transition from one stage to another. This has created confusion among leaders themselves, and problems for the women who, having thought they were called by God now face turmoil. This needs to be dealt with since the majority of people

21

attending today's worship services and meetings including other additional church activities are women and children. This writer would simply state that the reason for the problem is that once the church had taken decisions towards the ordination and induction of women, a deep exegetical and theological task remained.

### The significance of the biblical term of equality for ni-Vanuatu?

God's divine image engraved on Adam from the very beginning was created into two component parts, male and female (cf Gen 2: 21–23). From then on God established a relationship between them and called them Adam (man) and Eve (woman). In terms of equality, they had the same status, rights and responsibilities. However, how do we qualify this terminology of equality with the way ni-Vanuatu people see it? Let me take an example of this cultural view from the village of Erakor in the island of Efate where I was born.

In the traditional cultural belief of the people of Erakor, the equality of both sexes (male and female) is understood in terms of a complementary team, with man and woman having the same status, rights and responsibilities and yet they have different forms. In other words, a man and his wife are two separate beings, male and female, but they may be spoken of as having the same quality, for one cannot exist without the other. These two component parts or differences of humanity are to be taken as belonging to one whole body. This is most clearly seen in child bearing which requires the uniting of the two separate beings together. In our traditional culture the equality of the two sexes was both distinct and connected. For example, men would strictly keep themselves from the practice of clothes washing and women would agree that to wash the clothes would be their responsibility. Most women in that village are breadwinners for the family. They would spend the majority of each day in town working and raising money for the family while husbands would do other domestic jobs such as gardening and fishing just to pass the day. Wives, after having gone through a busy day of work, would return home and do the laundry without complaint against their husbands. This practice applied until the early 1970s within the domain of each family without anyone having a thought of bringing change to the situation. According to Jean-Marc Philibert, 'Far from considering themselves agents of change, they perceive their role essentially as a conservative one'.[13] Philibert explains further, using a metaphorical form of reality, to show how the people of Erakor (male and female) treat each other in terms of equality: 'Raising crops and bearing children are the main ways

---

13.  *Ibid*, 170.

through which the complementary relationship of each sex in the conjugal unit is expressed. Crops, like children, belong equally to both spouses because they can only be produced through their combined action'.[14]

However, at the end of that period of time practices began to change because women began to accept and take up a lifestyle from outside influences. Philibert as a person coming from outside can clearly see the changes taking place. He states, 'The complementarity of male and female is expressed today in a reduced form . . .'[15] Philibert deals mainly with the issue of land and how in the future people in that particular community will reap the consequences of losing their land, because women are choosing to marry men from other islands and are bringing their husbands back to the village. This practice is contrary to the tradition that when a woman gets married, she leaves her parents and moves out to live with her husband's family. The major problems in relation to land in the village are caused by women. These women were the first to lose sight of their cultural identity and chose to modify their own ways of life with foreign ideas. Their decisions challenge the status quo and display a competitive attitude towards men. One of the main reasons for this new approach is that some women have been able to gain a high level of education and think that changes should be made within the village about how women should be treated. They see equality as a term that puts men and women on the same scale not wanting them to be treated as inferior to men. The traditional and cultural lifestyle that they used to appreciate has become unacceptable to them. They criticize men not because of their failures but because of their lack of wealth and education. 'They point out that a good number of Erakor men have been out of work for some years and lack any realistic prospect of employment in the future'.[16] Should women complain about men because of men's lack of wealth and education?

In the early days, although men were not well educated in western cultural terms, they were able to live peacefully with their wives and keep their status free from conflict. However, as Philibert would say 'no blame is to be attached to Erakor women for being the vector through which important social relationships are no longer being reproduced in the same form as in the past'.[17] This writer would argue that although these women should not be blamed, the speed of change would possibly be reduced if they were to show respect towards the cultural and spiritual values of the community. Actually what is considered by women nowadays to be

---

14.  *Ibid*, 171.
15.  *Ibid*, 171.
16.  *Ibid*, 169.
17.  *Ibid*, 170

appropriate steps for change is contrary to past practice. This has placed them in a risky position as some of these women have found it so difficult to follow their husbands to the outer islands. This is the main cause of the problem occurring in the community when these women returned to the village with their husband without considering this as a threat to the whole system of communal ways of life.

However, men or women who originated from Erakor and got married with spouses from the same village would realise that arguments from either genders against the roles of the other would mean a loss of trust. In the past people held tightly onto their roles and would expect each married couple to do the same. They knew that they could not exist without the other. It requires the commitment and full submission from both men and women towards each other. This fits well with Paul's teaching in relation to the establishment of marriage between a man and a woman, and what it means in relation to the usage of the term, 'one flesh'. In fact, two separate beings, one with features different from the other, one formed weaker than the other and yet they are described as having formed into one flesh through marriage. There is a strong relational idea of equality based on their union with God and with each other.

In Paul's letter to the Ephesians, he addresses the idea of equality in the husband and wife relationship. Here Paul affirms that God's word in Genesis 2:24 is to be respected by all generations. As Paul writes, 'For this reason a man will leave his father and mother and be joined to his wife, and the two will become one flesh' (Eph 5:31). Paul emphasizes the importance of the relationship of oneness that a man and a woman have to maintain without question.

## The value of Jesus' teachings on women's ministry role

The teachings of Jesus concerning the roles of women in the New Testament make it clear that women's status around the world must be treated as significantly important. Although, there are certain standards of prohibited authority appointed only to male headships which must be respected by women, they are not strictly prohibited from sharing the good news of Jesus. As Jesus told the Samaritan woman, 'Yet a time is coming and has now come when the true worshippers will worship the Father in Spirit and truth, for they are the kind of worshippers the Father seeks' (John 4: 23 NIV). The text does not specify who the true worshippers would be, but it has a clear connotation of inclusion of men and women. In other words, Jesus used this text in a particular context where, as Messiah, an open door was promised to the Samaritans, male and female alike.

This divine declaration builds the confidence of the woman as she realises Jesus' words and begins to share her testimony with whoever she meets on her way. The woman tells the news about the love of Christ who transforms her life. She had confidence to go beyond any cultural barriers that drew lines between the different racial groups, and to share the good news that can unite them together. The men who witnessed the event then spoke of their transformation through the woman's testimony. "They said to the woman, 'We no longer believe just because of what you said; now we have heard for ourselves, and we know that this man really is the Saviour of the world'. (John 4:42 NIV). The role played by the Samaritan woman might not be equivalent to the ordained pastor's role, but she publicly presented a dynamic evangelistic message to transform life. The writer believes this to be a really powerful testimony by the men with whom the Samaritan women had shared the good news of Jesus Christ. The news which this woman shared had greatly impacted on them and had totally transformed their lives. There was no part of their testimony that spoke about a Samaritan woman being a hindrance to the ways of their transformed lives. Is this an illustration of the way that we are to look beyond our cultural understandings and fix our attention on Christ? Or do we see our cultures as obstacles to the ways of Christ? The writer feels that each Christian needs an eye of faith to see and acknowledge, with God's guidance, the roles that women are effectively carrying out and treat them as co-workers in the ministry. This means that although women may not go as far as becoming ordained to be pastors or elders, they should be given full recognition of their roles as commanded by the Lord.

## Conclusion

This paper tries to help us understand the different roles played by men and women in the church, roles which should be respected and appreciated. The differences between these roles are given powerful historical significance both by the Scriptures and by our cultures. It is not valid for us to change the whole system of leadership by men and women to suit our interest, but we must patiently abide by the differences and maintain them for the extension of God's kingdom. We need to gain understanding of and appreciate the differences between the roles men and women have played in the church. There will need to be more discussion in the future. Let us not lose sight of the significance of the biblical teachings but uphold and apply them in every real life situation.

To conclude, I would simply state that to lead is to risk one's life in a commitment that should make people who follow build their trust and confidence in the Lord Jesus. In most places in Vanuatu, the public leadership role is taken as a male responsibility. For some cultural contexts in Vanuatu, it would be awkward to see women playing such roles, but instead they are regarded as followers of men, with limited room provided for leadership. If this is the case, they will only lead within their own domain but will be hesitant about usurping the men's roles. This is also an affirmation of what the Scripture teaches. It depicts the same procedure for all humanity to follow. Therefore the writer would like to appeal to all classes of people, male and female to maintain this in all church settings, now and in the future.

## Bibliography

Beck, James R. and Craig L Blomberg, editors. *Two Views on Women's Ministry* (Grand Rapids: Zondervan, 2001.

Earle, Ralph. '2 *Timothy'*, Kenneth L Barker and John R Kohlenberger III editors. The *Zondervan NIV Bible Commentary* (Grand Rapids: Zondervan Publishing House, 1994).

Grudem, Wayne. *Systematic Theology: An Introduction to Biblical Doctrine* (Grand Rapids: Zondervan, 1984).

Keener, Craig S. *'Women in Ministry'*, In *Two Views on Women in Ministry*. Edited by James R Beck and Craig L Blomberg (Grand Rapids: Zondervan, 2001).

Philibert, Jean-Marc. 'A Case Study of Proletarianization of Peri-Urban Villages in Vanuatu', *Oceania* Vol 58, No 3 (1988).

Schreiner, Thomas R. *'Women in Ministry'*, in *Two Views on Women in Ministry,* edited by James R Beck and Craig L Blomberg (Grand Rapids: Zondervan, 2001).

# The Ordination of Women
# in the Church of Melanesia

## Sharyn Wobur

### Introduction

This is an attempt to examine the status of women in the ministry within the Church of Melanesia. I will seek to establish the equality of women and men in the ministry of the church. I will be dealing specifically with the case of women in the ordained ministry since that is one of the major issues in the church today. I will also indicate the church's main approach to this topic. The purpose is to address some of the concerns about the topic and to contribute to what is a big and sometimes tough debate today.

To examine the status of women in the church and their gifts and faculties we must recognise women's unlimited potential in life as children of God. Both men and women have been redeemed by Jesus Christ and restored to God as a partner and friend. This has implications for the various issues and arguments.

In this presentation there are seven sections. First there is a section on women in the church followed by a section on the initiatives that women contribute in the work of the church; thirdly some negative views on the ordination of women; the next section discusses cultural perspectives with ideas on helping people prepare themselves for the ordination of women; the next session deals with biblical approaches and then a section on biblical perspectives, then finally my own point of view with a conclusion.

### Women in church

In the present situation women are in the church as helpers; they take part in various church activities, they are involved in choir, in reading the lessons, being preachers of the Word and a range of other things.

In addition to this they have set up women's organisations like the Mother's Union which is a world-wide organisation; some are in religious communities based on the Benedictine rule of life meaning there are vows to take while in the service of these religious orders. These vows are strict and kept in a way similar to someone who makes a commitment to the Lord and has surrendered their life to the Lord in helping others.

Women were limited in their roles in the earliest history of the germinating church. Women were not permitted to give any public leadership or taking part in anything like speaking in church. This led to some attitudes which really restricted women and tried to keep women in their particular status, and not to be transformed.

Most women today have learnt to recognise and to affirm their equality with men, the dignity of their personhood, and their own divine purpose in God's redemptive plan. In our own church (The Church of Melanesia) we realise that the church is made up of both men and women. In our cultures women have their own identities, even in the nation, and socially in the church as a whole. In this way, women make a significant contribution to the completeness of the society and of the church. Ministry then means community because it is made up of both genders, who believe in the one body which is the church where Jesus Christ is the head.

## Some initiatives that women take that contribute to the work of the church

The working together of men and women in the church with equal participation is in fact a strength rather than a weakness.[1] 'The reality here is that God has given gifts to both men and woman regardless of gender'.[2] Therefore men in the church have no right to place themselves above women in any way at all. Some men have the false belief that they are wiser, more intelligent, and are socially and spiritually superior to women. This is not true. Men should be ready to accept this fact since today women do everything that men can do. In what ways will men take the initiative to be different?

Someone may say, 'I like women being ministers in church because they are caring people. They can care for the work of the church better than men do, and they are also good at speaking and organising'.[3] This may not always be true but often it is. Men are hard at times, and cannot easily understand a woman's problem; because his wife does understand and is a gentle and welcoming lady, a woman will go to share her problems with the wife. The problems of a woman are normally best addressed by a woman rather than a man.

Consider also how the lives of people in need are mended. It is normally through the work of women. Despite these things, men argue strongly against the issue about women being ministers in the church. They seem to be addicted to their opinions on this issue; they close their ears to these kinds of statements.

---

1.   Gender Equality, Seminar by URE Stanley Lecturer at Talua Ministry Training Centre Vanuatu 2002.

2.   *Ibid.*

3.   Option from Fr Benjamin G Diocese of Bank/Torres Vanuatu 2002.

Some women hold positions in churches as church leaders and take part in most activities of the church. Why are women allowed to participate in some aspects of the life of the church while other practices are strictly forbidden to them? Why not even consider the possibility that women may participate in these forbidden activities as well, and that they have the potential to do them well?

Giving dynamic leadership, women have initiated women's organisations and run women's programs and conventions; they have taken the role of preacher, evangelist, church builder, conductor, community promoter, home builder, school and health organizer. They have been given the rights to dedicate their national women's headquarters, building and teaching centres. These activities and roles are a mixture of church and government; some are both at the one time (eg work in schools) because some organisations are run by the church for the government or with government support.

The women have done these things in such a way that most women are now encouraged to work in employment rather than being house mothers. Most churches even now are recognizing how important it is for women to contribute as helpers and leaders in most church organisations.

In the church the main work of women has been to do things like sweep the church, arrange the flowers, teach Sunday school and join in the youth groups. In the Church of Melanesia there are other things that women are required to do. All these contribute to the growth of the church. These contributions that women make show their faith and love towards God the Father and the church (Luke 12:8).

Here is a particular minister's argument giving his view about women being ministers in church: Practically it is not a man's job to prepare food for the family but it is a woman's job. In the same way women must not be ordained because it is men who are ordained to do certain rituals within the church, in particular the holy eucharist.

In addition to this point, he added another: the example of courage set by the women in searching for Jesus after his death makes me feel that women can be ordained since at the same time, the men who followed Jesus in his ministry were behind locked doors (John 20:19).

A further view came from another church leader saying we should encourage women being church ministers since 'Ordination reflects not only theology but also our culture'.[4] It is wise to encourage women to be ordained rather than just giving women limited areas of service in Christian

---

4.   Church of Melanesia Newsletter, Sis Ellison Pogo Archbishop: Issue No 5 December 2002.

churches; to limit them is to limit the ways in which they can express their faith and love for Christ (Rom 8:28–29):

> And we know that in all things God works for the good of those who love him, who have been called according to his purpose. For those God foreknew he also predestined to be confirmed to the likeness of his son that he might be the first-born of many brothers.

There is a collect which a priest says before offering the gifts to God and giving thanks; it is like a confession prayer. He prays to God for forgiveness and for God to look mercifully on his iniquities. God's power and love for us in our iniquities is great. If we believe God removes and forgives our iniquities then why should we still have doubts here; both men and women are equal in being forgiven? What is the difference at this point? There is nothing beyond God's reach. Our understanding is limited by what is familiar rather than looking at this matter in a more relevant way (Rom 8:30–31):

> And those he predestined, he also called, and those he called he also justified, those he justified, he also glorified . . . what then shall we say in response to this? If God is for us, who can be against us.

## Some negative views about women being ordained?

'In the evangelical church in Melanesia, the view is that women are to be dominated and inferior and must sub-ordinate themselves to males'.[5] In the home, church, education and media, women are treated as inferior. Only men are engaged in theological studies; women are forbidden to do theological studies. Men are often said to have a divine call from God to the ministry, but the women do not.

It is my view that in fact women also have a divine call from God to do ministerial work and it is a role to help men too. Talking about the Church of Melanesia, we still maintain this hierarchical and male-dominated system in the church. Women can hold 'lower' positions, ministerial posts but it will take time for women to participate in the liturgical practices such as baptism, marriage and other sacramental acts within the church.

---

5. Seminar on Gender Equality by Lecturer Fr Ure Stanley at Talua Ministry Training Centre Vanuatu 2002.

Another man has said regarding the above statement: 'women can't do sacramental work because women are sinners'. He continued on to say that it was the woman who ate the fruit from the forbidden tree and that is the origin of sin on earth, and it has been passed onto all mankind. Because of this she is unworthy and it is not right for her to perform liturgical activity in the church. This is nonsense; in relation to the event when the first male and female were created, no one is righteous in God's sight.

Here is another person's view: 'Gender equality today makes a lot of mess in our community and societies. Now we have in our society women dressing as men, which really goes against custom. Then for a woman to become a minister, how much more will that cause arguments?'

Another person argued that gender equality is a western idea and doesn't belong to our culture. So the idea for a woman to be an ordained minister has originated from western people. The people of Melanesia have their own context and it is foolish for us to adopt western ways. Within Melanesia, men and women have their responsibilities and roles to play, and they are not the same.

Most people argue strongly that in Old Testament times, there is no record at all or any text which indicates that women were made priests. 'Who was ordained into ministerial service?' people ask. The argument here too, which is in line with this thinking, goes: God gave men and women different abilities to become who they are. Women are really below men. God is wise and he knows there would be many consequences and many obstacles that women would encounter in the ministry. Everyone is called to belong to God but in different ways (Rom 1:6). God will reward each of us according to what we have done.

The other problem facing women in ministry is within the Anglican church, and specifically within Melanesia. The Holy Eucharist is to be regularly done every Sunday within the year, and also on holy days or saint's days during the week. This holy sacrament is the most important and highly respected. There are some who argue very strongly asking what will happen if a woman is a priest and becomes pregnant—she will not be able to perform the tasks of ministry.

Most people discuss this very important issue and point out clearly that our Melanesian people are not yet prepared for women to become priests. For a woman to be ordained, this will involve a lot of issues, and a lot of consequences would follow from this. There must be very good grounds which are really needed before going ahead.

The idea here is that we should take a closer look at the context of Melanesia itself and not be influenced by the modern world. Most people who go along with this idea might have some option somewhere at the back of their mind. If that is the case, what are some ideas to help our Melanesian

31

people to be prepared to accept the ordination of women? What are some programmes, or some useful means to help equip our people to be prepared for this issue, or to help them be more aware.

## Some cultural views

There are some people who argue strongly against Melanesian women being ordained. They argue against others who support the ordination of women, and they do so on the grounds of their culture. 'The issue of women's ordination is currently a controversial one for some people in the Melanesia context'.[6]

Many people say our culture doesn't allow at all for the leadership of women. In keeping with the place of women in our cultures, women should not be ordained.

This is not a good argument; most cultures today are being transformed since we are living in a changing society. Take for instance our way of dressing: if we do not want to accept the current way of dressing, maybe we should wear custom dress—that is to be bare or to have grass skirts. In Bislama we called this 'dressing Nambas' or 'Kabilato'.

My point is this: there are some customs and traditions which we really are to value and keep. But there are some which are transitory and we should do away with them.

If people say we should stick to our traditional culture, then that is nonsense since much of our traditional culture is not kept anymore. For example, in our culture, women who are bleeding or who are menstruating are not able to take part in preparing meals, but this has changed since we have been baptised.

## Biblical approaches

'The church should take a leading role to show the world that men and women are equal and truly can work together to complement each other in terms of shared responsibilities'.[7]

Women in the early Christian communities shared with men a vision of the kingdom of God. Active in ministry, women exercised significant leadership. Anyone who trusts in Christ will never be put to shame. There were missionaries and apostles, church leaders and leaders of houses. This

---

6.   Church of Melanesia Newsletter, Archbishop Sir Ellison Pogo, Issue No 5 December 2002.

7.   Seminar on Gender equality by Fr URE Stanley lecturer at Talua Ministry Training Centre Vanuatu 2002.

shows that the kingdom of heaven is the kingdom of equality, free from all forms of discrimination and oppression (Rom 10:11).

But God's plan for every person is that Christ came to enable each person to attain life to the full—men and women alike. 'Christ through his saving attitude, encouraged women to move from the side to the centre, despite the social, cultural and religious restrictions of our societies.[8]

Men at times have thought to themselves that only they, and not women, have a divine call from God, to do ordained ministry. However, men have forgotten that it was women to whom Jesus appeared first after his resurrection, and it was the men who crucified Christ, who betrayed Christ and killed him. Despite this, men have argued strongly that women should never be involved in liturgical leadership although the gospel clearly demonstrates that women form part of the community of the kingdom which Jesus established (1 Tim 3:2).

True success and true happiness begin by discovering the way to God. Women were created in God's image, to be man's friend and partner in life (Genesis 2:6). God never planned for women to be alienated from men. When Adam and Eve sinned in the Garden of Eden, the sentence of death came on them both because God had said they shall die. The bible says that our iniquities have separated us from each other and from God; our sins have hidden his face from us. Yet 'God loved the world so much that he gave his only son, that whoever believes in him, shall not perish but have everlasting life' (John 3:16). That is why Jesus said, 'I am the way, the truth and the life' (John 14:6). He came to remove all our sins and to endure the punishment for us, so we all could stand before God, justified and restored to him as though no sin has ever been committed. Christ's blood has been honoured before God as a proof that the penalty of death has been paid not by us but by our substitute Jesus Christ (1 Pet 2:24).

There is nothing in Christ's ministry or in the Bible to indicate any difference in value or status or activity or effectiveness of one gender over the other. Christ places no more limits on the ministry of women who follow him than he does on that of men who follow him. Women around the world are becoming aware of their freedom in the body of Christ and to the equality in God's redemptive plan for all human persons. The ministry of Christ is an encouragement and enlightenment for women in any culture, any race, and any nation. For we are all Christ's body in the world sharing in God's service. We are his hands and feet, his mind, his heart to love, his mouth to proclaim his holy message. If we are shy to be Christ's proclaimers of his good news, he too will be ashamed to declare our names at the last day.

---

8.    *Ibid.*

We cannot continue to avoid this issue since women do almost all the same work as a man. People try and put a limit on women about performing the sacraments but that is not valid. If we come out strongly saying that our culture says this or that, in reality we have to admit that in many ways we are not people who hold on tightly to our culture.

Our traditional cultures are disappearing from our sight as the society around us is changing with the influences of science and technology in the part of the world we live in. Slowly but surely our cultures are fading away and we are adopting many changes. But all the changes blindfold us because of the experience and exciting ideas around us. Pressure is on us to grasp all these new ideas and as we look into it we turn to adopt the ideas little by little. Yet we still want to say that we belong to our traditional culture.

## Biblical perspectives

Genesis 1:28 states explicitly that God created women and men as unique persons, unique in themselves and in relation to one another, equal in dignity and co-responsible for the earth. This uniqueness and dignity of each person comes from being made in the image and likeness of God.

In Luke 11 there is a story about a crippled women. This story firmly points out that Jesus Christ, the fulfilment of all the prophets in the past, was concerned for women; he had compassion for women. Let women then assist in doing God's service.

In 2 Cor 2:14 Paul writes: 'But thanks be to God for, in union with Christ we are always led by God as prisoners in Christ's victory processions.' God uses us to make the knowledge about Christ spread everywhere like a sweet fragrance. This should cheer the hearts and uplift the lives of women who have a desire to serve God.

When living our lives in God's service, it is essential that we must be committed, giving up all for the sake of God. 'Offer yourselves as a living sacrifice to God, dedicated to his service and pleasing to him. Do not confirm yourselves to the standards of this world but let God transform you inwardly by a complete change of your mind then you will be able to know the will of God' (Romans 12:1–2). This is both for men and for women, since we are all called by God and are God's predestined children.

Since the salvation which has been offered to all is full and free, there is complete grace to all who believe in the risen Lord Jesus. Therefore men must not boast against God's will and women should let God's perfect will be fulfilled in their lives. How great are God's riches? How deep are his wisdom and knowledge? Who can explain his decisions? Who can understand his ways? For all things were created by him and all things exist through him and for him. To God be glory forever Amen. For who is able to give him advice? Who has given him anything he could pay back? For we are many parts of the one body of Jesus Christ (Romans 11:33–36).

It is time for Christian women to question the unreasonable traditions which contradict redemptive principles and which oppose those who believe in redemption through the blood of Christ. Jesus' stories and teachings are not only for men but women as well. In Luke 8:42–48 we read how much Jesus felt for women equally to men. The gospel of Luke recorded this because of the importance of noting that Jesus' attitude towards men and women was always to treat them as people.

Other miracles of Jesus were also performed both to men and woman. Luke's gospel is unique in the sense that it records what Jesus did to women more than the other gospels, perhaps because the author was a doctor who had concern for both men and women. Luke records the stories of women who were in relationship to Jesus, so men today must see that women are to be treated as important. Jesus never makes the male appear wise or good over against the female appearing sinful or foolish. If there are foolish women in the story, they are balanced by others who are wise (see for example, Matthew 25:1–13).

There are many stories about women and their involvement with Jesus which Luke has recorded. For example, in Luke 10:38–42, there is the story of Mary and Martha. Jesus says wonderful things to Mary for choosing what was better. She was listening to Jesus rather than being busy doing house work. Well what is our response to this? Men should understand for themselves the importance of women in leadership.

Women are able to work assisting men in the church. According to 1 Corinthians 15:58 we are to keep busy always in our work for the Lord, since we know that nothing we do in the Lord's service is ever useless. This issue never concerns one's gender or one's race. Jesus Christ and his ministry are totally relevant to women today.

## My personal view

What we should bear in mind and remember is that we are not competing in doing God's work but showing how God's work has good quality in it. However, what happens is that men underestimate women in most of their decision-making and in leadership roles. One interesting thing to consider is that: 'We have two distinct genders, male and female, but in every man there is a female side and in every woman there is male side. Neither gender is complete in any way without the other.'[9]

---

9.    Archbishop Sir Ellison Pogo, Church of Melanesia Newsletter, Issue No 5 December 2002.

Two matters raised strongly in opposing women's ordination are pregnancy and menstruation. Regarding these two points, 1 have already touched on them above. On menstruation, it is very important to bear in mind that is natural; it is God's gift in the lives of women and is special. We cannot ask God to prevent this?

In relation to all the above arguments, if the reality is that God the Father gave gifts to both men and women regardless of gender, then I see no reason why women should not be fully admitted into the ordained ministry of the church. The greatness of a person's power is the measure of their surrender. It is not a question of what you are or who you are, but whether God controls you.

Genesis 1 states very simply: 'Then God said, "Let us make man in our own image, after our likeness and let them have dominion over all the earth . . . " So God created man in his own image, in the image of God he created him, male and female he created them . . . and God saw everything that he had made, and behold, it was very good' (Genesis 1:26–31). The first 'man' carried the sense of 'mankind'; in Hebrew, mankind was created in duality, male and female and together they constitute mankind and together reflect the image of God and together exercise dominion over the earth.[10]

According to Genesis 2–3, woman was created from man's rib to be his helper. It is noted that first she was created after the man in time, secondly she was taken from him, thirdly she was named by him and fourthly she was created as his helper. However there is no explicit statement on sub-ordination in this passage.[11]

Some people argue very strongly that is a western idea for a woman to be ordained. Whether this is true or not, Melanesian society today is already influenced in many ways by western values. What is important is whether these influences are good or bad. We don't have to copy western society but we can do things in our own way. We shouldn't simply reject things because they are western. Some people stress very strongly that gender equality is creating many problems in our society, but disagree with this opinion. What we should bear in mind is that the chief aim of human life is to glorify God. Therefore we should not prevent women from being ministers of God's work. It is God's service in leading people to God, not for us to boast about it.

It is raised by some people that there is no record at all of a woman who has been ordained as a priest. However, there is no record too of saying that only men are worthy and pure enough to be ordained. In relation to this argument God gave ability to both men and women.

---

10.   Edited by Shirley Lees, *The Role of Women,* Great Britain 1984, 73.
11.   Edited by Shirley Less, *The Role of Women*, Great Britain 1984, 74.

The idea of women being ordained is not to put women above men, and men must not have the negative view that women who are ordained are above them. The idea here is to share in God's ministry, but the value of men being the head is always there since men are the head and women are to be always below men. Women are men's helpers; really they are men's right hand, meaning partners, not only in parental roles or partnership in marriage but in God' service.

## Conclusion

The journey of the ordination of women is like going through a long tiring adventure. The issue here is not that women are fighting for gender equality. If Christian teaching says that men are the head of women, then women are to keep that teaching. If it is recorded in the Holy Scripture that husbands are head in a home, then so it should be. Despite this, the reality in relation to serving God is that women can do what men do.

It is important to have a goal in mind, accepting the fact there will setbacks and obstacles, but if we continue to visualise the goal and walk towards it, then one day we will achieve it. The goal here is the ordination of women as priests, but it will only take place after a lot of discussion, the sharing of insights and the contributing of different views. This is all necessary.

As Christians we cannot speak about the goodness of God and continue to live in an 'unbalanced' condition. Therefore for Christians the matter of women in the ministry or having an equal status in the church shouldn't be a questionable issue. Christian faith is rooted in Christ Jesus who brings new life, new possibility and hope to all people in helpless situations.

In supporting women in ministry, it does not mean that we neglect responsibilities in the home. Christian responsibilities cannot be fulfilled if the basic duties at home are not attended to. Our Christian witness to God must begin at home. It is important as we pray for good health and safety to take action to tidy up our home. It must be a balance in the mind of Christians to see both the importance of women in the home and the importance of women in the ministry.

# Cultural Barriers and Women's Ministry in the Presbyterian Church of Vanuatu

## Mary Luan

### Introduction

It was at Bethany that Jesus warned Martha of so heavily committing herself to her domestic roles that she did not bother attending to the ministry of the Word. In praising Mary who had chosen the right thing, Jesus was affirming that attending to some form of Word ministry was significant. Thus just by being present and listening to the word of Jesus was a primal role. 'Mary has chosen the right thing which will not be taken away from her' (Luke 10:38f).

This is a symbolic truth for women and mothers in Vanuatu today. Many are so tied down to domestic roles at home that they have overlooked their primal role in Christian life which is to give their time to the Lord in utilizing their gifts of ministry in the service and the extension of God's kingdom.

Although women's participation in leadership capacities and other ministries is recognised and supported by the Presbyterian Church of Vanuatu, there are existing social and cultural barriers hindering women from exercising their gifts of ministry to their full potential. This is the core issue which this paper intends to address.

Furthermore, in no way does this paper attempt to promote the contemporary feminist independent approach, which consequently destabilizes the traditional and cultural values of family and community life in our day and age. Nevertheless, it seeks to consider and suggest ways in which existing barriers affecting women could be dealt with, and that women can be encouraged to respond effectively to their call to discharge their ministerial gifts in order to serve Christ.

### Biblical basis of women in ministry

*The place of women in ancient Rome*
In ancient Rome a woman was regarded merely as a piece of property, completely under the control of the husband. However, the wife was not kept in hiding; rather she shared her husband's life.[1] Nevertheless, her freedom was to some extent restrained. Thus, in 331 BC Roman rule made a

---

1. Charles, CR, *The Role of Women in the Church* (Chicago: Moody Press, 1958), 5

provision that every father and husband possessed legal rights over their wives.[2] This legal provision was abused in that husbands took advantage of their legal rights and ill-treated their wives. Consequently there was a mass poisoning of husbands in the same year (331 BC).

However, in 215 BC the Roman Empire went through a financial crisis. As a result, another law was issued that 'no woman should be allowed to posses a half ounce of gold, wear a part-coloured garment or ride in a chariot within the city of Rome'.[3] This consequently led to the increase of immorality as women sought to escape from the control of their husbands. Divorce became a common thing.[4] Seneca, in AD 54, described the situation in this way: 'Women leave home in order to marry, and marry in order to divorce'.[5] As a result of increased immorality and degradation the law was rectified during the reign of Emperor Marcus Aurelius, elevating the position of women and allowing them freedom to participate publicly in religious duties. This situation assisted the growth and spread of Christianity because women now participated more freely in religious activities.[6]

*The place of women in Judaism*

It generally seems that the position of women in Judaism from the biblical account is contradictory. On the one hand, women are regarded as inferior and secondary beings like the gentiles. This idea is clearly expressed in the daily prayers of male Jews, which states: 'Blessed art thou, O Lord our God, King of Universe, who has not made me a woman'.[7] In addition, there are related passages such as Leviticus 12, which shows the distinction and inferiority of a female at the time of birth: 'A woman who gives birth to a son will be unclean for seven days . . . if she gives birth to a daughter she will remain unclean for two weeks' (Leviticus 12:1ff).

Furthermore young girls were educated separately from boys and the rabbis would not give the same amount of work and instruction to girls as they did to the boys. The girls were strictly forbidden from being taught legal studies because the rabbis thought that women were not intellectually capable of pursuing such studies.[8] This cultural demarcation determined the role of a Jewish woman in public life. She was regarded as inferior and her

---

2.  *Ibid*, 5.
3.  *Ibid*, 6.
4.  *Ibid*.
5.  *Ibid*.
6.  *Ibid*, 7.
7.  sThe Autorized Daily Prayer book in *ibid*, 8.
8.  *Ibid*, 9.

role in the religious realm was of passiveness and submission to male leadership.

On the other hand, the Old Testament contains certain passages which speak positively and elevate women in the service of God's people. For instance, Proverbs 31:10, 25–28 speaks of the wife of noble character as 'worth far more than rubies. She speaks with wisdom and has faithful instruction on her tongue' (Vs 26).

In addition, there are other biblical accounts where women effectively engage in the leadership positions within the religious and political life of Israel as a nation. Hannah and Peninah who attended the gathering at Shiloh every year were examples of women participating in public prayer.[9] Miriam who was the sister of Moses and Aaron assisted her brothers in the leadership role as a prophetess.[10] Deborah was a prophetess as well as a judge.[11] From these few examples we are reminded that despite the inferior standing of women in the cultural ethos of Jewish society, they were still part of a 'covenant community'[12] and on that basis they had the privilege of participating in some of the religious activities.

*Place of women in the New Testament*
In the New Testament, most of the disciples and members of the crowds who followed Jesus were of the Jewish male-oriented cultural background. John gives us several accounts of women breaking the racial and gender barriers in order to communicate with and serve Christ (John 21:1–8, John 4:1ff, 12:1–8) which simply affirmed that there were existing cultural barriers in Jesus' time which hindered women from directly and openly relating to him. The way in which the Syro-Phoenician woman in Mark 7:24–30 related to Jesus and how Jesus responded to her is a clear example of the cultural separation that existed between male and female as stated earlier.[13] She attempted to break that cultural barrier because of her personal concern over her sick daughter. Verse 27 says: 'Let the children eat first, for it is not right to give the children's food to the dogs,' an indirect challenge made on the basis of Jewish male-female cultural separation. It was like saying to the woman 'you are like an animal and you do not deserve to be attended to properly'. Jesus' approach here reflects the Jewish attitudes towards women and gentiles. The woman, however, did not retreat in silence at this confrontation but had the courage to accept the challenge

---

9. 1 Samuel 11:ff, 2:19ff
10. Exodus 15:20; Numbers 12:2; Micah 6:4
11. Judges 4:4
12. Being members of the Covenant community
13. Stated in Section 3

and the insult that was put on her by that culture, and persisted until Jesus attended to her need.

On the other hand we observe that women were warmly accepted as followers of Jesus. They travelled with Jesus, learned from him as did other male disciples and they supported Jesus.[14] The teachings of Jesus were inclusive in the sense that they included the experiences which were feminine-related, such as wedding feasts, child birth, sewing and grinding corn. On one occasion Jesus used feminine imagery to speak of God.[15]

In response to Jesus' acceptance, women became some of his devoted followers. They demonstrated courage to be present with him during his persecution, trial and crucifixion.[16] Women were the first to arrive at the empty tomb after his resurrection.[17] Furthermore, Mary Magdalene who was considered a prostitute by some, was probably the first one in the Gospel to treat Jesus with respect and love.[18] In the epistles of the New Testament, we are also exposed to passages regarding women who played key roles in the spread of Christianity, such as Priscilla the wife of Aquila who opened her home to be used for worship (Acts 18, Romans 16:3, 1 Corinthians 16:9, 2 Timothy 4:19)

So far we have explored the biblical accounts of the basis of women's ministry in the service of God, both in the Old and the New Testament. We have discovered that it would be biblically inaccurate to make the point that women would not or should not be involved in the ministry of the Church, because there were great and godly women in the past who have been involved in the ministry of serving the people of God.

However, it is also clear that there have been cultural barriers of separation between men and woman, Jews and gentiles, slaves, and free, which to a certain degree have degraded women and affected them so that they may not be able to be confident in fulfilling their potential.

## Barriers affecting women in the Presbyterian Church of Vanuatu

*The place of men and women in Vanuatu society*
Vanuatu traditional society is similar to Jewish society in terms of having a male-oriented culture. Women seem to be located at the bottom of the religious and social structure, whereas men are always placed at the top. For example, in most island cultures in Vanuatu, a man is appointed as the chief of the tribe and community at large (although there are few exceptions to

---

14. Mark 15:40–41, Luke 8:1–3
15. Luke 15:8–10
16. Mark 15:40–41
17. Matthew 28; Mark 16:1–2; Luke 24:1–12; John 20:1–9
18. Luke 7:36–50

this). The male figure is regarded as important, superior, as the boss and decision-maker. The female figure, on the other hand, is regarded as less important and inferior, whose only roles is to listen and comply with male directives and dictations in all aspects of life.[19]

*The role of men and women in Vanuatu society*
This cultural mentality subsequently demarcates the role of men and women in Vanuatu traditional society, which simply means that there are only certain roles in which the women are culturally permitted to engage, and in particular domestic roles. On the other hand, men are expected to carry out heavy public responsibilities.

Women begin to exercise their domestic (so-called female) function[20] within the family household at a very early stage in their life. In most island cultures young females who have reached the age of four years are expected to learn from the mother their roles as a female, and they are even advised to behave in a 'female manner'. That means not to take the lead in any household affairs ahead of their brothers.[21] The 'female manner' in culture means to listen, to be quiet and to obey the male figure.[22] Women are placed in secondary positions in all aspects of human life, ranging from the kitchen to schools, community and even in the church.

This belief has permeated practically the entire social and religious ethos of traditional society. This has affected women's participation in the church in the sense that any aspect of church ministry is considered as a public ministry and women are not culturally permitted publicly to teach or advise, but are required to listen and obey. This does not mean that women were not allowed to teach or instruct in the private environment. Mothers were and are great teachers in their homes as they instruct their children with the help of the father in their up-bringing.

*The impact of cultural mentality in the church*
This type of cultural mentality outlined above permeates the islands of Oceania, in that women are not permitted to participate in certain forms of church ministry, in particular in the ministry of ordained leadership. In 1990, Roina from Western Samoa became the first woman to gain entry to

---

19. Interview with Pastor Johnny Naual, Talua Ministry Training Centre 23/06/2000
20. The domestic function in this context referred to what is known as the female roles, understood in Vanuatu as 'wok blong woman'.
21. Interview with Ps Simbolo Sanaku, Wala 2002
22. Interview with Ps Johnny Naual, Talua Ministry Training Centre, 12 June 2001

theological education and as women were not permitted to train as candidates for official ministry, Roina's journey was not an easy one. Tessa described Roina's admission to the college as a struggle in this way:

> The struggle against the traditional way of thinking has had a wide front. She (Roina) has met opposition from the church, from other women and from the students with whom she has studied. 'I don't blame them all', says Roina, 'after all, I had the same understanding: It's not a woman's world'.[23]

Young women in Vanuatu have been raised in a cultural environment which has shaped and moulded them to see their place and role as secondary in all aspects of traditional society. Therefore, when a village community turned to Christianity, the women automatically saw their role in the church as secondary. They were not to take leadership roles; they were to be silent and obedient to the elders who were men; they were to submit to male leadership, even if there were decisions made which directly or indirectly offended the prerogatives of women.

Culturally, when young girls become teenagers they begin to assume the role of adolescence and motherhood in terms of domestic responsibility, such as a pig-raising, poultry-farming, cultivation of land, planting and weaving; this was their designated role in the society.

However, this traditional mentality has been changing over the years. Women have been encouraged and given the freedom to administer their gifts as servants of God in specific church ministries, to which they feel they have been called.

### The constitutional basis for women's ministry in the Presbyterian Church

Although, there is no specific theological provision or statement of belief which affirms women's participation in the ministry of the Church, the Presbyterian Church of Vanuatu believes that the Scripture declares the covenant made between God and his people. As people of the covenant community, regardless of race and gender, it is a rightful duty for each person to show humble accountability in service to God.

Hence, on such grounds, it is provided for in the constitution of the Presbyterian Church under the title 'Servants in the church' that 'all

---

23.  Tessa, *M Roina pioneers theological education,* Journal of Theology, Series II No:4 SPATS, Suva, Fiji: 1990

believers' (regardless of gender) are servants, and that the Church has a primal role in nurturing and encouraging its members to discover, explore and utilise their gifts of ministry in the service and extension of God's kingdom. When Christ ascended on high he bestowed gifts of ministry to all his people, which included women.[24] God, therefore, also equips women with gifts of ministry, and they should be allowed opportunity to discharge them.

Thus, on the basis of this provision, the first female Pastor[25] in the Presbyterian Church of Vanuatu was trained, graduated and was ordained in 1994. According to ministerial records there are three female pastors currently in the field[26] and over six official female candidates currently studying for Pastoral Ministry at the Talua Ministry Training Centre.

## Core issues and existing barriers

Although the traditional mentality of inferiority and superiority between women and men in Vanuatu has gradually changed over the years, and women have advanced to leadership positions in the church, there still exists a stigma of female inferiority between husbands and wives, in community relationships, in church relationships and in society at large. This has made it difficult for women to participate fully in the ministry of the church today.

Within different contextual settings in Vanuatu contemporary society, the nature of these core issues and the existing barriers to women's ministry varies. Hence, I have attempted below to present two case-studies on certain issues affecting women's ministry, which I believe portrays the whole picture of barriers hindering women's ministry in the Church today.

*Case study one: Women in cultural society*
Lyn is from Benaur village in the North West of Santo. She is a well-educated lady whose educational background reaches secondary level. She is a talented young lady who has the qualities of leadership and could contribute to the leadership and development of the Women Missionary Union. Due to Lyn's educational background, the women in the Parish trusted her to be a good leader. Therefore she was appointed to the position of secretary of the Women's Missionary Union (PWMU) in her parish. Lyn was faithful in discharging her given roles.

However her husband Alfos was not very supportive. When she came home late from a meeting, he often quarrelled with her. He raised all sorts of

---

24. Ephesians 4:12ff
25. Pastor Mary Ioulou Hapina, wife of Robsin Hapina of Futuna Island.
26. Interview with Ps Fiama Rakau, PCV Clerk, Vila, 2002

complaints that his wife was concentrating too much on the work of the church and not carrying out her domestic roles at home sufficiently, such as weaving, cleaning the house, gardening, feeding the pigs and chickens and getting food from the garden. Once, during a PWMU meeting,[27] correspondence was received from Alfos, addressed to the President and Secretary. The content of the letter read:

> Lyn is my wife, and you must understand that I bought her
> at my own expense (bride price). She is my property, and I
> own her. The PWMU did not spend any money on Lyn's
> bride price. Therefore, 1 am advising you to make sure that
> Lyn comes home before five o'clock (5pm) this afternoon.

However, the meeting went on until 5.30pm I felt that it was my role as the Pastor's wife to accompany Lyn to her home in order to offer some explanation on her behalf to Alfos; not only that, but I thought I would have the opportunity to attend pastorally to their marital conflict. I discovered from my visitation that the heart of the matter was the lack of trust between the couple. Alfos did not trust his wife to be away from him for even two days. He had a jealous attitude towards his wife.

Despite my pastoral attendance to the couple, Alfos decided to punish his wife for coming home late from the meeting. He made Lyn follow him to their garden. She was then given a knife and forced to clear the bush for a new garden by herself. Alfos then stood by and watched her do the work by herself. Lyn was pregnant at the time.

At the following meeting of the PWMU, Lyn submitted her letter of resignation. In the letter she stated that she loved her Lord and wished to be given the opportunity to serve her Lord happily. However, due to her husband's cruel attitude towards her, she felt that if she attempted to continue ignoring and resisting his inane directives, she ran the risk of either losing her life or being divorced by her husband.

In the relationship between Lyn and Alfos, it was obvious that there was no trust. And most importantly, Alfos was not a committed Christian; therefore, he was not able to see the importance of supporting and encouraging his wife to fully exercise her potential in leading the women in that given ministry. Here we see an example of barriers to women's ministry today, which can emerge within marital and home relationships between husbands and wives.

---

27. This meeting of the PWMU was held at Valbay Village within the bounds of Nogugu session, which 1 attended.

*Case study two: the experience of the first female pastor*

Pastor Mary Hapina, known by her maiden name as Mary Iou Iou, originally from the island of Tanna, is the first female Pastor of the Presbyterian Church of Vanuatu. Upon graduating from Talua in 1994 she was appointed by the Ministry and Missionary Committee to the Southern Islands Presbytery. She was then ordained to the ministry of word and sacrament and inducted into a parish.[28] In the three parishes where she served, she encountered several demeaning experiences.

In her second parish, during a session meeting, differences occurred among the members regarding a motion, which was resolved at the ruling of the Moderator. For a woman to give a ruling which the men are to consent to is not accepted in Tannese traditional culture. Hence, in this situation those who challenged the Moderator were not looking at the roles and status of the Moderator as a person of authority who has the right to rule. On the contrary, they were looking at the status of the Moderator as a female, whose cultural prerogative was not to rule but to listen and obey. Thus, the Moderator was challenged in the Moderator's seat with the following remarks: 'Mifala ino wantem woman i lidim mifala. Woman ino mas lidim mifala' (that is: 'We don't want a woman leading us. Women cannot be our leaders.').[29]

## Identifying the barriers in the case studies

The demeaning and degrading experience described in the two case studies above indicates that, although the Presbyterian Church of Vanuatu encourages women for Pastoral ministry and other church leadership ministries, there is still a great need to educate the members of the church to gain respect. Acceptance and recognition for women in ministry is a major issue.

*Lack of trust and commitment*

There is lack of trust between husbands and wives. Husbands and wives do not show Christian maturity in their Christian life, in the sense that they are still gripped with the attitude of jealousy. There have been cases in which tension has arisen in major church meetings and functions between husbands and wives due to mistrust. This is an indication that Christian couples and Christian leaders in the Presbyterian Church need to reconsider their relationship, with God and in their commitment to each other.

---

28. During the period of this interview, Ps Hapina has already served as a Pastor in three different parishes.
29. Interview with Ps Mary Hapina, Isangel, Tanna: 12 February 2002

*Planning for understanding and communication*

There is lack of planning, communication breakdown and misunderstanding between men and women. Conflicts arise when there is no mutual agreement and understanding between husbands and wives.

In the first case study, it was very clear that there was not mutual agreement and understanding between Lyn and Alfos about what each one was going to do that day. This is typical of Vanuatu traditional culture, in which men and woman live in an easy-going life style. This life-style means that there is no need for planning a day's work. Another day will bring along its own agenda. Hence planning is not considered essential.

*Taking advantage of traditional values*

In the first case study the following statement 'Lyn is my wife, and you must know that l bought her at my own expense. She is my property and l own her . . .' indicates that there are traditional values such as the bride price which could be used by some Christians and even church leaders as a means of controlling and discouraging women in the ministry. The idea of ownership within this context often results in disrespect. Punishment takes the form of violence, control, dominance and manipulation. Within this line of thought the man often considers that he has the right to stop the woman from serving the Lord. He forgets that he will have to give an account to the Lord for his actions.

*Accepting the gospel from a traditional perspective*

In case study two, the demeaning expression of rejecting a woman's leadership ('we do not want a woman to lead us . . .') indicates that there is a danger of our cultural appointment system of leadership being imposed onto the vocation system of the church. For example, in culture, a leader is appointed by the elderly people through a form of heredity, gender or hierarchical system, whereas in the ministry of the church people sense a 'call' to serve in leadership positions; some of these could be young people, disabled people or women. Many women today in Melanesian societies, especially in Vanuatu, have sensed the call and are taking up new positions in different areas within the church. Many believe and are convinced that this is where God wants them to serve. Therefore Christians in the Presbyterian Church of Vanuatu should be warned not to read the traditional cultural mentality and philosophy into the theology of the church so as to jeopardize the participation of women in Christ's service.

The statistical records from the PWMU Head Office in Port Vila confirm that there are one hundred and eight (108) female ruling elders and three female pastors serving in the Presbyterian Church of Vanuatu.[30] How should the church help these women who have sensed the call to serve God in a leadership capacity in the ministry of the church, to develop their leadership potential and discharge their gifts without interference?

## Possible ways of removing the barriers

The previous sections of this paper have discussed various barriers which hinder women from ministering in the church. I will suggest possible ways to resolve the grave situation that women are trapped in with their ministerial pursuits. I will also propose the application of love in Paul's letter to the Christians in 1 Corinthians 13 as a solution to these barriers. I believe this passage is foundational and could assist in strengthening Christian couples, communities and society at large to gain a deeper respect for each other, and assist each other to serve Christ in the ministry, while fully and devotedly fulfilling the purposes of their vocation.

### The place of love in gifts of ministry 1 Corinthians 13:4)

The passage in Corinthians 13 is placed between chapters 12 and 14. In 1 Corinthians 12 Paul describes spiritual gifts, offices & responsibilities, the Body of Christ and the place of the gifts and offices in the Body. In verses 4 & 6, Paul begins by laying a foundation that the spiritual gifts have their source and creation from the spirit of God. Paul continues to reinforce the source of the gifts in verses 7–11, by stating repeatedly the words, 'by that one spirit . . . '[31] Paul continues his teaching by using the analogy of the body to speak of the church. In his analogy Paul clearly states that no one part of the body is dispensable: 'The eye cannot say to the hand, "I do not need you!" And the head cannot say to the feet "I don't need you!"'(1 Cor 12:21)

Paul is clearly stating that each function and gift within the church is necessary; one with gift of tongues cannot say to one with the gift of prophecy, 'I do not need you!' Just as the body depends on all its parts acting appropriately and according to the person's will, so too the church of Jesus Christ requires all the gifts to be utilized appropriately and according to his will. The conclusion of this argument is in verses 27–30 where Paul states that the offices or ministries established by the spirit of God each have their place and are all required to function with each other in cooperation and unity. In 1 Corinthians 14, the apostle Paul addresses the issues of

---

30. Interview with Deacon Ennie Kellen, Port Vila: 14 March 2002
31. 1 Corinthians 12:8, 9 & 11, The NIV Study Bible (Grand Rapids: Zondervan Publishing Company, 1995).

speaking in tongues and prophecy; he contrasts them, compares them and affirms the necessity of both gifts. Paul defines the basis for the manifestation of the gifts to be the edification of the body. In verse 4 of chapter 14, the role of edification is identified as follows: 'He who speaks in a tongue edifies himself, but he who prophesies edifies the church'.[32]

By using the word 'edifies' after the verb 'speaks', Paul is making edification the foundation of prophesying and speaking in tongues. Again in verse 5, in order to reaffirm the goal of edification he finishes the verse with the words: '. . . so that the church may be edified'. Further on, Paul addresses the issues of what appropriate and orderly operation of the gifts in the church entails. Within the teaching on the importance of the gifts in building and edifying the church and their operation in entirety and unity, Paul addresses the driving force which he says is 'love'. He speaks of love in critical terms and with the highest accolades, stating:

'And now three things remain: faith, hope and love; but the greatest of these is love' (13:13).

Paul here contrasts love with the spiritual gifts and ministries he has listed as being most necessary of all for the edification of the body. To prove that love is essential, Paul introduces his chapter on love with the words, 'And now I will show you the most excellent way' (12:31). He follows up this introduction to love by stating that without love, all gifts are just empty words and the people who exercise them are nothing and gain nothing; that acting in love is more important than the gifts and their exercise of them. He states that edification of the body is the reason for exercising the gifts and having them given to the church, and then states that without love these gifts and their exercise mean nothing. Paul is making love the essential element of any ministry and the absolutely necessary ingredient for edifying the body. This is seen in the following verses: ' . . . but have not love, I am only a resounding gong or a clanging cymbal' . . . '. . . but have not love I am nothing,' and '. . . but have not love I gain nothing' (13:1–4)

Love therefore is the only basis for any ministry, no matter which office of the church, which part of the body, or which gender it is that exercises the ministerial gifts.

*Appropriating the principles of love in the church's ministry*
To apply the principles of love in the context of husbands and wives, or men and women serving together as partners or a team, Paul clearly spells out the following characteristics to create a healthy working relationship.

---

32. 1 Corinthians 14:4, The NIV Study Bible (Grand Rapids: Zondervan Publishing Company, 1995).

(a) Love yields patience

Patience is defined as being calm and persevering[33] in times of anxiety and trouble. Due to our human nature, we complain and blame each other when we are confronted with a crisis. For husbands and wives to be effective partners in Christ's mission, they ought to learn to be patient and know when and how to approach or respond to each other so as to continue building and cheering up each other in the faith. The psalmist in his prayer for God's deliverance in time of trouble asked God to grant him patience.[34]

(b) Love yields kindness

Kindness is more than just being good or polite. It is a demonstration of love which accommodates the attitude of considering others better than yourself. The opposite of kindness is cruelty. Cruelty is a behaviour which creates a condition of pain, distress, worry and suffering.[35] There are many Christian sisters in the Presbyterian Church of Vanuatu, some of whom are wives of church leaders, who live in a family environment of pain, distress and worry because their husbands do not treat them kindly, especially when they attend women's meetings and arrive home late. Some wives are even bashed for attending church functions and for not cooking for their husbands. Paul stated: 'Husbands love your wives, just as Christ loved the Church and gave his life for it.'[36] If there is kindness in the home between husband and wife, the wife will be active and fulfil her role in the church effectively.

(c) Love yields generosity and humility

Humility and generosity are Christian principles and we are encouraged to imitate Christ's humility and generosity. In Philippians 2:5ff Christ is our model of humility in that for our sake he laid aside his divine attributes and assumed our human limitation, that through him we might be saved from death. Jesus was concerned about us. Therefore we are encouraged to consider others better than ourselves and look not only to our own interest but also to the interests of others. Many times in marriage relationships husbands seem to be blind and stubborn towards their wives' interests particularly in terms of church ministry. A sister once came to me and said

> My husband is a kind guy, and he supports our kids very
> well. There are many times we discussed how we should

---

33. David, B, editor, Macquerie Pocket Dictionary (Sydney: Griffith Press Pty Ltd, 1998), 768
34. Psalm 27:14
35. David, editor, Pocket Dictionary
36. Ephesians 5:25

live our life together in the coming years but I have never
heard him ask what my ministerial gifts are and what my
areas of interest are in the church.

It is disappointing to observe that some Christian husbands are ready to attack their wives for coming home late from church meetings and functions but are not ready to encourage and build them up in their service for the Lord.

(d) Love yields mutual submission

Paul stated that love is not self-seeking. In other words he was saying that there is need for mutual submission. Husbands exist for their wives and wives exist for their husbands. Many marriages are broken in our day and age because one spouse does not understand the interests of the others and when expectations are not met, tensions creep in and eventually destroy the relationship. In Ephesians[37] Paul mentions that husbands and wives are bound in mutual submission. 'Submit yourselves to one another in the fear of the Lord'. In the case study two above, we discovered that the members of the session were not humble enough to submit to the moderator-ship of a woman. It is a great lesson and a challenge to those who are in a leadership position as a pastor, chief, or a teacher to learn to submit to the ruling of a woman pastor or teacher.

(e) Love yields forgiveness

It is interesting to discover that 'love does not keep records of wrong' (1 Cor 13:6). I remember a young pastor who had just got married and after his graduation he was appointed with his young wife to a new parish. Before they went to that parish the wife learned that her husband's former girlfriend lived in the parish. The wife of the pastor then refused to go to that parish and the pastor withdrew from the appointment. In many relationships the good things done are forgotten easily, but failures and wrongs are remembered. This is an issue which is also affecting the marital relationship of church leaders and other Christian couples. Whenever there is tension people accuse each other of what they did in the past. Paul is reminding us again that if there is true love, the 'records of wrongs' each of us possess should cease to exist.

(f) Love yields truth

It was identified in the first case study that there was lack of trust between Mr and Mrs Alfos. The bible clearly states that where love is operative there

---

37.  Ephesians 5:21–23

is trust. Where there is absence of true love there is no trust. Christian couples therefore should be truthful and committed to each other. They need to be faithful to each other and develop confidence in themselves. This will assist them to be free from guilt, and jealousy. Many women (as well as men) do not attend meetings and church functions nowadays without their spouses because of lack of trust. It is important for Christian couples to pray for their growing confidence in each other.

In his final words, Paul states that love always protects, trusts, is hopeful, perseveres and never fails (1 Cor 13:7). Husbands and wives are to protect each other from sickness, hunger and poverty. Husbands must protect their wives and rule over them with love, dignity and respect. Christian wives are to protect their husbands by zipping their mouths from matters which could directly or indirectly jeopardize their self-image and relationship. Christian couples in their work as partners in the Lord's service must continue to trust in God in all they do. Jesus said, 'without me you can do nothing' (John 15:5).

**Conclusion**

In the service you are rendering for the Lord, set your hopes in God. The writer of Hebrews expressed this concept of hopefulness in these encouraging words:

> Since we are surrounded by such a great cloud of witnesses, let us throw off everything that hinders and let us run with perseverance the race marked out for us. Let us fix our eyes on Jesus, the author and perfector of our faith, who for the joy set before him endured the cross, scorning its shame and sat down at the right hand of the throne of God. (Hebrews 12:1–2).

It is encouraging to note from this text that we are not alone in our struggle to serve Christ and walk in his ways. To you my sisters in the Lord who are still under some form of cultural and social control, you are not alone in your struggle. You are surrounded by a great cloud of witnesses; therefore endure everything that hinders you from participating fully in the ministry that God has called you to. Run with perseverance and live up to the standard of your calling in Christ. Fix your eyes on Jesus, for his love will never fail you.

# Bibliography

Charles, CR. *The Role of Women in the Church* (Chicago: Moody Press, 1958).

Dowle, A and Goodwin John NS, editors, *Concise Dictionary of the Bible* (London: Luther worth Press, 1996).

Kathrine, M. *Women as Leaders: Accepting the Challenge of Scripture* (Monrovia, California: Marc, 1973).

Malin, I. *Christian Marriage and Family Life* (Wewak PNG: Christian Books Inc, 1987).

Osborn, WD. *Women Without Limit* (Tulsa: CSFO Publishers, 1973).

Tessa M. 'Struggle with Tradition', in *Journal of Theology* series II No 4, Suva, 1990.

# Interviews

Elder Aiong Iatonga Ifira 2002.

Joseph Wial Village, Malekula 2002.

Kaiar David Lawa village, Malekula 2002.

Pastor Johnny Naual Talua Ministry Training Centre, Santo 2001.

Pastor Fiama Rakau PCV Clerk, Port Vila, 2002.

Pastor Simbolo Sanakau Wala, Malekula 2002.

Pastor Selerick Michel Port Vila, 2002.

Deaconess Eni Kelen Port Vila, 2002.

# Part Two


# Other Issues Of Gospel And Culture

# Part Two

# Other Issues Of Gospel And Culture

# Marriage in Toga Island

## Winston Elton

### General comments

This paper attempts to explore the traditional ways and values associated with our cultural celebration of marriage, with special attention given to the people of the Torres region of Vanuatu. It is a call to the churches, especially to the Church of Melanesia to rediscover the traditional values of celebrating marriage in our culture.

The overall emphasis of the paper is that it recommends the recognition, especially by the Church of Melanesia, of our traditional values and customary practices. The church can continue to witness faithfully within the context of the traditional values of her own members. The paper also suggests that shared team ministry involving all believers should be encouraged in the church if she is to be effective in her mission in the world.

### What is marriage

Marriage was instituted by God and not by man. It was instituted by God at the very beginning at the creation of the first man and woman. A marriage is the act of uniting two people, or the ceremony at which this is done. It involves a decision made by two people, a man and a woman, to come together in union. Marriage and the customs associated with it differ in every culture. Differences occur in both the practices and the motives. It is said that in general there are three different types of marriage structure, known by their technical terms as polygamy (that is several wives to one man), monogamy (one man to one woman), and polyandry (that is several husbands to one woman).

All three of these are called marriage. When people have decided to live together and through certain public ceremonies are united (whether in traditional custom, in the church or in a civil ceremony) we call it marriage.

### Introduction

In traditional culture, in the time of our ancestors, the marriage ceremony was a very important ceremony which involved not only the couple but the whole village community. The people were born and raised within a culture and traditional environment where community life was central to the culture and steered by it. I feel compelled because I have discovered that as days go by and the generations multiply in number our cultural life is being changed through the impact of different cultures and the people are being led away from their own cultural context.

It is my understanding that God has created human beings and has blessed them with their cultural settings; there is a way of life which God has blessed and which people are called to live in order to please God. This way of life includes the cultural context of people. The marriage ceremony of our church teaches us that

> Marriage is an honourable state of life instituted by God Himself from the very beginning. It signifies to us the spiritual union between Christ and his church and the unending love of God for his people. It is therefore not to be entered upon lightly but with careful thought and with reverence for God, considering the purposes for which it was instituted.

We are told that marriage was instituted so that those who are given the gift of marriage might live a holy life; it was instituted for the proper expression of natural desires and affections which God had given us; it was instituted so that men and women might join together in life-long union, to give themselves to each other in body, mind and spirit and to grow in mutual love and knowledge of one another to the glory of God; it was instituted so that those who are given the gift of children might bring them up to know, love and fear the Lord to the praise of his holy name.

Therefore from the very beginning marriage was instituted by God, and with that understanding, people from the past, especially our ancestors, had the view that the marriage ceremonies were very important in the life of the community. Marriage was celebrated in a proper and orderly way, suitable to the traditional context, and this was followed by tribes, lines and the related clans as the way marriage should be celebrated.

Marriage can be discussed and explained in a variety of ways within the context of our many different cultures in Vanuatu. This paper will cover only three different kinds of marriage in Vanuatu today, as follows: Custom Marriage, Civil Marriage and Christian Marriage. These have become the main practices in our culture and we have used them whenever there has been a marriage ceremony among our people.

## The cultural perspectives on marriage

In traditional culture, marriage was an honourable state of life where the peace and joy of life was experienced and shown. Every marriage that was celebrated had to be marked by certain traditional ceremonies, and there was a proper process for marriage whether the marriage was by arrangement or by the couple's own choice.

The cultural perspective on marriage was laid down at the beginning in the context of each island community. This means that even before people were born, there was already a traditional settling for marriage that had been laid out. People were born into already established tribes and lines and clans, and they were brought up in the understanding of how marriage should be carried out. If the people in the community followed closely the traditional cultural pattern and perspectives of marriage, then this ensured the good development of the people and a good environment for the community; their well-being was sustained and they continued to live happily together in a peaceful and joyful environment. Therefore when we explore the cultural perspective on marriage we see that marriage was not only a matter of personal choice, but it was a setting for a proper and orderly pattern of community life, it was the foundation upon which the good development of the people was laid, and through it the people experienced joy and peace. So the cultural perspective on marriage was that in the very beginning, God created the first human beings, male and female; he blessed them with their cultures and when he instituted marriage, it was within their traditional cultural context and their ways of life.

## The modern perspectives on marriage

Through migration, people moving from one place to another, the world is changing and now there are changes taking place to the cultures of the islands in Vanuatu and to the life-styles of the people. Many people today are entering married life simply as a way of fulfilling their own personal interests. The fulfilling of love is becoming the fulfilling of lovers' own interests. Many marriages have become a matter of personal choice, and people choose partners for themselves whether on a traditional basis or not.

In this new context, natural sexual attraction plays a significant role in the expression of love. People are making their own choice of a future partner from any sect, any race, any religious group, from different cultures and different backgrounds. The result is that when there is love between two people, male and female, then they get legal papers for a civil marriage or they seek a pastor or priest to bless their living together, even when according to their culture, the marriage is forbidden or not appropriate. The couple simply do what they want to do. When there is agreement between them, they arrange certain ceremonies to make their living together legal. This is exactly what is happening today. However these modern practices and modern perspectives contradict the traditional cultural perspective on marriage.

**Arranged marriage**

Since the introduction of Christianity, polygamous marriage has been abandoned, leaving only monogamy as the form of marriage. Among the people of my island of Toga in the Torres, the monogamous form of marriage was practiced in the past. A man was only allowed to have one wife and a woman was only allowed to have only one husband. However today there are three forms of marriage ceremony: custom, church and government; all are connected with each other in the celebration of marriage. The people of Toga in the Torres are now following the teachings of the church and also observing their own cultural customs.

At this point, I want to consider the concept of arranged marriage in our traditional culture on Toga Island. However I do not intend to look at 'Legia Urve' (as such marriage is called in my language) in a destructive way, suggesting that everything belonging to our tradition was demonic and all must be put away. Rather I want to looked at the situation as it was and consider the elements which may be good or not so good. The things that are good may be adopted and the things which enslave people may be rejected.

'Legia urur', in which most marriage partners are chosen by the parents, was the common practice in Toga in the past and remains the main practice also today. However today, the practice is declining as young people prefer to choose their partners for themselves. Some people refer to this recent practice as 'Own Choice' while others call it 'Love marriage'.

'Legia urur' actually means more than arranged marriage. Legia Urur has a beginning, a middle and an end. It has its beginning through dialogue between the father of the boy and the father of the girl, or between the families related to the two parties. Once the agreements are made in this first encounter, other things then progress through various stages to the climax of marriage.

*The process of arranged marriage*

a) There are some specific processes involved in arranging a traditional marriage. In our culture, we have two 'lines' within which the arrangements for marriage must take place. The first line is called 'natumor' and the other is called 'negemelset'. Whenever the arrangements of marriage were made, it had to be across the two different lines and not on the same line. To explain, it means that if the boy is on the line naturmor then the girl must be on the line negemelset, and vice versa. There were also particular restrictions which were applied to the lines of the mother and the father which were laid down at the very beginning and were not to be contradicted. For example, a father cannot marry a daughter and a son cannot marry his mother or aunt. The genealogy of everyone was observed closely and the traditional guidelines were there for everyone to follow.

b) The arrangements for marriage were normally made when the boy and the girl were only babies, and so when they grew up the parents of both families let the children know about the arrangements. Having due respect for their parents, the two children accepted the decisions made for them. As part of the arrangement, sometimes there was an exchange of gifts between the families, and the boy may be required to do something to support the girl's parents for example, cutting firewood, fishing, gardening. In doing these things there is mutual benefit and support for the couple and for their parents. The parents who made the arrangements join in the celebration of the marriage with their children together with the whole village community.

c) An alternative way of arranging the marriage took place in the later years of the life of the boy and the girl. The girls were kept under the care of their mothers at home, during the period from their teenage years to the age of early twenties. While the girl was at home, she learned weaving, how to prepare food and various other skills taught to her by her mother and by the older women of the community in preparation for the time when she moved away from her parents' home into the marriage home.

d) The same thing happened to the boys. They were kept in the village nakamal during the same years in order to receive certain teachings. They learned carving, gardening, how to hunt and various other custom activities; they were taught by their uncles and other older men in the community. In doing so, they became fully prepared to be independent and responsible when they married.

e) During the period when the boys were being kept in the nakamal and the girls were being kept with their mothers at home, the parents made the arrangement about which boy should marry their daughter or which girl should marry their son. Normally, the parents of the boy negotiated with the parents of the girl. Once the agreements were made, there would be a custom marriage ceremony to celebrate the union of the boy and the girl.

f) Marriages were arranged through these procedures explained above. It was important that the plans be based on the cultural practices with the couple coming from the two lines mentioned at the beginning of this section. The parents of the couple were glad to celebrate the marriage and the whole community rejoiced together in the celebrations. The traditional procedures guaranteed the involvement of a large community of people, and when the arrangements were accepted by the couple, it laid the foundation for a happy life together, not only for the couple but for the wider community.

## The positive effects of arranged marriages

There were some obvious positive effects of an arranged marriage. There was continuation and strengthening of relationships, maintaining of rights to land, to properties, fruit trees, beach or reef, and also the use of family names. The couple received help and support from their families and offered help and support to the relatives. The couple's home was open to their families and friends, and to the wider community, all of whom happily celebrated the marriage of the couple.

The very positive experience of the marriage celebration which marks the climax of the arranged plans is something which is remembered and passed on to later generations. The community itself is enriched by the event. Once married, the couple will now contribute to the community and participate in its activities, gatherings and events, which is part of their obligation as a married couple.

Traditional cultural weddings are a good example of the way the whole community celebrates and comes together. There is cooperation and involvement by the whole community in the various aspects such as feasting, dancing and gift-giving. The whole event links up the past to the present, and the present to the future. The children who will be born into the family will benefit from the context into which they are born and what has been provided for them. In arranged marriages the community sees a meaning beyond what marriage means merely to the man and the woman. Arranged marriage has a significance for the life of the whole community as well as for the couple involved, and it is a contributing factor to the stability and growth of the marriage and the community.

Therefore arranged marriage that is accepted by the boy and the girl as planned by their parents has some clear and important positive aspects.

## The negative effects of arranged marriages

Apart from the positive sides of arranged marriage described above, there are some negative sides also. These are apparent especially when the intention of an arranged marriage is not followed properly. For example, an arranged marriage requires the acceptance of both the boy and the girl and this may not happen; this can cause problems. Further problems can occur when parents have made arrangements, but later the girl is 'stolen' by somebody else. This may happen if everyone is not aware of the arrangements because they were not told, or if people were trying to make their own choices. When this happens, the situation creates tensions and problems in the community.

Sometimes a couple are forced to marry even if they do not accept each other. Their rights as people are not respected. This means that their marriage is missing an important unifying factor. Their unwillingness to live together brings about quarrelling, rebellion, wife beating and unhappy homes. Even if children are born into the family, the wife will be left alone to care for the children while the father does whatever pleases him. Arranged marriages, when the intended processes do not work, can bring about conflict and fighting between individuals, families and even villages.

Another problem associated with arranged marriages today occurs when a couple begin to live together without any ceremony to mark their marriage, even though they have already arranged with their parents to marry. In this case they will be guilty of the practice of fornication.

With the changing of cultures and the influence of education in today's world, the structure of arranged marriages has brought about other problems such as the increasing incidence of 'bush marriages' where a couple live together 'in the bush', that is by their own choice and without the proper cultural ceremonies. One of the consequences is that today there are many children born outside of marriage.

These are some of the weaknesses or problems associated with arranged marriages. However these are not present in my island now but they may be in the near future. It is better for us to acknowledge these weaknesses and problems which sometimes enslave people, before they happen so that we can think about what is the best way ahead in the future and what practices we need to adopt for the good of the people.

**Own choice marriage**

'Own choice' literally means to do what you like. Many young people today follow this practice of 'own choice' marriage; they do what they like in choosing their own partners.

Own choice is not something new; it was also practiced in the past alongside the practice of arranged marriage. But in traditional culture our ancestors practiced own choice within the limitation of following the two family lines which I have mentioned in the beginning, 'natumur' and 'negemelset'. In other words, the person who chose his wife or her husband followed the processes of the cultural system. This also meant they did not marry within the very close family such as a brother marrying a sister, but for example, a boy could choose as his partner his uncle's daughter. In this way, own choice was also practiced in the past and is still continuing today.

However own choice is becoming the accepted practice among all young people and it does not follow cultural processes. There are many factors that lead people to the practice own choice. In fact it is not possible to enumerate all of them because they are almost as many as the persons who choose. Also the weight given to these factors may change according to the characteristics and personality of different people. Both cultural environment and physical aspects play significant roles in the practice of own choice. In particular cases there may be one factor or a combination of factors which contribute to the decisions which are made.

In general, there are three factors which have led to the increase of own choice marriages and to the decline of arranged marriages among young people in the Torres islands. These may or may not apply to other islands in Vanuatu, depending on whether arranged marriage is required or freedom is given to young people to choose for themselves.

The first of these factors is that the practice of arranged marriages tended to be applied as an oppressive law. From the point of view of parents who arrange marriages for their children, there is flexibility and choice, but the children must fulfil their parents' demands when they are old enough to get married. From this point of view, for children who are subject to the arrangements, the marriage may seem to be forced on them and it may no longer be something which brings happiness. In response to this, young people seek freedom from traditional processes which seem to them to enslave and force them.

The second factor is island isolation. In the past young people lived within their own communities and did not travel to other islands. Today there are means by which it is easy to travel from one island to another. There are opportunities for people to undertake education beyond their own culture and environment. Young people from different cultures and different backgrounds come together especially in the urban areas. This gives a chance for young people to select their friends and companions for themselves, irrespective of religion, race or cultural background. This then leads to marriages between different people. At present, however this is not true in my island of Toga, but it does apply to almost the whole of Vanuatu. Today an Anglican can marry a Presbyterian, or a ni-Vanuatu can marry an Australian or a French person, whereas in the past, it was not possible. The movement of people and education gives rise to the growth of own choice marriages.

The third factor is the concept of 'I love you'. This is the most highly acclaimed motive for own choice marriages. One person may say, 'We are in love with each other so we must marry; I love her and she loves me and we cannot be separate from each other'. These are the sort of statements made by lovers. However the word 'love' has a much deeper meaning and definition in the teaching of the bible, far beyond the ordinary use of this word in the personal relationship between a boy and a girl. For them, the word is used to express merely warm feelings for one another.

There are many reasons for the attraction of boys and girls to each other. The facial appearance of people, the way they dress, the way they perform in the field of sports, arts, music, and education all play a part. For example a good educational qualification helps to get a good job, and this leads to better living conditions. Apart from the above reasons, there are some people who claim to make their choices through prayer. And of course the natural sexual attraction plays a significant role in expressions of love.

These are some of the influences involved in the concept of 'I love you' which gives rise to own choice marriage. These are natural human elements or forces that are part of every human being.

The traditional practice of arranged marriage means that people are restricted to marrying one person. Those who are under arranged plans and who are in love with somebody else do not welcome the arrangement and are likely to keep to their own choice rather than to the arranged plans. As a result, there are problems between parents and young people over their differences of opinion about arranged marriage and own choice marriage. There are no easy answers to the problem; it requires dialogue between parents and young people so that the young people can understand the factors involved in their parents' preference to have an arranged marriage; on the other hand parents need also to understand the factors that motivate young people to choose their own partners.

*The positive effects of own choice marriages*
The choice of a suitable partner is not an oppressive law but it offers the freedom to respond to oneself in search of the other. There are some people who wish to marry and there are those who wish not to marry. It is a decision which every mature person has to make. The persons who decide to marry do so in freedom and face the task of finding a suitable partner. A good deal of careful thought is given and considerable anxiety may be created because upon this choice much of the future happiness of a person depends.

The relationship between a boy and a girl initiated through love brings a uniting factor into the marriage. A boy and a girl who love one another do in some way communicate with each other. The relationship of the two makes them want to meet and talk with each other, to give gifts to each other and to borrow each other's belongings, and they may send letter to each other when they are apart.

There are many who speak about their loved one or the one they have chosen when the love between them is strong. A young man once said about his girlfriend, 'Even a high barbed wire fence and my girlfriend's dog could not keep me away from her.' However the love which a boy and girl have for each other can give rise to this sort of statement. When people are in love, they have a feeling of adventure and risk about their life together.

As the boy and the girl relate together in their love, they develop a better understanding of each other's personalities and expectations. A close understanding of each other is very important because they need to consider their love for each other, and whether it is right to get married or not. Marrying in a hurry is a big risk, a game of chance. It is gambling with the happiness not only for the two concerned but also for children yet to be born. A couple are likely to see each other in proper perspective only over a period of time.

It is good for young people to choose for themselves because they will do so when they think the time is right. They take responsibility for establishing the relationship by any means suitable, normally either by letter writing or through a friend who acts as a messenger. They can seek the advice of parents and friends or pray about it. In doing so they discover and develop for themselves their own standards and ethics. They are responsible for their own actions, either to suffer the consequences or to benefit from them. They cannot blame their parents or become irresponsible about the relationship as sometimes happens in an arranged marriage. In an arrange marriage some couples blame their parents for their own actions; this is a way of avoiding responsibility. In a situation of own choice relationships, learning about limitations and making mistakes are part of the reality of the world people live in, so to have he experience of this and to face the consequences of this is a healthy way to develop a person's character and patience.

One of the other positive aspects to own choice is that it establishes dialogue and communication before marriage. Through their communication a couple reveal their expectations about their future life as husband and wife in the area of sexuality and family planning and about their home and occupation. Through communication they become aware of each other's expectations and establish a means to use to solve conflicts in married life. In other words, they are able to talk to each other well and prepare well before marrying.

Young people may be distressed and unhappy when they face certain situations. If they are free to choose their own partners, they will act without pressure, and develop values and principles upon which their philosophy of life will be based. They will seek to have the same fundamental attitude and outlook as their partner.

Today young people are fortunate to be able to read and write. They have access to books that give instructions and information on relationship matters. There are also opportunities for attending seminars and workshops to support and to guide them, to make things better or to explain why they are not. Unhappily, it does not always work out that way; people are inclined to create more problems without finding suitable solutions for themselves.

*The negative effects of own choice marriages*

The negative sides of own choice marriages come about when choices are made but the right processes are not followed or people do not marry along the right tribal lines. The boy who is on the line Natumor will choose a partner who is on the same tribal, or the girl on the line negemelset will sometimes choose her partner on the same line.

When such choices for a partner are made then there may or may not be a proper celebration of marriage. If there is not, then it may creates shame and disrespect for the lines which they belong to. The community will not want to celebrate the wedding together with the couple but will create problems for them. If a celebration is held in these circumstances, it will be a most unhappy celebration and the whole community will be involved in the tensions and problems about the marriage. There will be destroying of properties such as gardens, plantations of coconut, cocoa, fruit trees, and any property of the couple who wish to marry.

In the case of a marriage between people of the same tribal line (a forbidden marriage), there would need to be a custom peace ceremony of reconciliation of the families and lines and the couple will be required to distribute mats, pigs, yams and poison arrows to show that there is a maintaining of custom laws. The custom ceremony in response to the breaking of tribal lines and the opposing of the traditional cultural practices must take place before the marriage that was forbidden by custom occurs.

The breaking of the cultural system in this way by own choice marriage will also mean that the children of the marriage lose the right to land and any other custom right.

One of the other effects of own choice marriage is that children are often born outside of marriage. This happens particularly when the couple are aware that their parents want to arrange their marriages. In this case there are no arrangements for marriage and the couple just live together, that is they create a 'bush marriage', outside both Christian and custom marriage. The couple also lose the support of their community.

In today's world of education and change, there has a mixing of people from different cultures and races and lifestyles, and in this context, own choice marriage has brought about various personal and social problem. There is a big role for parents and young people to think about the changes and the motives of own choice marriage. It requires a dialogue between older and younger people to sort out the best way for the future.

**Traditional ceremonies of marriage**

The traditional ceremonies of marriage are the custom ceremonies practiced in the past. These ceremonies had an important place in the life of the people of Toga Island in the Torres and involved the whole community including men, women, and children, and the couple and also the chief and custom leaders who were appointed to conduct the marriage ceremonies. In traditional cultures from the time of our ancestors until now the marriage ceremony has been a big and important ceremony respected by all the people.

The custom ceremony of marriage could take place only when all the arrangements had been made according to the traditional laws and practices of the people. Before the marriage ceremony could take place, the right decision about who was to be married had to be made by the respective families. The process of marriage was followed either by arrangement or by choice, depending on the situation. Either way, the marriage must follow the lines and clans and must not be forbidden by the traditional laws. When all the arrangements were made then there followed a ceremony which marked the coming together and the living together of the husband and wife.

Of course, before the actual marriage ceremony took place, there were various activities involved in the preparation, for example the cutting of firewood, the collecting of items of food, pigs, yams, kava plant and mats. When the things required for the celebration were ready, and everything was well organised, then the preparation of the food took place. At the time of the ceremony, the couple were placed at the front in order to witness the ceremony. The paramount chief stood in front of the gathered community and the families. The families exchanged their gifts such as mats, pigs, kava, yams, and other custom items to show their appreciation of the marriage. There was no specific bride price, only the exchanging of gifts between the two parties. The gifts were arranged in rows and also announced by the chief who conducted the marriage ceremony. The family of the girl gave the girl to the family of the boy, and the boy took her as his wife in marriage. The ceremony of giving and exchanging was done in order to show that the couple were joined together in marriage; it was done publicly for the whole congregation to witness. During the ceremony the chief who conducted the marriage gave his speech and also the families of the couples offered their final speeches to the couple who were now independent. After the feasting and the speeches, there were custom dances involving the couple with the whole community. At the end of the celebration the man took the wife to his house and they lived together.

**The practice of marriage today**

Today there are various practices of marriage among the people of Vanuatu. Many people prefer to choose for themselves what kind of marriage they want, whether by own choice or by arrangement made by their parents.

Since the introduction of education many people have become well educated and the practice of marriage has become diverse. People who move away from their own communities are exposed to many different views on the way of marriage and also develop many different views of what marriage should be.

In the normal practice today, people refer to three kinds of marriage: Cultural Marriage, Civil Marriage, Christian Marriage. These are the main practices celebrated today. I want to consider each of them.

## 1. The cultural marriage

Today the traditional marriage ceremony is not practiced as it was in earlier days; there have been many changes. The place of traditional marriage was strong in our culture but the impact of the missionaries and of modern education has given rise to various changes.

There has been a loss of the values associated with marriage even though the missionaries allowed some of the early traditions to continue as well as introducing some things that they thought were important. These changes meant that the people began to lose their own traditional cultural way of life. As a result, today many young people getting married make their choices about how their marriage should be in ways which oppose their tradition.

The traditional cultural ways of celebrating marriage involved a respect for and obedience to the community's way of doing things. Things were done peacefully, cooperatively, smoothly, joyfully, and easily, without complaining, and everyone was happy when participating in or contributing to the various activities and responsibilities in the celebrating of marriage.

## 2. Civil marriage

For the purpose of his own glory and for the good public life and order, God who is the world's supreme Lord and King, has ordained civil authorities who are answerable to him to rule over his people. To accomplish his aims, God has armed them with his power of the sword to defend and encourage those who are good and to punish the evil-doers. It is lawful for Christians to accept and carry out the duties of public office when called to do so. In carrying such a task, they ought to uphold justice and peace in accordance with the laws of the government they serve. Civil authorities are not permitted to administer the word and sacraments, or interfere with the spiritual life of the church, yet they have authority and it is their duty to see that unity and peace are preserved in the church, that the truth of God is kept pure and complete, that all blasphemies and heresies are suppressed, that all corruption and abuses in worship are prevented or reformed and all the ordinances of God are duly administered and observed.

In regard to these civil authorities, the government does have legal papers authorising civil marriages for a couple, with the choice of the two witnesses to sign. The papers for civil marriage are used in order to help keep order in the society and stability in living conditions. Special attention is given when children are born outside marriage in regard to meeting the child maintenance responsibilities and in the use of family names in registration. This applies especially to people who live in urban areas. Today the cost of living is getting higher and there is the possibility of a couple living together without a ceremony of marriage. People who live in towns especially are involved in this practice.

The signing of civil marriage papers encourages people to acknowledge that their marriage is real and that they have a responsibility to each other in the way they live. Civil marriage is often used for people who are involved in own choice marriage or are from different religious or different cultural backgrounds. Today the practice of civil marriage has also spread widely to rural areas. It requires three months and three weeks notice in public places before the marriage ceremony takes place; this is actually a legal requirement for civil, custom and Christian marriage.

## 3. Christian marriage

The most common marriage practice today is Christian marriage. Christianity is widely spread and the knowledge of marriage with its biblical teachings are known to everyone, and Christians know what Christian marriage means. Marriage is between one man and one woman. It is not lawful for any man to have more than one wife or for any woman to have more than one husband at the same time. God ordained marriage for the mutual help for husband and wife, for the lawful increase of humankind, to provide the church with children and for the prevention of moral impurity such as adultery and fornication.

Christians teach that the couple being married ought not to be within those degrees of blood relationship or kinship forbidden by the Word of God; there are particular Christian values which are important for how marriage should be celebrated. Christian marriage demands a lot of dialogue between couples and parents, and also the support and help of the community in doing things, especially when there is no priest or pastor available to conduct the marriage ceremony.

The negative feature of the Christian marriage is the financial cost. There is too much money involved not only in the purchase of food but in other requirements needed in the ceremony. Many costs are involved such as obtaining enough pigs for the celebration. These are part of the overall ceremony widely practiced among Christians.

## Biblical teachings

In Genesis 1:28 we see that God blesses man and woman and commands them to be fruitful and have many children, not simply for the purpose of having children, but also to preserve history and sustain culture and everything in it. God gives marriage as a gift for everyone.

However the bible does not indicate which man should be married to which woman. God invited us to trust him and to share all our decisions with him. The bible is the Word of God and offers guidelines for men and women to think about their appropriate marriage partners. In the bible there are various examples of how marriage may take place. In Genesis 24:1ff we are told how God helps the servant of Abraham to arrange the marriage of Isaac. In this chapter we see an example of how true love many grow for a couple in an arranged marriage. In the case also for Jacob we see how Jacob with his father arranged the marriage with the daughter of an uncle. There is nothing in the bible to suggest that an arranged marriage is wrong. Also, it is not wrong for a boy to marry a girl from different backgrounds, even if this may require some difficult adjustments to be made. God is the God of every culture (Ps 22:27ff). We are not told that one tribe or group has the right to choose partners, but also the traditional practice of choosing marriage partners is not wrong. In Christian understanding, a man and woman are able to find their own way to be married depending upon their own context.

When we look more deeply into the bible and its teaching, we find that there are certain things which are not permitted, for example, polygamy where one man is married to more than one woman. In Christian marriage, one man and one woman unite and the two become one. In Proverbs 5:15, men are instructed to be faithful to their wives and to display their love for them in every way.

## Future directions

As church leaders we have special responsibilities and must consider how we live our married life. Marriage is a precious gift from God but unfortunately in Vanuatu today marriage is taken up for selfish reasons ( for example to gain wealth, to gain authority or reputation or for sexual satisfaction). In marriage we expected to build up relationships with each other through love and respect. The church today is committed to dealing with and getting rid of the problems and bad practices that spoil marriage (for example adultery, and fornication).

Divorce is also a problem today. The separation of a man and woman creates hardships in many homes. Prostitution is another problem. The church opposes the practice of prostitution where people sell their bodies for money. This is a rapidly increasing problem. We are commanded not to associate with prostitutes.

However there are several other issues that the church will need to face in the future in order to build up marriage and create a good environment for children to grow up. We must strongly discourage the practice of bush marriages. We should do this by running bible studies with young people to educate them about the meaning of marriage. There is a need for church leaders to help people to explore appropriate cultural ways of life, and perhaps preserve or reintroduce some of the traditional customs. If people ask the questions, 'Why should the church preserve traditional customs?', it is because some of the great values of our custom are related to the biblical teachings. In the life of the church, we have to consider both 'gospel' and 'culture' together.

## Conclusion

With this topic, we have explored many things about marriage, and there are many other things which people will have observed as well. The traditional culture continues to be the very foundation of the life of our people in the Torres. Man-Torres was born inside this cultural way of life, and everyone who loses his or her cultural heritage risks the loss of their birth rights. Today, there are many forces that challenges and change the values of our culture in Vanuatu, including Christianity, migration, and education. In the face of all these changes, Man-Torres, and Man-Vanuatu must stand firmly on their own traditions. God has made all people and has been kind to all. As part of this kindness he has created us within our own cultures. God blesses is with our cultures so that we might have life and preserve our birth rights. Culture is the life-blood of Man-Vanuatu.

## Bibliography

Fountain, O & J, *et al. Marriage is for Life* (Wewak Papua New Guinea: Christian Books Melanesia Inc. 1993).

Mason, PJ. *Pastoral and Occasional Services* (Honiara: Provincial Press 1996).

Prior, R. *Gospel and Culture in Vanuatu 2: Contemporary Local Perspectives* (Melbourne: Gospel Vanuatu Books 2001).

Rakau, F. *Christian Marriage Makes a Difference: An Exploration of Custom, Civil and Christian Marriage in Futuna,* Paper October 1982.

# The Importance of Youth Ministry

## Edward Meswia

### Introduction

Today in Vanuatu the development of young people is very highly regarded by people in our communities. As the population of young people is growing very fast there are also problems which are arising, especially in our two towns, Port Vila and Luganville.

There are so many young boys and girls who just spend their time drifting in these two urban centres, unemployed and with nothing to do. These are students who are pushed out from the education system because they have not been able to carry on to further studies in any secondary schools. The problem of urban drifting among our young people today is causing major problems for them, for their families and for the country as a whole.

The chiefs, the church leaders, as well as the government are finding it very difficult to control these young people or to influence them as to how they should live, how they should relate to their own community, to other people and to God. The Government does not have the resources to offer employment to every young person since the economy of our country is not strong enough. The chiefs are concerned mainly about justice and culture in our country, and this does not offer any help to employ these young people. This also applies to the churches, especially to the Anglican church of Vanuatu which doesn't support or encourage its members or communicants in finding a job or in becoming a priest. The same is probably true for all the other churches such as the Presbyterian church, Churches of Christ, the Protestant Church, and so on. The important question is, what can be done to solve this problem?

As priests or pastors we must be very sensitive about controlling young people today. It seems to me that the best option for giving direction to our young people is through the structures of youth ministry within our churches. Through the church's youth ministry we may find that we can hold young people together and prevent them from drifting to towns and creating social problems. Such a ministry carried out by the church could be a very important and powerful ministry to young people who are unemployed, and would contribute to the government and to our village cultural life.

Since youth ministry is my own special area of interest, I have chosen to write on the topic, 'The importance of Youth Ministry'. In my view it is important for churches to recognise and develop their youth ministry.

Through the development of youth ministry at the local congregational level, we may be able to help our young people at this time. As a future Anglican priest the reader will identify that my focus is on the Anglican youth and follows my interviews with our youth workers and coordinators of youth ministry.

## Definition

It is important that we begin with some form of definition. We can define 'youth' from a number of different viewpoints. Without depending for our definition on any well-known theologians, let me offer some definitions which I have collected from my interviews.

A young man named William defined youth as 'a group of young boys and girls in a society from the ages of ten to thirty-five years old. This group of people share things together including religious duties and social ceremonies.

Still another person defined youth as 'a group of young people from under-privileged backgrounds who meet together and take part in various activities. They teach each other and learn from each other. They help and support each other in their work and they work for the benefit of their group.

Rosalyn, the wife of a priest said that, 'youth is a group of people in a community who have joined together as an organisation for various activities such as work, games, cultural and other things. She went on to say that youth are formed in the context of a community and that without the community then youth cannot exist. They are the group who evolve from children and who move towards being the old people in a society.

Finally my own definition is given from the perspective of youth in the church. Such youth are defined as men and women aged from twelve to thirty years of age. Normally it would be those who, in this age group are in confirmation class or are already communicant members. From my theological understanding, the term youth is defined with reference to age groups, not marital status. They are in the natural human transitional period between childhood and adulthood. And so this definition allows for people who have committed any crimes or made any mistakes during the course of their lives.

## My aim

When we want something to develop amongst us we must have our aims by which we seek to achieve certain goals. Today the youth departments in our churches in Vanuatu have a special ministry to the whole population of young people. Recognising this, I have built my work on the following aims:

- To encourage and promote the active participation of young people in devotional life and church activities which promote spiritual, cultural, social, physical and economic development in their own lives, within their families, their communities, their islands and the nation as a whole.
- Spiritual development promotes and teaches the Christian faith and provides activities to enhance Christian life among the youth.
- Cultural development promotes and encourages cultural values.
- Social development promotes and encourages participation in social activities and community services.
- Physical development promotes participation in activities which lead to a healthy environment.
- Economic development encourages participation of youth in economic development for self reliance.
- To develop an effective ecumenical relationship and worship with youth groups from other churches
- To promote the level of understanding of the gospel and bible study.

**Summary of Anglican youth**

For the Anglican Church of Vanuatu (as part of The Church of Melanesia), youth ministry had its beginnings around 1973, some thirty or so years ago. It began to grow and be recognised widely in the Melanesian Church in the year 1975. The strongest influence came from the Solomon Islands where the seed of what is called, 'the Melanesian Youth Mission' was originally planted and from there was taken across to Vanuatu. The church of Melanesia currently has a numerical population of more than half a million adherents, of whom around seventy-five percent are under the age of thirty.

Although the Church of Melanesia encouraged youth ministry to develop within its own Melanesian soil, it did not provide any real approach about how to do this. As a result, many extreme interpretations and confusions arose in the Anglican Church of Vanuatu.

Today the Anglican youth ministry in Vanuatu has a special ministry to young people of our time. Its purpose is to involve the youth of Anglican families to participate fully in church activities and in the communities where they find themselves.

The Anglican Church of Vanuatu has now been divided into two dioceses, each with its many districts and many ministries. Youth ministry is one of the ministries in every district and every village churches.

There are a large number of young people aged from twelve to thirty years who are proceeding towards the goals of youth ministry. It is important, not only for the Anglican Church but for all Christian churches in

Vanuatu to work together to build youth ministry and to help young people to move towards the one main goal which is to be a servant of Jesus Christ.

## 1. The importance of youth ministry

Many of our Christian churches today may not understand what is involved in youth ministry or have any policy about the importance of youth ministry. This is also the case with individual Christians; many do not recognise or understand youth ministry and its importance. But as we carefully consider the situation of young people, we discover how important it is. In my view it is important in many ways. And in many of our villages, the youth realise the importance of youth ministry and are exploring creative methods of youth ministry. Even so, many people still do not recognise this and are ignorant about youth ministry in churches.

There are also misunderstandings or wrong ideas among young people in our youth groups. Some young people may join in a youth group with the idea that it is a place to enjoy themselves with the opposite sex in the group. Others may think it is a good place to meet friends and to tell stories. While these things may happen, this is not the point of youth ministry. The purpose of youth ministry is beyond our own interests and desires. Its purpose is to gather young people together, especially those involved in urban drifting, and those who have had no chance for expanding their education to grow in fellowship with God and with other Christians in the church. Youth ministry should be appreciated by young people because of the valuable help it gives to them and to others in their life.

*1999 Census*

The general opinion among the people of Vanuatu, around the islands and most especially within the churches is that Vanuatu has a very youthful population. The results revealed in the 1999 national population census confirm this. From the census data, I have extracted the following information which is relevant in helping to understand the situation among young people.

The total population in Vanuatu in 1999 was 186,678 and out of this population 95,403 (equivalent to 51.1%) were under the age of thirty years.

Of the 89,727 who were under the age of thirty and were eligible to go to school, 48,885 were males and 40,842 were females. There were 2,872 who never attended any schools, 1,814 males and 1,058 females; they were left in their villages because no opportunities for education were given.

And during the same year 1999, out of the total of 23,747 students who completed primary schooling and sat for the secondary entrance exam, only 12,617 managed to secure a place for further education while 11,130 missed out. Out of the 12,617 who started secondary school, only 2,980 went through to form 5 and 9,637 were pushed out. Out of the 2,980 students in form 5, only 713 went on to form six and 2,267 missed out.

Despite the many students unable to continue their education in the schools, the vocational schools enrolled only 266.

In Port Vila, the youth population was 17,335 of whom 15,918 were males and 1,417 were females. Many of these young people were not employed and could not continue their education.

*Problems caused by young people*
We are aware from the data of the number of young people who are unemployed. We know it is important to hold those young people together in mission in youth ministry. It is an important and challenging ministry. Because of unemployment, the problems are increasing very fast in our country as a whole; young people, boys and girls are becoming trouble makers.

One good example of this is in the Solomon Islands, where a majority of Anglican youths in Malaita and Guadalcanal have joined in the recent ethnic tension as Militants. In Vanuatu, we find other problems caused by young people who drop out of the education system. These problems impact on their own level of personal satisfaction since young people are in search of a better life. This also has an impact on their families.

Here are some of the problems I have noted in relation to young people today and it is important that we develop more understanding about such problems and their solutions.

- Teenage pregnancy is growing at a faster rate in both the rural and urban communities.
- There is a fearful escalation of substances abuse around Vanuatu (such as marijuana, home brew, alcohol, tobacco) spreading from urban areas to rural communities.
- Young people are moving away from the Christian faith.
- Youth, especially males are using violence to threaten communities when disagreements arise in villages.
- An increasing number of street gangs are found in urban areas.
- There is widespread incidence of sexually transmitted disease experienced among the youth.
- Young people are very mobile and are searching for a better life.
- Prostitution is increasing. In some circumstances, young girls as young as eleven years old have been found to be selling their bodies in exchange for cash or food for survival. Some young boys have also been involved in prostitution.

*Urban drift*

Since the time of the last census on youth population in Vanuatu in 1999, there is an increase in the number of youth involved in urban drifting. As a result of unemployment, young people are going to the towns and forming little groups who call themselves by the term 'SPR'. Those young people have nothing to do during the day except spend their time drifting around the towns; rather, they should be doing something back in their home islands or communities. Urban drifting is most common in our two towns: Port Vila and Luganville. It involves young boys and girls who have been pushed out from the school system; they go to the towns in search of work because they have not being able to secure a place in any secondary school or in any vocational school in Vanuatu.

Many of these young people become trouble makers in the towns and end up in jail. They break into stores and steal things for their own living. Sometimes they go back to their homes and adopt the same urban style of living which they have come to know in the towns. In doing so, they find themselves in conflict with their cultural leaders.

The following are some of the problems related to urban drifting which I have noted:

- Today the unemployment rate has increased to 60% among youth, hence young men or even women are forced to steal or commit other crimes in order to survive.
- There is an increasing number of young people who are moving away from the Christian faith. Some have turned to pagan and or ancestral beliefs. Some who claim to be born-again Christians, because of a lack of understanding of the Christian faith have joined various sects.
- In countries outside Vanuatu, lawlessness is one of the main areas of concern among the youth. For example, young men have taken very active roles in implementing the political decisions of those national leaders who initiated the war between Guadalcanal and Malaita.
- Migration of youth from rural into urban areas has led to an unfair concentration of services in urban areas and a lack of services to rural areas.
- Many young people migrate to urban centres in search of social life and modern entertainment, where these can not be found at their home village.
- Politicians have deprived youth of their rights and their freedom to speak and do things with a clear conscience. Many of the resources and services provided have price tags or conditions associated with them. This is a deprivation of human rights by those wishing to benefit at the expense of youth.

- Young people in the urban areas of Luganville and Port Vila grow weak in their Christian faith and live in a world of corruption.
- Many young couples who are newly married are now living together but without a proper church sacrament or holy blessing.
- Some urbanised youth return to their rural communities with new lifestyles that oppose Christian belief and the cultural practices of their own communities. They show a lack of obedience to and respect for Christian values and do not attend Sunday church services.

## 2. The importance of youth in the cultural context

Each of our individual cultures has its own youth group. The cultural youth group is another special group of people within our society. This type of youth group we find only in villages where they perform certain functions during cultural ceremonies. This kind of youth group includes the leaders who are the chiefs, and is identified by their valuable contribution to ceremonial life. They are well organised and well respected by members of their local communities for their commitment to follow the traditional practices. They live under and according to what the cultural tradition requires of them and they uphold their trust in their leaders.

It might be that sometimes this youth group does something which is opposed to what the church teaches. But because it is likely to be a matter of our cultural identity, the people accept it and it remains as part of our cultural life. Overall the cultural youth group helps greatly in encouraging a way of life marked by respect and good behaviour.

For example, they perform tasks to teach people to understand their own culture; they teach other young people about such things as the Nakamal and how to observe cultural taboos; they teach cultural wisdom sayings and songs, and they conduct concerts for people in the towns to show them how to live in a way which upholds their culture and which is also based on Christian doctrines. They don't receive any pay for their work and are viewed as good representatives and teachers of our culture. Because of their free will in doing this kind of youth work, they receive certain honour in cultural ceremonies.

But our question is: How do the cultural youth and the Christian youth cooperate and what is the importance of their ministry? Christian youth and the local cultural youth actually work in a cooperative way. Each of them works with youth, supporting young boys and girls in their development. They help them live and work within the context of both the culture and the church, and to cope with the changes of lifestyle, now that some of our cultures are changing with the impact of western lifestyles. I have spoken about the importance of the community in our traditional ancestral culture;

although this is threatened by western lifestyles, both the cultural youth and Christian youth seek to maintain this communal aspect of our culture.

It is also true that the cultural youth groups in our villages help out greatly in bringing many people to live godly lives. In this way, they help young people both to uphold the culture and also to live according to church teachings.

*Strengths*

This is the way in which the local communities view the importance of Christian youth ministry. They appreciate the way the Christian youth operate with their programme and activities, and demonstrate a good example to the young people in their community.

To give an example, they help young people in dealing with some conflicts which exist between aspects of our traditional culture and the ways of Christian life. To illustrate what I mean, in a small community in Torres islands, young boys (aged twelve years and upwards) went to the nakamals and learned both good and bad teachings from the old people. Their ancestors taught them about using 'black power', killing people with custom magic and many other things. As a result, these young people didn't attend church services for a period of some months. Members of the youth ministry then went into the nakamals and converted these young people. Now, having been converted, they have decided to rejoin as members of youth ministry and the church.

Sometimes when touring from island to island Christian young people learn about and adopt good cultural practices from other islands and they then teach them to young people in other places.

A chief of one community said that he looks at youth ministry as a real strength because of what its members contribute to the community in the way that they observe both cultural traditions as well as a Christian lifestyle based on the doctrines of the church. 'They follow what our culture requires and teach it to others. They learn from people who know about our culture, they teach it in their youth group and they demonstrate it to others in their lives.' He went on to say, 'I am very pleased with what the church youth in my village are doing. When we, chiefs of the village teach about cultural things, especially about respect, they always observe it. And when new generations join in with the youth group, the older members who observe such teaching pass it on to them and help them to apply it in their life.'

In many communities, youth ministry is strong and has an important role in the development of the local community. For this contribution, the chiefs, church leaders and the people are very grateful. I observed a good example in some of the little villages on a small island within Torres. For these villages, Saturday is the day which the chief sets aside as a community day of work. The aim of the day is to keep the village in good condition, to help with any building, to do maintenance, to clean, and to help any who are in need. On each Saturday, it is the youth members who are the first to arrive and to begin the work. Other people follow afterwards. This indicates the strength of youth ministry in the villages; and it is viewed by the people as supporting the real progress of developing their village, their church and the country as a whole.

*Weaknesses*

Our culture with its valuable teachings is a powerful ministry of our cultural people. In our societies, we believe that our own people are identified by cultural appearance, by language, by certain practices and many other things. This is what makes up our identity within our communities and islands.

Many young people in youth groups today are well respected people by their communities. Some members in a youth group may also be respected in the wider society beyond their own communities. However, we could make the claim about every youth group that not everyone in the group is well taught to be a good young Christian, especially the new members who have come in more recent years. Also, they have been taught well by their parents but sometimes in ways which may be against their own tradition. For example, many young people who are new members to a youth group sometimes behave in wrong ways or come with a wrong attitude. Some join only to enjoy themselves with other young boys and girls, and this has led sometimes to sexually immoral acts being performed in the youth groups. Sometimes in a youth group a boy may be having sex with his own cousin sister, or a daughter with her father, and so on. Such behaviour is a very bad example to others and is against the cultural teachings in our communities.

When such bad behaviour is discovered by other youth members, it is then reported to the youth coordinators of that particular youth group. But the youth coordinators may not report the problem to the chiefs, church leaders, other community members or the parents. Later the family of the girl involved may find that she is pregnant. The result is that the girl's parents, and other parents then do not allow their children to attend youth ministry and they keep them at home. Some parents may not even allow other young people to enter their homes unless peace ceremonies take place first. This causes a major blockage for youth ministry and it seriously weakens youth ministry in the community.

Another weakness of young people in youth groups is laziness, perhaps caused by too much drinking of kava by some youth members. I have observed, in some youth groups, that some members are addicted to kava drinking or to other alcoholic drinks; they sleep late in the mornings and generally the community work in their island. This is true in the youth group of Banks and Torres where many young boys drink too much kava, wake up late at night in the nakamal and become lazy in their responsibilities to the community. When chiefs or church leaders ring the bell for church services, these young people do not attend, and neither to they attend other community activities. When I see this happening, I ask myself the question; what is going on here and what can I learn from this?

In 1998 on the island of Mota-lava, youth ministry had been a powerful ministry for young people. They learned about Christian principles, how to live a well managed life and other Christian teachings. However, it was reported by the youth leader that during that same year, young people did not show respect for each other nor for other members of the communities. There were some who were living wild lives - stealing people's property, committing fornication and adultery, and sometimes quarrelling with their own parents. Because of this bad behaviour, three members from the youth group ended up in jail, and six of the young girls became pregnant. The chiefs had to deal with the problems and the ministry of the youth was seriously weakened.

As a result of these sorts of problems, people may question the importance of youth ministry in our culture. In some cases, it may mean that there are no longer any effective youth programmes and activities developed in the communities, and any ministry among the youth is seriously delayed.

*Suggestions*
Our culture in Vanuatu is a well managed structure with its vision of and commitment to cultural teachings. The organisational structure begins in the most taboo places in nakamals, and extends to the village, to the homes and to the individuals. So when there are problems which threaten our way of life, we must suggest ways of dealing with them.

There are my suggestions:
- The community must have a plan which implements youth development policies. For this to happen, the chiefs and leaders of the community with the youth coordinator should provide opportunities for young people to undertake cultural programmes. These programmes would instruct the youth in the structure, the policies and the particular teachings of a particular community.
- Leaders should provide cultural activities for young people to help them become aware of and committed to cultural teachings. This should happen before they enter youth ministry and receive Christ Jesus as their personal saviour.
- Youth members, and other young people who are not yet involved in youth ministry, should be encouraged to participate fully in church

services on Sundays and to mobilize their skills to support both church and cultural activities.

- Young people need help to understand the significance of moral development for their own lives and for their culture. This instruction which begins in their homes, enables them to grow with the character of divinity; it will shape the future of the youth and family, the community, the island, and the nation; it will lead to the fulfilment of church and cultural teaching and uphold both respect and peace.
- There should be teaching given to young people about self-reliance and about serving God, so that they become effective contributors in their community and their family in the future.
- Each diocese should have its own cultural values and ethnic differences, according to the will of God, and these must be respected.

## 3. The importance of youth in the church

The most recognised group in the Church of Melanesia is the youth, and youth ministry is one of the most important ministries in the church, being recognised for its creative programme and leadership every year. Youth ministry is an important form of evangelism, of proclaiming the word of God. This happens through religious activities such as dramas, singing especially with action songs, choirs, teaching in family homes, leading worship and so on. By their behaviour and example, Christian young people are seen to be religious, living their cultural lives according to Christian doctrines.

It is with these activities that Christian youth in churches need to be occupied so that the Christian teachings remain central to their lives. As the church continues on, its commitment to the importance of youth must remain strong, and influence its ministry.

*Strengths*
The youth in our church are the most important group of all the identifiable groups; youth ministry is helpful in developing and supporting all young people, the educated and uneducated, in our villages and in the country as a whole through their programme. It is a ministry that helps brings up young Christian to be mature and to follow the Lord as personal saviour in their life. Today the church has now come to understand the important role that the youth is performing within homes and churches.

The first and most important responsibility of the church is to preach the word of God. However, we must recognise that in most of our churches, church leaders do not make their teaching clear or easily understood by everybody, especially in their sermons. As we know, in many Christian churches half of the people who attend church services are not well educated, some are not good hearers and some are still children who do not understand much. The problems arise in many Christian congregations because priests and bishops use theological language in sermons. As a result of such theological sermons, not many Christians understand the preaching of the Word. In villages there are many young people; if they do not understand the teaching and preaching, then no matter how well and how much a priest preaches, they will never be able to follow what the church teaches. The blame rests with church ministers.

In contrast to this, we can see how effective and important youth ministry is for many people. Its aim is to help people to understand. This means that everything in youth ministry is done to the best of their ability, using creative and helpful methods such as dramatizing bible passages, action songs, games etc. By doing such things, many young people become interested in finding out more; many become converted and have an interest in joining youth ministry. Some uneducated people who come to understand do not join because they are older, but they grow to become strong in their faith and they live for Christ. From the time of their conversion, they become good godly people, living for God alone.

I quote from one man in a community who said, 'I saw the good work of youth ministry in my community and I decided to join because I was converted. And as I shared with youth ministry in their campaigns for one year, I really learned about the power of youth ministry and I began to understand fully what youth ministry is about now I that was mature in Christ.' After a long time of discussion he then said, 'in my own life, I am now very interest in spending time in youth ministry, especially in outreach and evangelism, reaching un-evangelised areas. In my own life now, I live in dependence upon Jesus Christ who guides me by his Holy Spirit.'

Youth ministry is sometimes viewed in the church as mass evangelising or group evangelising. This is said because in our local communities youth take up important roles such as reaching out to people in prayer, leading worship, witnessing to the Gospel in urban areas, visiting the needy, helping those who are helpless, and upholding those who are without hope. In these and other ways, youth build up and strengthen both the physical and spiritual life of people. And this is done at any time according to their programme.

So through such good works, the young people in youth ministry witness to the goodness of life in Christ as revealed in his gospel. In what they do within the church and within the community, they speak words that are powerful and converting to other people. This is especially clear in the way that they proclaim the good news to all people and offer service to everybody, whether poor or rich, sick or healthy, needy or not.

Because youth ministry is done in the context of the life of a Christian congregation, it can be understood as group evangelism. Despite some instances of misbehaviour in youth groups, they do carry out the good works that youth ministry was created for.

To illustrate what I mean, I asked one youth worker, 'How would your youth group reach out to people who are far away from you? Have you done this or not?'

His answer was that despite his youth's lack of finance, they are able to reach out to people in their homes through the power of prayer. They also have a mission offering to help people in need in other places, and by doing this they strengthen many believers by their example.

*Weaknesses*
The diocese of Banks & Torres has taken up youth ministry as one of the priorities in development for the year 2002 and beyond. In the diocesan head administration in Vanua-lava it has provided office space which is manned by a diocesan youth coordinator. This Anglican youth ministry in the diocese is a special ministry aimed towards young people in order to encourage the youth of the Anglican family to participate fully in their local church and in their local community. The youth coordinator helps the youth to carry out the aim and objectives of their local youth groups throughout the diocese of Banks & Torres. He promotes and develops their program according to the four principles of devotion, education, recreation and service, and in this way helps young people both in their spiritual and physical development.

However, despite the above new development in the past few years, and the overall strengthening of youth ministry in each island of the Torba Province which has resulted from the work of the coordinator, many young people in our communities are growing weaker in their Christian life. Apart from the strengths in youth ministry, there are also some weaknesses among the local youth group in many villages. There are many options and temptations for young people today, and these are weakening Anglican youth ministries in our diocese. There are some groups which are weak and the coordinator is not able to help every group.

Let me say more about some areas of weakness in the Anglican youth ministry in the Torres islands. What I want to say comes from my experience and observations during the years 2001–2002. During this time, youth workers in several places never met together to talk about the work they should do among the youth members. Many of them did not hold bible studies, lead prayers or arrange games or sports, and this had consequences for the young people. Many young people left their homes to go to other islands or to urban areas. Some fled from their homes and travelled from island to island just searching for something to satisfy them; many finished up living in the towns and joining other drifting youth. Young people were restless; many created problems in their homes and in their local communities, and quarrelling developed among them. Many became involved in drinking alcohol or kava, to the point where they became sick or developed a lifestyle of laziness.

In my work among youth in the year 2003, I observed that youth ministry had been weakened for some months throughout the diocese of Banks and Torres. This was due to lack of support from the villages and from individual people, as well as lack of supported from the diocesan youth coordinator. Out in the rural areas of some islands, there are not good communications, and there is a lack of resources. Youth ministry had not visited any of these places to provide ministry because the youth coordinator did not keep in touch with them or offer support to them. In some of these rural groups, there was little organised activity for youth and many of the young people in these areas lost interest in attending the youth programme. In some communities, there was no active youth ministry.

In the month of June 2003, leaders of youth ministry had to attend a special regional congress. Because of a lack of finance, the youth leaders had to do fundraising to get enough funds to be able to go. On being asked for help, many communities did not respond. Many people did not even help in buying or selling things; it was often only the youth members in a youth group who did the work to get the support. The young people were discouraged by what they saw and experienced. It led to the weakening of youth ministry in some areas.

*Suggestions*

Because of the demanding task of youth ministry, it is important that the churches always concentrate on strengthening the young people in the community. Before the inauguration of the province in 1975, the Church of Melanesia did not have any idea about how it would manage youth ministry; it did not consider putting down any policy guidelines to assist in the development of youth ministry. In the early years, the church with its two diocese was only slowly developing policies and providing structures for youth ministry. The Church first received the idea of youth ministry as a foreign idea, and therefore there was a lot of resistance to it at first, especially from the rural communities.

So, with the absence of any policy documents, the dioceses have taken initiatives to set up their own operational structures and shape of the youth program which they see to be appropriate to their situation. In this context of the development of church policy for youth ministry, I want to offer some suggestions. These suggestions are designed to give guidelines in matters related to youth development in the Church of Melanesia. In formulating their policy, the department of youth in the Church of Melanesia should recognise the following points:

- The Church of Melanesia has a very strong membership of youth and if these young people are not cared for, there is likely to be a very unpleasant outcome for the church in the future
- Youth development must teach the fundamental core elements which concern the life of young people, taking a holistic approach for a balanced youth development
- The youth policy must include a good definition of youth so that there is no confusion in the church over this
- The basis of the policy must include a call for full recognition and empowerment of young people in the church and their respective communities. Also, church leaders, politicians, community leaders and village chiefs will have to see that young people enjoy the services of the church, the government and communities.
- Each diocese should have its own program on a regular monthly basis in order to maintain the interest of the youth in participating and in joining. The program ought to include spiritual activities, educational training, health education, sports and recreational activities, vocational training, community services and opportunity for voluntary service, youth partnership in mission, youth conventions and rallies, law and order education, contact with other religious communities and other church groups.

The above suggestions are made to develop young people to become mature Christians with a strong commitment to a high moral life to be lived out in daily public life in adulthood, and to nurture young people in their spiritual, physical, social and moral well-being without depriving them or abusing them of their rights for personal gain. Therefore youth leaders must be known as trustworthy people, who can be regarded as having a role as parents to the young people.

The purpose of the statement is to provide common respect for young people and harmoniously create a firm relationship leading to mutual respect between the young people and adults.

## 4. The importance of youth in government

The government has its own involvement with youth and its own youth organisations. These young people associated with the government, who are of varying ages, have their own distinctive views about the country and what is important for the country. Their views are not necessarily the same as the views of church youth or village youth. They work under the guidelines of the government and are accountable to the government. The government and its political leaders also recognise the importance of the church and its youth organisations and the views that church youth have about the country. What follows are some perspectives about church youth ministry which are held by the government.

*Strengths*

The government considers that youth ministry in the church makes a significant contribution in support of the work of the government and of the country as a whole. Church youth ministry helps out in so many important ways. The government welcomes this contribution recognising the commitment of church youth to demonstrate its service to the whole country.

For example, youth ministry always reaches out from local churches to the wider community, including in urban areas. They provide a range of special activities which are aimed at helping out young people. This demonstrates their sharing, loving, humbleness, peace-making and other virtues which not only assist people but convert them to a new way of life. This has been so for many people throughout our country, and this indicates the strength of church youth ministry.

Church youth are also active in working in urban situations to assist people in need to live together in peace and harmony, to have happy lives rather than broken homes and corrupted lives. This is a fine example of the nature of Christian living and an indication to the Government of the role of Christian leadership in a Christian country. We are aware that nowadays there are Government leaders who are not committed Christians and never attend church services on Sundays to worship God or to hear Christian teaching. Church youth, in their evangelism, reach out to such leaders to change them. I quote one representative in the Government to whom I spoke:

'Youth ministry is very important in the life of Vanuatu today. Since many rulers in the Government are not good Christians, they ignore rural communities, they have hard hearts and are not generous in their giving; they divorce their wives, they commit adultery, they misuse money, and other things. Youth ministry is simple in its teaching, but it helps those of us in Government so much. It gives clear direction to the ways of peaceful living and a good life. In the Solomon Islands in 1996, the Government was challenged by what the young Christian people were doing, so they united and created within the Government a 'One-ness in Christ' movement. As a result, many have decided to follow Jesus Christ and have become mature Christians.'

The Government of Vanuatu has its own constitution which covers every ni-Vanuatu citizen, within and beyond the church. Further, as part of its structure, the Government has its own military forces and police to maintain peace and order, to protect the people, and to ensure that the constitution is kept by the people of Vanuatu. However in practice this doesn't seem to help much. Many problems arise in our country because of law-breakers, most of whom are actually young people. They commit all sorts of crimes — they steal, they murder, they practice sexual immorality. Government forces attempt to stop them but the problems seem only to increase more and more. Through the work of youth ministry, these problems are now being reduced across our country. Church youth are evangelising these young law-breakers and converting them so that they follow Jesus Christ and join in with the youth ministry. This does not mean that the problems have disappeared; there is a need for more youth to be involved in this ministry and support the others already involved.

Youth ministry has also been effective in tackling the growing problem of 'urban drift'. Urban drift refers to the problem of young people coming from the villages into the towns in order to get further education and jobs but finding that the government does not provide a place for them in schools or any jobs for them. Youth ministers go to the towns and through the churches make contact with these young people and convert them with the help of the Holy Spirit. They encourage them to return to their home villages where, through the development of youth ministry across our islands, interesting programs and activities are being established for young people. When they return to their island villages, they join in with the youth ministry and then are able to help their other friends who are in a similar situation in the towns. I quote from one of our youth workers:

'Youth ministry is like evangelising in the sense of going and converting many young people who are urban drifters and trouble makers. Before, I myself was one of the urban drifters and trouble-makers in the town, but when I met people involved in youth ministry it was a turning point in my life. I decided to return to my village and to live a Christian life. It was like a new birth, a new life.'

*Weaknesses*

Youth ministry in the Church of Melanesia today is an important ministry – for the Church itself, for the society as a whole, and for the Government. I have outlined some of the strengths of this ministry in the section above. In this section I want to refer to some of the weaknesses which can be observed in youth ministry. Some of these were raised during the youth leadership and development workshop in Torba Province held from 1520 October, 2001 in Sola Parish, Vanua-lava. They refer to weaknesses in youth ministry

89

which are common in local district areas and are observed as weaknesses by some Government leaders in the Province.

i) There is sometimes lack of oversight and support for youth ministry from the local priest-in-charge, from parents, from other church leaders, and from community leaders. In some cases this means that some members of youth ministry move around the towns or villages and behave in a way which does not demonstrate a good Christian example. There are many young people who only pretend to be Christians, while following life-styles which are of their own choosing. They are involved for example in sexual misconduct, addiction, drunkenness and black magic, and return as 'backsliders' to their islands around Vanuatu.

ii) The district priest is responsible for the whole youth group of his district, in teaching and advising them about the Christian faith in Anglicanism. Often, this does not happen as it should and the youth leaders can become the only ones involved in evangelism with their members.

iii) There is a lack of leadership planning and management skills among the youth of the church. A Government worker observed that this is the main reason why youth ministry does not work well in local areas. This leads to some groups operating for a few years and then dying out; there is a lack of good skilled leadership.

iv) Some people in Government consider youth ministry to be a problem because it focuses only on the negative sides, for example on the way some youth demonstrate bad behaviour within their youth group (immoral sexual relationships within the group, etc). This reflects badly on youth ministry and gives a bad impression in the eyes of others.

v) Childhood is not being spiritually nurtured and developed at basic levels within the life of the family. Parents are failing in their duty. When a child is born, it is not being taught spiritually about good behaviour and obedience and the ways of Christian life. When these children later enter into youth ministry, they display the same lack of obedience and disrespect towards Christian teachings, as well as a disrespect for the ways of our culture and the rule of the Government.

vi) Church and community leaders have not been addressing youth social problems. When problems occur, and when youth are involved in un-Christian behaviour or activity, the leaders fail in their duty to try and provide a helpful or good solution. Instead, they gossip about the person involved and make the situation worse, which is itself against Christian teaching.

There are other weaknesses which could have been listed but the above six I have identified as the main ones viewed by the Government as an obstacle to effective youth ministry in the church today.

*Suggestions*

To help youth ministry to grow, we cannot depend on only one person; it depends on the whole church. The strengths I have listed above must be encouraged and the weaknesses must be addressed. Leaders of the churches, youth leaders and all youth members must cooperate in doing this. Therefore it is important that leaders of the church and government must share their ideas with youth leaders and offer their own support to youth ministry. The following is a list of my suggestions about the way of developing youth ministry and addressing the current weaknesses.

- Leaders should provide religious programmes designed as a means of teaching, to enable young people to grow more deeply in love and respect for God and for their neighbours. Young people need to become daily readers of Scripture and good examples of Christian living in their daily life.
- Government leaders need to allocate time to developing their own ideas about what good Government leadership requires of them, and to appreciate what is good about their own country.
- Leaders of the church should provide opportunities for individuals to make a commitment of their lives to Jesus Christ as Lord.
- There needs to be provision of bible studies which challenge people about the new way of life with Jesus Christ as their personal Saviour, and which informs them about the assurances which come to them when they follow Jesus.
- Youth need to be encouraged to be involved and to participate in helping out the Government in terms of its social services, and offering their skills to support the Government especially in fund-raising, etc.
- Prosperous youth ministry needs to begin in the home by providing a spirit of divinity which shapes the life of the family, the community, the island and the nation as a whole, in the ways of respect and peace.
- The diocesan youth coordinator should have an action plan to create more youth rallies, seminars and awareness activities that would address and focus on the idea of the moral life and support of communities.
- All district priests who are concerned about youth ministry ought to work directly with youth leaders, and become involved in youth ministry whenever a youth ministry team tours around their area.
- Productive leadership comes from people who have developed the skills for good leadership. Leaders need to be trained in the skills which will make them good leaders so that they can sustain programmes for youth.
- Youth ministry needs to provide teaching to encourage youth organisations in local churches, communities, church schools, and

91

religious communities to work together, to study together the Word of God and to learn how to live with and have respect for one another.

- Youth ministry needs to encourage all youth to be law-abiding citizens, to have respect for the Government Constitution, for their culture and for the cultures of other people, and to honour differences.

## 5. Christian perspectives on youth ministry

*Biblical views on the importance of youth*

The Bible doesn't offer any clear insight about youth ministry as such. What I mean is that the Old Testament and the New Testament writings do not clarify for us the particular importance of youth work. However we read references to youth, for example in the apostle Paul's instructions to Titus: 'Urge the younger people to be self-controlled. Show yourself in all respects a model of good works and in your teaching, show integrity, gravity, and sound speech that cannot be censured' (Titus 2:6ff). We could take this passage as a general instruction about how to treat young people.

We can assume that youth of course existed from the earliest times of the Old Testament as part of the people of God. There were youth among the chosen people of Israel to whom God promised a land, a people who were led by special leaders (e.g. Moses, Aaron) appointed by God.

We can of course make the same assumption for the New Testament times. We may even assert that the group of twelve disciples who followed Jesus in ministry from place to place, preaching the gospel, was a group of youth. Beginning from the period after Jesus' ascension into heaven, the early church community comprised young people who took up the ministry to which Jesus commissioned them. This group of people did exactly the same as youth today in carrying out Jesus' ministry. The only difference is that when we use the term 'youth ministry' today, we are referring to a particular age group of young people.

Although there are no specific references to youth ministry in the Bible, there is a clear assumption that young people should be taught a good example. In the Old Testament it is the requirement of the people of one generation to pass on to the next generation the works and teachings of God. And in Paul's instructions to Titus noted above, we see an expectation that young people should be given a good example in Christian life, to live with respect, self-control, etc.

Therefore, when we ask the question about how we bring up young people, we can find a basis in the Bible.

*What does the Bible say about young people?*

First we must understand that young people, indeed all people, are interwoven with and dependent upon the environment in which they live. This is clear in the biblical stories of creation (Genesis 1–2). Therefore, it is important to promote the preservation of the environment and this could be done by deepening awareness of the Bible through talks, dramas, etc based on particular biblical insights.

Many young people today shape their lifestyles on the basis of personal satisfaction, and for many, this leads them to desires and decisions which are contrary to Christian living. How might we address such a problem? In Paul's letter to Timothy, the apostle says: 'Let no one despise your youth, but set the believers an example in speech and conduct, in love, in faith, in purity'(1Tim.4:12f ). This means that it is very important that we teach young people by giving them a good example in Christian life, by helping them to turn from any destructive desires and to build their lives as Christians. It means that we must teach them to realise that their youth is a gift from God and inspired by the Holy Spirit. They must be taught well with solid biblical foundations in order to grow in faith and to achieve what is good for their life, and so to set a good example for others to live in peace and holiness of life.

They must be discouraged from building on the evil desires of youth and from living foolishly; they must be self-controlled and flee from all evil desires; they must live according to the love that comes from God, the peace that comes from Jesus Christ, the righteousness and faith which comes from the gospel (2 Tim.2:22f). They must learn to confess the name of the Lord to all people, and to turn away from any wickedness, showing a good example to all ages.

It is also clear from the bible that all ministry is a ministry of God and therefore all youth members should acknowledge that youth ministry is also a ministry of God. This implies that the relationships between youth members is important; youth members from all Christian groups should treat each other as brothers and sisters; they should treat each other with a pure spirit and not be harsh with each other. In this way, 'our youth will be renewed like the eagle' (Psalm 103:5).

Furthermore, we can learn from Paul's instructions to Titus (Titus 2:6–9): 'Encourage the young men to be self-controlled. In everything, set them an example by doing what is good. In your teaching, show integrity, seriousness and soundness of speech that cannot be condemned, so that those who oppose you may be ashamed because they have nothing bad to say about us.' Following this instruction, and the directions indicated already, we can see how important it is to bring up our young people in the context of youth ministry. It is important to encourage them to use the gifts given them by God through the work of the Holy Spirit, to be nurtured in the fruits of the Holy Spirit for good works, and to continue to be built up in the faith.

## Why should we teach the faith to our youth?

There is a great need for our young people to live a holy life and therefore it is important that we teach our young people within each youth group to grow together in unity as Christians. Some of the particular responses to the question of why we should teach the Christian Faith to our youth can be summarised as follows:

☐ To enable them to set a good example for others
☐ To continue to develop the work of evangelism
☐ To enable them to be guided in their lives by the Holy Spirit
☐ To build them up in the way of truth

The most important thing is that young people, by their words and deeds, show their Christian way of life. They need to convince everybody of their Christian living by showing, in words and deeds, their love for everybody and their readiness to share with all people; this will set a good example and prove that they are led by the Holy Spirit.

## Youth ministry strengthens young believers

Youth ministry gives strength to the young believers in the church communities in many different ways. When young people join in youth programmes, they experience a development in their belief. In particular, through youth ministry, young people

- gain strength and encouragement to believe more strongly in Jesus, and to live for him alone
- learn what it means to be led by Jesus Christ as their personal Saviour
- learn more deeply about the Gospel
- are strengthened in the principles of devotional life, in recreation and in service to the community
- are strengthened in their respect for other people, for their parents, for the community chiefs, for the church leaders, for older people and for the disabled.
- are strengthened to work with other believers by establishing and organising them to nurture their minds, souls and bodies in Christian living, by helping them to grow up in a healthy Christian environment.

In these ways, young people are enabled to use their potential, their energy, their talent, their skill and their knowledge, as individuals and as groups, to promote an active and meaningful devotional life, to develop a positive attitude to serving God's church, their families and their communities.

*Maturity in Christ*
Before we discuss this topic, we should ask ourselves the question: 'What are the qualities which make a young person spiritually mature?' If we consider this question carefully, we will discover that 'spiritual maturity' is one of those terms Christians use often and assume everyone knows what they mean. However, different Christians may have different understandings of what they mean by 'spiritual maturity'.

For a better idea of what we might mean by this term 'spiritual maturity in Christ', I want to propose seven characteristics which I believe are the best indicators of spiritual maturity in young people. They are:

- A willingness to encourage others to live for Christ
- Generosity in their behaviour
- Regarding other people with honour
- Devoting their own lives to Christ
- Wanting to develop their spiritual gifts
- A reflective thoughtful personality
- A desire for holy living

In conversation with leaders of youth ministry, many of them may choose quite different characteristics. Some may choose characteristics based on devotional bible reading, bible study and prayer; others may choose to emphasise loving relationships; others may concentrate on obedience to rules; others may focus on involvement in mission and service; others may want to speak of emotional self-control. Using insights from the bible, we can state that 'spiritual maturity in Christ' can mean different things to different leaders. However people want to define this, they should be clear about their particular ideas, and how they think about maturity in Christ.

*Biblical views about spiritual maturity in Christ*
In my view, there are particular priorities which we can find in the Bible about the qualities which display spiritual maturity in Christ, and which young people should strive for. The choice of selecting these qualities is of course influenced by other youth leaders who have been a model for me. Others may disagree with me but in what I say below, I am not setting down the sum total of all aspects of spiritual maturity, I am speaking of the priorities which I consider are important and which have practical implications for the way that young people live in their villages and their communities. They are as follows:

- Understanding the gospel: it is important that young people should discover their acceptance with God based on what Christ has done for them
- Commitment: we are to seek first the Kingdom of God and his righteousness, knowing that all things will be given to us (Matthew 6:33)
- Fruits of the Spirit: Spiritual maturity must be reflected in our relationships with others. Paul the apostle sums up what is required when he speaks in Galatians 5:22ff of the fruits of the Spirit: love, joyfulness, peace, patience, kindness, faithfulness, gentleness and self-control.
- Attitude of Servanthood: According to Paul in his letter to the Philippians (2:1ff), we should adopt the servant attitude of Jesus Christ. Young people should learn in the pressures of life that we are great when we are servants; we must serve our Christian brothers and sisters, and the world at large.
- Devotional Life: the spiritually mature person will develop a regular practice of bible reading and prayer as part of their relationship with God.

The above points from the Bible are those which I want to emphasise as indicators of spiritual maturity in Christ, and which ought to guide youth ministry in its work among young believers.

*Biblical goals for youth ministry*

From the Bible, we are able to identify what we could call goals for youth ministry. These goals are understood and shared by a number of people I have spoken to who are youth leaders involved in youth ministry. The main goal for a youth worker in youth ministry may be expressed differently, for example:

- To hold young people together in the church community of youth so that they don't leave their church tradition and join with one of the false denominations
- To hold young people together as a group in society and to keep them under the leader's control, so that they will not go to places or do things which are not appropriate for them
- To hold young people in a fellowship together until they are well grown up through the unsettling stage of youth, they can live responsibly and teach others about the Christian Faith
- To run a program for young people within the church and local community. (With this goal, there may not be much thought given to how good the program will be at developing those young people who

come along for their future; the focus is more on the activities of the program.)
- To maintain a particular method of youth work. (The leader's commitment is to a particular method of youth work which can easily over-ride the spiritual and emotional welfare of the young people in the community.)

The goals stated above are the goals of some youth leaders from particular village youth groups. However, there is another goal which I would choose which is biblically based and which would be the most important if I were to be a leader in youth ministry. I want to refer to the letter to the Colossians (1:28). In this letter, the apostle Paul states his own goal in ministry when he says: 'We proclaim Jesus Christ, admonishing and teaching everyone with all wisdom so that we may present everyone perfect in Christ.'

Following this claim, I would state the goal of youth ministry in this way: to preach Christ to everyone, with all possible wisdom, to warn and to teach them in order to bring each one into God's presence as mature individuals in union with Christ. Here, I am instructed by Paul's own goal in ministry. It is my view that every youth leader should be directed by this goal since it comes directly from the apostle Paul and it is biblical. It is the goal to bring everyone to Christ and to be in union with him.

There are all kinds of goals, as I have stated, but in the end, all goals are merely tools to achieve the true goal of leading people to maturity in Christ.

## Conclusion

Youth work in most of our Christian churches at this point of time has suffered a great deal from social, economic, spiritual and political issues impinging upon them. Some of these have occurred because of ignorance and lack of education on the part of youth, while other issues have come as a direct result of political decisions, and insufficient pastoral support by the church and other leaders. In the national survey, the Government and Non-Government Organisation researchers discovered that young people in our country are facing a lot of difficulties in their daily living and are involved in a lot of trouble-making.

Youth are active, energetic people. Their potential needs to be developed fully in a direction that can lead to a higher enrolment of young people in appropriate education and training, providing them with access to spiritual development programmes, community volunteer programmes, self-employment and entrepreneurship, recreational and organised sports, and health programmes with an emphasis on prevention activities. Having such activities included in youth programmes would produce positive results which would give strength to young people and develop them:

- as God-fearing citizens
- as highly committed and disciplined in Christian life
- as healthy and balanced in their Christian life
- as culturally oriented in communities, filled with respect
- as self-reliant
- to have respect for neighbours and people of both genders
- as peace-loving in community
- as economically prosperous

The churches must work to a policy for youth development. This commitment to youth ought to be provided in each provincial area. The organisation of this ought to exist permanently in our churches, and youth ministry should be coordinated throughout the provinces of our churches. In this way young people, both boys and girls, would be supported and encouraged to reach a high standard of living. It is the responsibility of the churches to ensure that young people have important duties to perform both with one another and with the wider church. This will encourage them to become future leaders and potential assets for the church, having both responsibilities and obligations.

I would conclude by saying again that youth ministry is a Christian ministry; it must be upheld and supported in all the churches so that it becomes a source of strength, hope, trust and encouragement for young people, to give glory to God in their lives.

## Bibliography

Richard, W. *The Church of Melanesia: Provincial Youth Document One* (Honiara, Solomon Islands, 2001).

Herman, A. *The Anglican Youth for Young People in the Local Church* (Diocese of Banks and Torres, 2000).

Patterson, W. *A Guide to the Understanding of Youth Ministry to Youth Leaders* (Diocese of Banks and Torres, 2000).

Derrick, H. *Out of Trouble, Theology in Youth Ministry* (Papua New Guinea, 1992).

## Interviews

Patterson, W. Diocese of Banks and Torres, Vanalava, Sola, 16 November 2002.

Joel, L. Torres youth worker, Hiu Island, Yugavigamena, 1 January 2003.

Judah, M. Hiu Island District Priest, Yuguana, 2 May 2003.

Cecil, H. Custom Chief, Hiu Island, Yuguana, 4 July 2003.

William, C. Loh youth worker, Loh Island, 1 August 2003.

Nathaniel, M. Village youth worker, Hiu Island, Yugavigamena, 2 June 2003.

Rosalyn, R. Priest's wife, Hiu Island, Yugavigamena, 3 November 2003.

# Migration on the Island of Tanna Today

## Simon Vani

### Introduction

Migration happens all over the world for many different reasons. People migrate from place to place, town to town and country to country. Tanna is an island where most of its people have moved onto other islands. They believe that the inter-island movement is important to their way of life. Their history shows different movements that have occurred in the past.

Today a large number of Tanna people have changed residence by moving to Port Vila, Santo and other islands of Vanuatu. They believe that in towns there is better education, employment and other benefits. Their movement today simply reflects what they believe in. The issue of migration is being discussed widely. Today according to Vanuatu's population growth and mobility, the government should have an action plan to help solve some of the problems that are being caused by migration.

The biblical story identifies the beginning of the covenant promise as an invitation to migrate for the sake of receiving the eternal promise. The wilderness suffering of Israel and the spread of the gospel in the New Testament came through migration. The point here is that migration belongs to the story of the people of God; people are called to migrate in response to the Word of the gospel breaking through in their lives.

### Section One

**Cultural Movement**

*Who started migration on Tanna* (Tanna's history)
Before the arrival in Vanuatu in the nineteenth century of the traders, explorers and missionaries, our beautiful and green land was full of varied cultures as a blessing from the Lord. The people on the islands lived in accordance with their cultures, where the traditional pattern of life was practiced by the people. Tanna itself is one of the larger islands of Vanuatu and has since become one of the main islands in the country in terms of its contribution to the economy and to other developments as well.

People have traced back their lives to where they were rooted—in their culture. Chiefs from different tribes or clans have exercised their power to rule and have maintained the good things in relation to language, land, name and other aspects. One valuable aspect is the migratory movement. It is not simply what we call migration today, but a movement that has taken place in the past. We called it 'Nawanien' (which refers to a person moving from place to place in search of something)

Around the fourteenth to fifteenth century before the Europeans came, the people of the island of Tanna were one. We called this era *Mipro* where people lived under the authority of our god *Karpapen* (meaning the Mighty God). The history shows that in the south, west and north of the island, there were no people; the area was totally empty. In the eastern part of the island where the great god *Karpapen* created his first human being named 'nassip', there was a community of people. Tannese believed that Nassip became the ancestor of all people and out of him different tribes were chosen. These people were the very first people to move around the island, to build new homes and to explore parts of land. Due to the low population at that time, the people were able to move freely anywhere they wanted to and have the right to choose any part of the land to occupy. The settlements were in groups and each of the clans was formed with a leader who exercised authority. There wasn't any historical law to stop this movement or intra-island migration, but people were allowed to move freely. The strong quest in their hearts was to find new ideas, new changes and to take advantage of other places.

*Different types of migration on the island of Tanna*
As the years went by, people began to settle in different regions, and different Nakamals were built with different rulers exercising authority. All societies were built based on necessity.

During the sixteenth and seventeenth century, two tribes, the 'Numrukwien' and the 'Kawiameta', made their way through the island. Each of them claimed authority over the whole island as if they were the very first people or race to move around the island. Chief Freeman Nariu, who said that 'Numrukwiens were called "Nassipmine" and Kawiametas were called "Nikimruamine',[1] went on to say, 'Their arguments went on because of different authorities, therefore fighting began and each was forced to live and move for the second time to find new residences. Poison was used as a weapon in fighting and making people move.'[2]

Today migration is important in the life of the Tannese people because of land issues. Many people move to find their own land or to find the land belonging to their own relatives or ancestors.

---

1. Interview, Chief Freeman Nari, Apostolic Church, Samaria village, South Tanna 2002.
2. *Ibid.*

Political migration brought risk, danger and changes in the life of the Tannese people as traders made their ways into the country. Chief Nama reported about one occasion, saying:

> During the night before, we heard the noise of a roaring volcano, (meaning a boat engine) coming into our harbour. We all ran down to see what it was. There were white people (Nipitonga) with their muskets and they were waving at us. At first we were frightened but later we managed to speak to them. They did many things but later fooled our people with tobacco, pairs of pants, knives etc, and many people were taken on board and never returned again. We did not know where they had gone.[3]

Traders caused disturbance in the lives of our people with their economic greed. Some of their trading goods were dangerous to our people. Our people did not know much about them; therefore they caused many deaths when used improperly. Chief Iata said:

> Around 1842–1858, over 100 vessels from Australia called in at Port Resolution, taking slaves to work in Queensland; twenty-six were known to have sailed to Sydney. In 1861, thirteen young 'Naraimine' (tribesmen) were taken by the whaler ship Southern Cross and turned up in Tasmania.[4]

This slave trade not only influenced the Tannese people but also the other islands. 'When we consider the practice of slave trade in some other countries in the world, for example Africa, Middle East and Europe, we learn that slave trade was widely practice for thousands of years and was a well established institution'.[5] In many other countries people were forced to migrate either by the state or by some other social institution that wielded power over them. One good example is the movement of some 150,000 British convicts to Australia between 1788 and 1867. Another instance is the exile of one million Russians to Siberia during the nineteenth Century. In

---

3. Interview with Chief Nama S Port Resolution, East Tanna 2002.
4. Interview with Chief Iata, Port Resolution, East Tanna 2002.
5. William Benton, New Encyclopedia USA 1943–1973, 187 Helen Hemingway Benton.

'the case of World War II, the Nazis deported 7–8 million people, including at least 5 million Jews who were subsequently murdered'.[6]

In Vanuatu as a whole, people were taken by force. A local music group in Vanuatu sang a song with the lyrics 'I pulum mi long wan bot, mi mi no wantem go, i no talemaot se mi go long kweenslan, long wan sugarcane plantation, Johnny Tanna'[7] (that is: 'He forced me into a boat; I didn't want to go; he didn't tell me that I was going to Queensland, to a sugarcane plantation, Johnny Tanna'.) Many of these victims of the slave trade are living in Australia and are citizens of Australia, and many are now wanting to return home. A local man Kaurua said to me, 'My ancestors were taken as slaves to Queensland for many, many years. Later we came to know that we are from Vanuatu, on the southern part of Tanna Island. I have come over to see our relatives to see exactly where we come from, as we had been told by our grandparents.'[8]

Tanna was greatly disturbed by the traders. However, during that same century, another influence made its way through the island and this was Christianity. It wasn't very easy for the Christian mission because of the disturbance caused previously by the traders, but slowly Christian life began to spring up like a little plant. The Tannese began to hear about this wonderful news of Jesus Christ. Elder Yapatu said:

> Due to this movement, our great grandfather Iaupia has left our home Yenkahar and has moved to Athness, Port Resolution, to receive this good news. It wasn't very easy because life was still in darkness. They spent six months living there waiting for an opportunity to return home safely with this wonderful message of God. Many of them became local missionaries and moved around the island spreading the good news; some were killed and buried. However, Tannese came to believe that this movement of the Christian Gospel brings prosperity into people's lives because of the impact of its message of peace.[9]

World War Two in the South Pacific caused many of our people to migrate to the town of Vila where many of them died. The war was part of

---

6. Ibid, 189.
7. Stonny Boys Local String Band, Ambrym 1990.
8. Kaurua Kisiai village, South Tanna 2002.
9. Interview with E Yapatu, Nepraintata session, Samaria village, South East Tanna.

the political power of the British and the American forces. Chief J Namuli said,

> When we heard the message about wanting labour to help during the war, we all left and boarded the ships. We were told we were to be paid with a pair of trousers and a shirt. We were very happy because we believed that something was about to change in our life. There were about a thousand Tannese who migrated to Port Vila during the war. However, there wasn't much to eat, but we thought of the changes and we believed that there will be a change for the better, even if there was a possibility that we might die.[10]

## Did the parents teach their children to migrate?

Tanna was radical in its traditional norms. As I have mentioned above, the very first thing that happened to the life of the people on Tanna was migration. We believed that the pattern of migration of our people is permanent because of the way in which migration brings changes to the people, to communities and to the province as a whole. Counsellor Wako said, 'Most business which is currently operating on Tanna is owned by the local people. And it is because parents have advised their children to migrate for better benefits'.[11]

Everybody's parents on Tanna teach their children to migrate and find something better which may bring development. Today many have migrated permanently to take advantage of opportunities in Vila and Santo to earn money and even to widen their horizons. These migrants carefully weigh up their options to build their nest and win the highest wages, but it is true that many have also migrated temporarily because they have opposed their parents' instructions. I will say more about this below.

## What is the chief's advice to their people?

Wherever you go within the country of Vanuatu, the chief plays a very important role in giving advice, teaching, and in promoting development in the society to help the people. Today, our Tanna chiefs are playing their role to help individual communities by giving them advice about what is right and what is wrong. Chief Kanker said:

---

10. Interview with J Namuli *Catholique Mission Imaki,* (South Tanna 2002).
11. Interview with Counselor Wako, *Tafea Province* (White Sands Tanna, 2002).

Migration is important today as in the past. But Tanna people should weigh up their decisions when migrating. They have to be careful and to select the best option because of the opportunities provided by western culture. People are free to do more things, and many help support their families with a source of income.[12]

However, chiefs hold meetings regularly also to remind their people that in these days, development should also take place on their own island.

## Causes of division

### Land disputes

Throughout Vanuatu from the North to South people live with different customs and cultures in relation to land ownership. In some societies, land is owned by men while in other societies the women own the land; therefore, intermarriage creates interesting situations. Elder Kiery, a member of the Apostolic Church on south-east Tanna, said, 'Today many men from Tanna have to ship their bags and go to live with their wives on her land; therefore, he becomes a partner in land ownership'.[13] Because marriages between island groups is more common now with people living in the towns, many of the men from Tanna as well as from other islands have moved to live with their wives.

Land is important to Tanna people because in the past one of the priorities for the migration of people has been for them to find land. Today we have land courts, tribunals and the Nikoletan Council of Chiefs, all of which have been set up to deal with land disputes. Chief Nowal said to me of his own situation, 'Due to land disputes between our families, we have intended to move to Vila so that peace might prevail between us. However, my sons have bought us a piece of land where we can survive.'[14] Today many Tanna people have migrated to Vila or to Santo because of land disputes. Many have heard about the selling of land in the towns and have come to buy a piece of land to live there.

### Disobedience

---

12. Interview with Chief Kauke, Ipuis village South East Tanna 2002.
13. Interview with El Kiery C. Apostolic Church Jericho South East Tanna 2002.
14. Interview with Chief Nowal, Ienamaliu village, White Sands Tanna 2002.

Today, most Tannese people migrate because they want to escape from problems. Disobedient people in our communities, both adults and children, are becoming a major problem, and it is because they do not want to obey the rules of the society or the instructions of their parents. Chief Iata said:

> My daughter went away to Vila, after being judged by the Chiefs' Council because she committed a crime. However, she was not happy with the judgment and two days later, we thought she was somewhere looking for the payment of her penalty, but then we heard that she was in Vila. She is now married to a man from Santo and they are living there.[15]

Today many people leave their homes because they are not happy with their families, with the chief or with other members of their communities. They are in Vila and Santo trying to earn some money and the move makes radical changes to their lives.

*Religious movements*

When Christianity arrived on Tanna, people were all worshipping within the Presbyterian Church of Vanuatu. This is because there wasn't any other church. Then later the Seventh Day Adventists (SDA) and the Roman Catholics came. But after independence in 1980, with 'Freedom of Religion' as part of the constitution, many religious movements have come into our islands. As a result, the spiritual life of our communities has become weak; many people have left their original churches and become members of other denominations. This happens because many have migrated into Vila and Santo and have been influenced by other religious movements. Today our children who grow up in our towns will eventually have no roots in their Christian lives; therefore, they will not be able to balance their life in modern Vanuatu. Elder Rassai J said, 'Many of our young people who have been to Vila have joined the Mormons because they believe that if they go there Mormons will bring good changes into their lives and their communities. However, it brings division in our society.'[16] Many of these people have migrated to Vila, leaving their home, parents and relatives, in search of employment, but then they became members of other religious movements. This sometimes brings frustration into the community.

---

15. Interview with Chief Iata, Lenakel West Tanna 2002.
16. Interview with El Rassai J-Nepraintata session, Imaio South East Tanna 2002.

## How do we solve the problem of migration?

Migration in Vanuatu today has grown so much that people from every island in the country have decided to change residence due to our economic situation. The security of families and communities in our rural areas is being seriously undermined by this steady exodus of people into the towns, especially the exodus of those seeking a formal education. This affects the size and composition of the family labour force in the communities, and influences the social dynamics and organisation of communities.

The Lord Major of Vila, Mr Patrick Crowby Manrewo is quoted in the Trading Post Issue No.810 saying, 'Leaders should agreed to an urgent review of the government decentralization policies, with an emphasis on taking investments with job creation to rural areas as essential. We can only stop urban drift by the creation of jobs within the provinces.'[17] Today people migrate because they want change; they think that these urban centres have jobs available. Therefore to stop this exodus, the government should act on the ideas of the Mayor.

*The parents' role to advise their children*

In our culture, parents are responsible for their children, to give them advice, to teach them and give them training to live and work. The purpose of this parenthood is to equip them for their future. Many parents have advised their children to migrate to find a vocational school which can assist them in their learning. Parents know that migration brings advantages, but may also bring disadvantages if their children do not follow their advice. Today, many young people from Tanna who cannot continue their education on Tanna have followed their parents' advice and migrated, while others have not. Parents advise them to get a job and get some capital for the sake of their own development and to be self reliant. John M said, 'My elder son is now working in Vila as I advised him to. He earns the money and sends it to us and now we have started our little business. This is because we need changes in our society as we adapt to the modern world.'[18] Today, people need changes but the changes depend on the way each parent gives advice to their children.

*The provincial roles*

From 1906 Vanuatu was governed by British and French authorities. They continued to rule until 1980 when Vanuatu gained its independence. Today

---

17.  Patrick Crowby, Lord Major Trading Post No.810v Port Vila 2001, 3.
18.  Interview with John M Apostolic Church, Jericho South East Tanna 2002.

our local authorities are trying their best to improve our province and to help people by creating more job opportunities. They work closely with our chiefs to make sure that local development may come and so help to solve some of these migration trends. The secretary of the local Tafea Province said, 'Today a large number of Tannese migrants have gone to Vila and Santo because Tanna itself has a history of people migrating. We can only stop this by bringing more investors onto our island. In this way we can provide a good living for our people.'[19] Today, on Tanna all businesses are owned by the local people. These changes have occurred because our people who migrated to Vila and Santo have returned home with capital and have started businesses.

## Section Two
### Migration in Vanuatu today

*Constitutional provisions*
At the time of independence in 1980, the people of Vanuatu as well as our Tannese people hoped for high standards of living, health, education and longevity as well as material comforts. This desire for high living standards has caused many Tannese people to leave their homes and island and migrate to Vila and Santo. However, the living standards of the people have stagnated or even fallen. Many men and women are unemployed in urban areas as well as in our villages. Therefore deep dissatisfaction has occurred and inevitably this has led to a culture of violence.

Today migration remains very high. In fact the problem seems to be growing because families cannot generate sustainable incomes from rural resources. Land pressure and the lack of quality services in rural areas, the wish to experience city life and other factors have led to the migration into towns. There are a great number of Tannese migrants among other island migrants who have moved into towns. These migrants are composed of many different age groups. The desire to change their residence has increased because there are improvements in economic conditions, in communication and in transport systems in Vanuatu today. Chief Katipa said, 'They tend to get their information from their neighbours, newspapers, offices, agencies such as labour exchanges, immigration offices and so forth'.[20]

However, there are other factors that have made our people decide to change residence. To fulfil the hopes of independence, the constitution of

19.   Joe Narua Secretary General Tafea Province Isangel Lenakel Tanna 2002.
20.   Interview with Chief Katipa Apostolic Church, Saralingi Samaria East Tanna 2002.

the republic has recognised the need for every citizen of this country to travel, to move from one place to another, within the provinces or even abroad. The constitution does not limit the type of movement that people can make, neither does it specify the time in which people may move and where or how they may move. It has rather broad provisions which empower every citizen to feel free to move back and forth from one place to another, depending on where they think it is good for their livelihood. The constitution encourages our people to look for the best option to live a free and peaceful life, generally feeling free to move whenever and wherever they think it is best for them, either temporarily or permanently.

*Employment*

Our educational system in Vanuatu does not provide adequately for our children's future. Many drop out at the end of class 6, others drop out later in their junior secondary education. Very few go to universities and are able to be employed at the end of their studies. Therefore many of our young people have decided to live in our towns rather than returning to our provinces, villages and communities. At a seminar on urban drift, the late Bishop Walter said, 'Parents see their children in schools as an investment; that is why they are prepared to pay high school fees. They hope that their children one day will return their investment by finding a good job and earning some money. Many have fulfilled their parents' expectations but in my view, the majority of these children do not.'[21] Today many of these school leavers are living in our two main towns (Vila on Efate and Luganville on Santo) and do not want to return home. But one important thing about them is that these migrants will still do work which others refuse to do.

*Wage cap*

Today, most of our Tannese people migrate, temporarily or permanently, to take advantage of opportunities to earn money and to widen their horizons. Some migrate to other countries. They carefully weigh their options in seeking the best opportunity and the highest wages, and compare this with opportunities and wages in Vila or Santo. They know that the best wages can be earned in towns rather than on our islands. New Caledonia is one of the countries to which many of our migrants have migrated. When we look at the world scene, many migrants know that the largest wage gap is between the two neighbouring countries, USA and Mexico. A search of the internet tells us that 'hourly earnings for US workers are around $15; an

---

21. Bishop Walter Siba, Lecturer at Talua Ministry Training Centre, Santo Vanuatu 2001.

average factory worker in the US earns around four times more than one worker in Mexico and 30 times more than a Mexican agricultural worker'[22]

## Education

Today our educational system has higher standards than in the past. The government is creating schools with better and more facilities and good teachers. Many of our people have migrated to towns looking for better education for their children. Joe Kamity said, 'I have moved to Vila to find better schools for my children's education because education in our rural areas does not provide good teaching facilities; schools have fallen down and teachers sometimes do not attend classes because they cannot find secure accommodation'.[23]

These educational migrants are not categorized because Vanuatu is a country with bilingual educational administration and some provinces are overseen by both administrations. Today with 200,000 people, Vanuatu has a heavy government burden complicated by the colonial history of the British and French Condominium known as Bilingual Administration which has imposed legal, government and educational divisions according to the two foreign languages, English and French.

## Push and pull factors

There are theories which try to explain the internal migration based on what are called *push* and *pull* factors. Push factors are those that push people away from where they are; pull factors are those that pull people to a new place. There are pull factors about life in the towns which attract our people to travel to these places. Pull factors might include better job opportunities, better access to good social services, leisure possibilities, peer-group pressures, mission work, business and other opportunities. Elder Sam Nato said, 'Normally Tannese move to town in search of something better and more exciting than what is happening in their own communities. They often come in search of work, or to visit relatives to strengthen family ties, and for young people, the town is a place of bright lights.'[24]

There are also the push factors that make people want to leave the rural areas. Joshua N says, 'Land shortages, the lack of regular income, the lack of a good education, poor health services, persecution and other important

22. Internet, Current Dynamics of Inter-nation labour migration, http.www.un.org. esa.pub.ittmig, 2002.
23. Interview with Joe Kamity Taxi Driver, Olsem Port Vila 2003.
24. Elder Sam Nato, *Vila North Session,* Olen Port Vila 2003.

factors compel people to move away and reside in town'.[25] The push factors are related to the local conditions in our rural areas. It is often such negative conditions that will compel a person to leave their home and move to town.

*Population growth*

Twenty-three years after independence, Vanuatu which is not a cash economy is growing very fast and has the highest population in its history. The nation itself does not have enough jobs to employ all ni-Vanuatu, whether they are educated or not educated; there are simply not enough jobs. But the major destination for all ni-Vanuatu as well as our Tannese people is Vila and Santo because people believe they can get a job there. Smile Johnson from the Statistics Office said, 'The 1989 census shows that internal migration is very high, in fact it seems to be growing because families cannot generate sustainable incomes through rural resources. Most migrants are in the age group of 20–30, followed closely by the 30–39 age groups, a pattern reflected equally amongst both males and females.'[26]

When we look at the 1999 statistical report (pages 22, 23), Tanna alone has a total of 5,225 migrants living in Vila while 335 Tannese migrants are in Santo. Today in Vila we have squatters living in the areas of Olen, Fresh Water and Blacksands, and most of our Tannese migrants are living in these squatter areas. But does this migration then mean a corresponding loss for the home island? Not necessarily so because migration is in some respects a form of trade, and fair trade allows all parties to gain. Father John Bani on the opening of the second session of Parliament on 24 November 2003 said, 'The growth of our economy is very slow but our population is growing fast'.[27]

There are concerns that are raised by the leaders as well as the chiefs that the number of migrants is growing rapidly. However, if there were more economic opportunities on the island of Tanna, there would be a reduction in the number of migrants to Vila and Santo. Therefore, most of our people need to develop their own lands in order to make a living rather than migrating. The high levels of migration have played an important role in helping the country and the government especially to create more jobs and to understand its population dynamics. However, there is no agreement in Vanuatu as to whether migration is good or bad.

---

25. Interview with Joshua N *Nepraintata session,* Imaio South East Tanna 2002.
26. Smile Johnson, *Statistics Office Port Vila,* Efate 2002.
27. Father John Bani, *President of the Republic of Vanuatu,* Port Vila 2003.

*The government action*

There is a rising concern amongst the national leaders in the country about how to deal with the consequences of urban migration. People have more knowledge these days about their individual rights as a legitimate claim strongly supported by the constitution of the Republic of Vanuatu and by other international human rights codes. Whether or not it is reasonable or necessary for a person to move from their island to any major town or centre, they know that nobody can oppose their constitutional rights by stopping them from migrating, permanently or temporarily into town. It is a matter of choice. But the question we perhaps want to consider is how we deal with the cause of migration instead of dealing with its consequences.

We all have to realise that urban drift is happening more and more than ever before. It may be good for business in towns as more people can mean a greater labour force. The businesses are only interested in having more workers, but all the burdens associated with managing the increasing number of people is left to the government. This becomes very difficult because the government has its own financial problems, and lack of good policies in this area will fail to deal effectively with this matter.

There are numerous difficulties associated with urban migration. Port Vila and Luganville are now witnessing more criminal activities than they have seen over the past decade. There is a high level of unemployment in the two towns so young people resort to crime to find ways to survive. Most criminal activities in the towns originate from the places where there are dense squatter settlements.

It is hard to send people who have already been established in town back to their home island, or to stop people from moving into town, because conditions and opportunities vary considerably in the islands, and people need to be given flexibility about deciding how best to meet their family needs. Good control and administration must be instigated and maintained, most especially by the local authorities in each of the provinces.

Investment into rural areas is an important economic activity which also has a social impact on migration of jobs. Investment should be generated into the rural areas more effectively. It will provide the possibility for retaining the young people. There is a general imbalance in the investment distribution in all provinces and islands of Vanuatu. Often we see the two major areas of Port Vila and Luganville as investment oases because of good accessibility to better infrastructure, telecommunications, utilities, and other services.

## Section Three
## Biblical aspects of migration . . . the Old Testament Perspective

*The beginning*

In the beginning, God by his sovereign power and will, created the universe. At first the earth was featureless and in darkness because of the mass of surrounding water. As God's creative activity began, he brought into being animal, plant and human life. Humans were made differently from all the animals because they were given power to rule over all God's created things. (Gen 1:24–34). The Bible shows us that the world was prepared stage by stage and was made a suitable place for man to live. Now man's status as being in God's image brought with it the responsibility to obey God's purposes (Gen 2:47). But man disobeyed the commands given to him by God (Gen 3:1–24), and therefore sin entered and spoiled the whole creation of God.

After some years of rebellion by man against God, God began His work of restoration (Gen 3:1–24). During the period of time between Noah and Abraham, the earth's population had increased greatly. 'People had migrated to different regions and many tribal groups and even nations had been established. It appears from this that there must have been far more than 10 generations, between Noah and Abraham. In that case the genealogy recorded here has been simplified, the ten names listed being the names of ten leading people of that period.'[28] (Gen 5:1–32).

*The beginning—a promise*

In the bible we see examples of people migrating. The book of Exodus is entirely a book on the topic of migration. It contains the moving out (exodus) of the people of God called Israel, about whom I will say more about later. In the scriptures we see God as the motivator of migration. He calls and directs people to move out of their situation and go to another place that he has destined for them.

In Genesis 12 God called Abram (later called Abraham) and his wife Sarai (later called Sarah) to leave their land, heritage and people and go to a new land (Ur) that God would show him.(12:1) God chose this one man out of all the nations because of his obedience to God, so that through him, God would build a new nation which would bring blessings to the whole world.(12:2–3) This call carries with it a great blessing through this one man Abraham. The bible states very clearly that Abram and Sarai, with his father and nephew, moved at God's direction south into Canaan (vs 4). God

---

28. Don Fleming, *Bridge Bible Handbooks (1)* Bridge way Publications, Brisbane, Australia 1990, 18.

promised to give Abram the land and make him into a great nation. Abram obeyed and migrated under the command and direction of God, to fulfil God's will in his life. Abram responded with a strong belief that there was something new from God, something that would bring a change in his life.

## Slave trade

In the bible, there is a lot about slaves; their stories are told in different chapters of different books in different situations. The long story of Joseph shows us how God takes the lead in moving his people from place to place to fulfill his pre-announced purposes. From his ancestors' land, Joseph was sold as a slave, not knowing that one day he would be prosperous in another country. In Genesis 46:1–4, it says that as they were leaving Canaan and migrating to Egypt, Jacob and his family stopped to worship God at Beersheba, the last town in Canaan. Here God told Jacob that he would die in Egypt. His descendants would one day return and possess the land. Jacob's family who at that time moved to Egypt numbered about seventy.[29] (46:27). The important thing in this movement was to fulfil God's will, but at the same time, another important factor is that the entire family had to move into Egypt because of the famine in their own land. They needed to push out to find enough food for themselves, and therefore they decided to migrate into Egypt.

## Suffering for the purpose

As I have already mentioned earlier, the book of Exodus shows us the migration of the Israelites from Egypt to the Promise Land. Movement from one place to another has been a major issue in human history. The Bible records the greatest collective exodus of mankind in the entire human history. The Israelites were on foot in the wilderness for over forty years before they finally reached Canaan, the promised land.

Various lessons could be taken from this account to summarize this significant movement. But the important point is that the movement of the Israelites is divinely stimulated by the strong desire for a better land promised by God. Canaan is a land chosen by God for his people, a land where they could enjoy abundant blessings and prosperity forever. It was a divine promise made to their forefathers by the almighty God. Despite the challenges and thorns on the way, the leaders continued to inspire their people to strive persistently for a better place where their children would enjoy a much better life.

It was faith in the divine promise that kept them going forward despite the extreme obstacles on their way. At times it appeared that they would

---

29.   *Ibid*, 40.

never reach the promise land because of their disobedience to God. But God knew well what he would do through his chosen leaders to keep the promise in their hearts and minds. Some leaders never got to see the promise land. Their great hero, Moses, died without having the opportunity to enter the land promised by God, but he did see it from a distance. This exodus event was a great movement of humanity but it was more of a controlled migration coordinated by their leader and master-minded by God. God promised to do so because for 400 years the people had lived in a foreign country. The people were in harsh conditions, but God through Moses liberated them and led them back to the land which he had promised.

## The New Testament perspective

The New Testament presents to us the accounts of Christ's life and the movement of the early church as directed by God. The first migration recorded in the New Testament appears in the gospel accounts of Jesus birth. He was born at Bethlehem in Judea (Matthew 2:1) and then escaped with his family to Egypt under the direction of God (2:13). From Egypt the family returned to Nazareth (2:19–23) and settled there. From there he began his public ministry when he was an adult. On the one hand, this movement into Egypt was ordered by God so that Jesus could accomplish his mission. But on the other hand Jesus migrated with his family because Herod was trying to kill him. Jesus needed security; therefore to prevent him from being killed he had to migrate to a safe place.

The book of Acts presents to us an historical account of the establishment of the early church and the Christian mission. The importance of these stories cannot be over-estimated because they present to us the founding of the church, the spread of the gospel, the beginning of congregations, and the record of the evangelistic efforts in the apostolic era. The apostolic movement provides a coordinated account of the church's beginning and the fulfilment of the teachings of Jesus in the four gospels. Ps S Kaltaliu said, 'The apostles were under the command of Christ; they moved from place to place with the gospel. The New Testament provides the record of this movement and of the impact of the Christian gospel through the power of the Holy Spirit in the heathen world.'[30]

The day of Pentecost (Acts 2) records the movement of people from many nations (Acts 2:8–10) as they assemble together in Jerusalem to receive the great power of the Holy Spirit, a power that will bring change in their life and will enable them to fulfill Christ's commands. As they

---

30. Interview with Ps S Kaltaliu, *Issue on Migration*, (Nepraintata session, East Tanna 2002).

witnessed to the gospel, many Christians were persecuted (Acts 7:54–60), facing hardship in their lives, but the struggle of faith was necessary. In (Acts 8) we see Philip and Peter migrating from their region of origin, Jerusalem, to the other places, spreading the gospel.

St Paul, once the great persecutor of Christians, after his conversion recorded in Acts chapter 9, has a strong desire to accomplish the mission of Jesus. We see in Acts 13–28 that Paul's first, second and third missionary journeys are to places all over the ancient world. His last missionary journey was to Rome where he was arrested and persecuted. Paul's missionary zeal enabled the church to grow.

The focal point for us here is that without migration in this apostolic era, there would be no Christian mission and faith today. There is a church today because the apostles had that strong desire to migrate with the good news of salvation to the whole world, as Christ commanded them (Matt 28:19–20). In the New Hebrides (Vanuatu today) in the nineteenth century, we had the London Missionary Society (LMS) with the Samoan teachers whom came as missionaries to spread the good news of Jesus Christ. Without these migrations, there would be no Christianity in Vanuatu today. The development of Christianity spread nation-wide and one of its achievements has been the political independence of the country.

*A personal view applied to Christians today*
The Christian view of migration can be best understood in the light of the great commission of the Lord in Matthew 28:19–20. Jesus with authority commanded his followers to go out with the gospel. The command was accomplished in the beginning of the first century. It is an on-going programme of going out with the good news to the non-Christian world to bring the lost people into his Kingdom of light and life.

**Conclusion**

The bible describes many different migrations. Some were for religious reasons, some for economic reasons and some for political reasons. Abraham was told by God to go to another land; Jacob and his sons moved to Egypt due to lack of food (ie for economic reasons). Israel left Egypt under Moses due to religious and political oppression. Vanuatu has experienced and is still experiencing the same sort of motivations for migration, for example, land disputes, education, economics, political oppression, religious movements.

The bible also describes some migrations that did not lead to God's blessing. Cain left Eden and moved east, Lot moves east because he wanted good land to pasture his flocks. The land where Lot settled was pagan and ungodly. Lot was influenced by his neighbours. He compromised his faith with the influence of the corruption of the people of Sodom and Gomorrah. Lot lost his house, possessions and even his wife.

Good migration occurs when God is the one who leads. Abraham migrated because he wanted to follow God. As Vanuatu today deals with the problems of migration, the first priority should be to serve the Almighty God. Migration that only focuses on economic concerns might not bring blessings. The leaders, churches, chiefs and families of Tanna and Vanuatu need to find ways to encourage only the migration that will honour God, and they should seek to discourage migration that is not God-centred.

If the root cause of migration in Vanuatu today is due to economic problems, then maybe the government, chiefs, and people of Vanuatu should find ways to expand economic opportunities on the island of Tanna as well as on other islands. Migration brings changes which can be good or bad. Let us pray that the people of Vanuatu will be able to experience changes that are good.

## Bibliography

Benton, William & Benton, Hemingway Helen, *New Geographical Britannica*, USA 1943-1973

Fleming Don, *Bridge Bible Handbooks: Genesis-Deuteronomy* (Brisbane, 1990).

Miller J, Graham, *A History of Church Planting in the New Hebrides to 1880* Live 1, (Sydney: The Presbyterian Church of Australia).

Stalker Peter, *The Non-sense Guide to International Migration* (UK 1994).

# Division in Vanuatu Communities

## Morrison Marcel

### Introduction

This major assignment is the outcome of my study during my field experience on the islands of Tanna and Erromango in the Southern Islands Presbytery. Seven months was spent on Tanna and three months on Erromango.

The focus of the assignment is the nature of division in local communities. At present, almost every community in Vanuatu has divisions and for this reason I have chosen it as an important topic to be addressed. Division in local communities throughout Vanuatu is becoming an increasingly important issue.

This study will look at the causes of division and its effects on the life of the people. We will also look at what the bible says about division and what the church could do to assist in solving this problem.

### Definition

The word 'division' simply means an act of dividing one whole item into parts. The term may be applied to numerous different things and situations. It may be defined in terms of separation or disunion.

### Cultural perspectives on division

Compared to the present there were very few divisions in our communities in the past. People in our communities had very strong relationships and a deep sense of unity. Their only major division in the past was associated with tribal wars which were typical in traditional Melanesian societies like Vanuatu. For instance, a tribe from one community might fight against a tribe from another community in order to secure as much land as possible. A practical example of this is the island of Efate where the paramount chief *Roimata* had to stop the constant tribal fights and restore peace and unity in the communities of his time.

In the past people in our communities all submitted themselves to one authority. They had great respect for their chief whom they regarded as their god. The procedure of passing on chiefly title and other traditional custom activities were always done in a proper and peaceful way. People always respected and abided by custom laws and rules laid down by the chief in their communities. They lived in peace and continued to uphold unity in their communities by observing the expected norms of behaviour.

## The causes of division

*Unrecognised resettlement*

Unrecognised resettlement is becoming a great issue in Vanuatu today. People travel from one island or community to another and settle in their new location without seeking proper permission from the chief. Most of these people have moved away from their islands and communities for some specific reasons, such as shortage of land or difficulties in finding money; some just move to other communities where they find life easier. Marriage between people of different cultures also leads to people moving into a new community. This includes inter-marriages where the groom lives with the bride in her community (rather than the other way round which is the normal practice). A good example is the late settlers on the island of Efate where men from various other islands moved to live with their Efatese wives on Efate, and have never thought of going back to their own islands. Migration from one island or community to another also applies to government and church workers. For instance, people may move with their job from one place to another or they move in search of a job; when their term of work comes to an end, these workers do not want to return to their communities but instead continue to live on where they are. Some might even have been given land to live on, while others may have purchased land, and others again have given their daughter in marriage to a boy in the community. They become settled in their new community.

Unrecognized resettlement has contributed a lot to the contemporary problem of division in our communities. One reason for this is that the 'newcomers' do not know the custom and traditional values and practices of their adopted community. . So when a community has a problem such as land disputes, the unrecognized settlers might give their support to the wrong people and the problem becomes even worse.

*Land disputes*

Land is one of the most important assets in our communities. People cannot live without land. Without land they may not survive. The importance of land is represented in the following quotation taken from the motto of the Melanesian Progressive Party (MPP), 'My land is my life'.[1]

In our communities today there are many cases involving land disputes. Speaking on this topic, Epeli explains that 'a people's interest in land is determined both by what they use it for and how much of it there is'.[2] Therefore people in our communities treat land as their security for survival.

---

1.  See the MPP Calendar 2004
2.  Epeli, H. Introduction to Pacific Studies Page 137

However, the availability of land is reducing as more and more people settle on other people's land, causing more division in the communities.

In addition to this, many people make the claim to be land owners. Maripong in one of our conversations mentioned that most of these land claimers are those who used to distribute land to other people but were not actually the rightful owners.[3] This has contributed a lot to the division among people in our communities 'since land in a traditional Melanesian society is not owned privately, but communally owned mostly by kinship groups'.[4] This means that a chief of a community is just the leader of a kin group who has the right to use land. Any decision regarding the distribution of land must not be done by the chief himself, but by the whole kinship group who own the land.

*Chiefly title*

In some of our communities dispute over the chiefly title is a major contributor to division. Many people want to be chief even if they have no right to claim a chiefly title. Moreover, some people make up false chiefly names and also perform unrecognized ordination of chiefs. According to our traditional Melanesian culture, a chiefly title is passed on to another person through heredity. There are two systems of passing on chiefly titles — patrilineal (through the father) in male dominated communities, and — matrilineal (through the mother) in the female dominated communities.

Today many people do not bother about our cultural values and practices regarding the chiefly title. They tend to do it in their own way. Therefore, the further they move away from traditional practices, the more division they cause in our communities. A good example is the ordination of the chief in the Paunangisu Village in September 1995. On that occasion, five men were ordained as chiefs but they were not the right people to be ordained.

*Wrong judgment in court*

Sometimes the divisions referred to above need to go to the courts to be solved. In our own communities, we have traditional cultural ways to handle such issues in meetings in the nakamal. Procedures for resolving division begin from the local village court and if necessary go to the Supreme Court. However, the court system may make a situation worse. The 'wantok'

---

3.  Maripong K.K. Chief Paunangisu Village, Efate. Interviewed by Author, January 2003.
4.  David, N. Geography teacher, Onesua Presbyterian College. Interviewed by author, December 2003.

system is very strong in our society (people being related to each other or speaking the same language are strongly interconnected). For instance, some people may have relatives who are judges in meetings and these judges may favour the side of their 'wantok' and so make a wrong judgment in their favour. Judging people unfairly can lead to further division which can then end up in violence or even death.

## Black magic

Black magic is also a significant cause of division in almost every community in our country. In the past, black magic or sorcery was used as a supplement to ordinary human effort.[5] Normally it was used as a form of social control, and it could be used only by certain people, usually one of the chief's assistants, who applied magic or sorcery to keep order and peace in the community. Today black magic is inclined to be used in the opposite direction, namely in ways to harm people or to disunite people in communities. People use it to kill or destroy another person's life, or to protect people. It is also used to control people's thinking, for example, if someone does something wrong, he may use black magic to defend himself in court or even to make other people forget about the wrongs he has done. In this way some people are able to use black magic to win cases in the court even if they personally think that they are wrong.

Black magic is also used to destroy the resources of communities. For example, Chief

Awia of South Tanna informed me that some people living on his island believe that they can use black magic to cause an eruption of the Yasur Volcanoe in order to destroy other people's property such as gardens, water supply and houses.[6]

The practice of using black magic is becoming a great tool in destroying our community livelihood.

## The effects of division

### Custom and culture

Division in communities affects the lives of people in many different ways. In such situations of division, people seem to manipulate or ignore the proper custom practices and values, of they make up false customs in order to defeat those with whom they are in conflict.

When a problem arises in a community people may decide to take their case to a court such as the magistrate or the supreme courts instead of to their local village courts in the nakamal. In our past, it was in the nakamal

---

5. Firth, R. Reasons and Unreasons in Human Belief. P.123.
6. Chief Awia of Tanna. interviewed by Author, March 2003.

where problems were solved where the unity of the community was restored. Today people do not respect custom meetings anymore. They see the ways of our traditional Melanesian custom and culture as inferior to the ways of Western culture. In fact, I agree with an opinion expressed in an interview with David[7] that the Melanesian ways of solving problems within Melanesian communities are much more powerful than other ways. The particular example given to support his argument was the Bougainville crisis in Papua New Guinea where members of the Bougainville Revolutionary Army (BRA) on one side, and the Civilians and PNG Defence Force on the other side, after so many years of fighting, were finally reconciled through the processes of traditional Melanesian reconciliation ceremonies.

### Community development

Many people today are suffering due to the lack of any real development in their communities that can assist in supplying their needs and wants. This is true of most communities in Vanuatu and the main cause is division. As stated by the former Prime Minister of Vanuatu, the late Father Walter H Lini, 'Divided we fall, united we stand.' When a community is divided, the government and other funding agencies often find it hard to develop that community. For instance, in the Paunangisu community on the island of Efate, development over a number of years had been at a complete stand-still. The reason for this was that there had been too many unrecognised settlers giving rise to land disputes, and there had been fighting over chiefly titles. These conflicts eventually divided the community into two groups under two leaders. Developments such as the building of a sports ground, extension of a primary school, donation of generators and lawnmowers to the community, church maintenance, telephones and the extension of the co-operative were just dreams during those years. However, in the last two years or so, there has been a reconciliation process to unite the people. As a result of this restoration of unity, there are now many developments taking place.

### Family relationship

In my study of the problem of division in our communities I have observed that many of them are started between close family members, and most often involve problems relating to land. A peaceful community is one with strong and stable family ties. However, when a community is divided, and family relationships are upset, then people no longer respect their other relatives. This then affects certain traditional practices which involve family

---

7.  David, N. Geography teacher, Onesua Presbyterian College. Interviewed by the author, December 2003.

members, especially the exchange of gifts during marriage or death ceremonies where people need support from their relatives. For example, the villages in North Efate are all interconnected in such a way that a person from one village has relatives in all the other villages. This means that if there is a death or marriage in that person's home then assistance will always come from all the villages. However, Kaltonga[8] expressed his concern that families and kinship group members are not giving the same level of support to each other during ceremonies when compared with the past. He went on further to say, 'The cause of this failure of family support is the many disputes among family members.'

Division in communities cause families to hate each other, to fight against each other, and to say foul words to each other, and the result is the loss of true family relationship values.

### Education of children

Division in communities also affects the education of children. For instance, when a division in a community becomes very tense, schools may be closed. School children may feel too insecure to attend classes. Hearing stories from adults about conflicts may lead children to act in a disrespectful manner and practise disobedience in the community. In some cases children grow up with division in their minds, especially when it takes a very long time to solve the problem. During a discussion, a villager from Kwamera in South Tanna stated that children's education should not be about learning the Western culture and ideologies alone, but also to learn the Melanesian ways. Learning our own culture and practices at a younger age will help a lot in maintaining peace and order for the younger generation since they are our future community leaders.

### Church and spiritual life

Division in a community is one of the strongest weapons used by Satan to destroy each person's spiritual life and the work of the church. In a context of division, church activities become weak since community members cannot worship together under one roof. That is why many churches are found in divided communities. People have bad feelings against each other and so they turn to other churches. But then this makes the division even worse and even harder to solve. Among other things, it has a big effect on the growth of the church because people do not want to contribute. I was able to meet with Pastor David Kaltapiri who at present resides at Paunanisu village. He gave a practical example where division in that community had

---

8. Kaltonga, K. Primary School teacher, interviewed by Author, January 2003.

affected the church (Presbyterian) and its members. He had mentioned that previously the village had only Presbyterian Church members.[9] Nowadays there are several new churches in the village. I strongly agree with him that the main reason for these new churches in the village is because people in the community are not united, there is division among them. Pastor David went on to share his experiences of the first year of his arrival in that community. He had observed that previous members of the Presbyterian Church had fled to other churches with bad feelings, and that strong Christians had become weak, leaving the church empty. He had done his very best, using the word of God as his tool, to unite he people and to bring more members back to the church. Today the church is functioning very well and has shown a positive sign of growth and development.

## The pastor's responsibility

In Vanuatu today division continues to exist in almost all communities. In the centre of these divided communities there stands the church. The church exists in order to speak out against injustice and to maintain peace and unity. However, in some communities the church is also involved in the problem. The church pastor should be very careful in all they do. The pastor should be very wise when required to live in a divided community. They should be neutral at all times and spend most of their time praying for the people and the situation.

The pastor should make sure that every member of the church is a faithful, committed and mature Christian. Communities to day are divided because there are a lot of 'skin' Christians, that is those who pretend to be Christian. The pastor has to ensure that everyone becomes a committed Christian through assistance in Bible teachings.

## Biblical perspectives on division

When we read the Bible, starting from the Old Testament and moving through the New Testament, we come across many stories regarding division. Right at the beginning in the story of creation, there is a division when Adam and Eve disobey the Lord God and are driven out from the garden. They were separated from God because of the sin of disobedience (Gen 3: 1–13).

---

9.    Ps David K. Pastor of North East Efate and Session Moderator, interviewd by Author, December 2002.

Genesis chapter 27 talks about the story of Esau and Jacob where Jacob stole Esau's birth-right and ran away. The two brothers were angry with each other and divided from each other.

In the period of the transition of Israel from the rule of the judges to the monarchy, there is a further division. In Samuel chapter 8 the people ask God for a king. God was already their king but they had rejected him. Saul was then chosen by God to be their king. However, some years later Saul was rejected by God because he was disobedient. God then chose David. Later Saul and David began fighting over the leadership of Israel.

The biggest problem of division in the Old Testament was that of the nation of Israel. The book of 1 Kings continues the story of the Israelite monarchy. It also talks about the division of the nation of Israel into two kingdoms, the Southern and the Northern Kingdoms.

## My personal view

In my own personal view, division is one of the powerful weapons used by Satan to destroy the lives of the people and communities. Although the people in the communities involved in division are often all Christians, Satan has won their hearts and used them to destroy the unity of their communities.

It may take a long time for the church to solve the problem of divisions. In doing so, the pastors should approach the problem only with the Word of God. The pastor cannot fight with their own words; instead they have to find the relevant powerful biblical passages to tackle the situation, since the Word of God is the only weapon that the pastor can use to restore peace and unity in the communities.

## Conclusion

Division in our communities is one of the hardest problems to solve. Some divisions take a very long time to be resolved. Division in a community is like a sickness. For a doctor to cure the disease, the causes and effects of the sickness must be identified in order to supply the right medicines. In the same way, in order to solve a problem in the community, one should take enough time to study it carefully.

To conclude, I would like to mention Genesis 13:1–13, the interesting story about Abram and Lot. They went north out of Egypt to the southern part of Canaan with their wives and everything they owned. On their way quarrels broke out between Abram's men and Lot's men. Then Abram said to Lot, 'We are relatives, and your men and my men should not be quarrelling, so let us separate. Choose any part of the land you want. You go one way, and I will go the other.'

This is a peaceful separation. To solve the division problems in our communities in Vanuatu today, this story is a good example. The parties who create the division in communities should take people to their own land since land is very important in a traditional Melanesian society. In doing so communities will always live in peace.

## Bibliography

Epeli, H, *Introduction to Pacific Studies* (USP Suva, Fiji: University of the South Pacific, 1994)..

Firth, R, 'Reason and Unreason in Human Belief', in *Human Types* (New York: Mentor, 1958), 123-125

## Interviews

Kaltapiri, D, Session Moderator, North East Efate Session, 2003

Koukari, D, Village Chief, Larke Village, White Sands, Tanna, 2003

Kaltonga, K, Student Teacher, Vanuatu Teachers College, Port Vila 2003

Maripongi, KK, Village Chief, Paunangisu Village, North East Efate 2003

Awia Village Chief, South Tanna 2003.

David, N, Geography teacher, Onesua Presbyterian College, North East Efate, 2003

# The Traditional Concept of Peace
# in North Pentecost

# Benjamin Tosiro

## Introduction

As one born and raised within a traditional environment where culture and
custom are strongly emphasised, I am very happy to write on this topic of
peace, because I have observed the traditional concept of peace in my
culture and have researched how it was understood and practiced in the past.

In this paper, I intend to explore the issue of the restoration of peace
from a North Pentecost perspective. The focus will be on the traditional
concept of peace in this area. Traditionally, the principle of peace served as
an internal phenomenon, within a person—it is basically the goodness
within oneself, the virtue of respect, dedication and patience that externally
is expressed through certain values.

I will also be exploring the biblical concept of peace following the ideas
of some biblical scholars about peace. Finally, theological reflection will be
offered on how the traditional concept of peace relates to scripture.

I shall begin by looking at the etymology and the definition of peace in
North Pentecost then I shall move into the details of the peace process.

## Etymology

Peace is known as 'Tamata' in the North Pentecost Nonda language.
Tamata is a traditional term derived from the root words '*Tata amre i ata*'
which mean 'Father in heaven and on earth'. Tama is derived from the root
word '*Tata*' which means Father; '*Ama*' is derived from the root word
'*Amre*' which means 'up there', 'higher' or in other words, 'heaven'; '*Ata*'
can mean 'down', 'below' or 'earth'.

All this etymology arises from the single word '*Tamata*' which means
'Peace'. It is in a sense a symbolic term or an image used to describe an
invisible quality on earth which is connected with heavenly matters.

## The traditional concept of peace .
### The definition of peace

The Oxford Advanced Learner's Dictionary (sixth edition) has three
definitions of peace. The first one is 'a situation or a period of time in which
there is no war or violence in a country or area'; the second is 'the state of
being calm or quiet'; the last is 'the state of living in friendship with

somebody without arguing'. All of these definitions refer to the phenomena of calmness, harmony, accord, and agreement.

When interviewed, an old significant figure of North Pentecost, Uloi Wanga (otherwise known as Thomas Liu) defined peace according to the culture and environment of North Pentecost as 'a living phenomenon that exists within us; it has a bodily structure that can eat and breathe. It is comprised of three different colours—black, white and yellow with the end of yellow turning more orange-red'.

What does Uloi Wanga mean by this representational definition? Let us look at a very simple example of restoring peace and how the definition fits in before we look in greater detail at exactly where peace comes into play in the lives of the people in this area.

First of all, as for all other societies, there are certain unwritten norms of behaviour that exist as rules within the society of North Pentecost. For example, going into other people's gardens and digging the crops without permission is regarded as wrong. Such norms of behaviour exist as traditional values and they are the basis of the societal way of life. They vary from island to island but with small differences. Most societies also promote gender differences (for example, in our society women are not allowed in the kava area of the Nakamal).

On North Pentecost there are certain chiefly ranks that have authority to put a taboo on certain things, such as trees with fruit. This is usually done to let the tree bear its fruit before harvesting. It is done by putting a Namele leaf on a tree. If a Namele leaf is on a Navele tree, and along comes a young man who, when he sees the Navele tree full of nuts, decides to ignore the taboo and climb the tree and starts picking the nuts, if he is caught, the matter automatically becomes a topic for discussion for the next village meeting called by the chief. Why? Because the boy's behaviour is against the norms of the society. The Namele leaf means that the tree is taboo.

This type of incident would normally create uneasiness between the person who has initially put the leaf on the tree and the person who picked the fruit. A quarrel or row usually breaks out, leading to violence. Though the young man may have his reasons for picking the nuts, something must be done in order to keep this type of taboo effective. This will be resolved in the meeting at the Nakamal. This example illustrates Uloi Wanga's definition of peace above. Let me explain.

*Peace: a living phenomenon that exists in us*
What Uloi Wanga was trying to put forward here is the fact that peace is not a physical matter that you can see walking towards you in the form of a human being or machine. It is more of a desire within your heart, a desire for harmony and happiness for you and other people or the environment

around you; it is not something that you can touch but you can see its effect and you can feel it inside you.

## Peace has different colours

If peace is a living phenomenon within you, it is then displayed in physical phenomena. With our example of the young man picking the fruit of the taboo tree, the physical phenomena of making peace include the giving of traditional mats, killing of the pig, the pig's tusk and so forth. These are the traditional items of cultural value. Any fine is given in the form of these things. They are exchanged during the peace ceremonies.

In referring to the colours, Mr. Uloi Wanga was trying to express the various colours that are displayed or exchanged during the peace ceremonies. These colours are important in that they are the representation of peace colours. We have noted that peace exists within; externally it is represented in these colours.

## Peace must be fed

If peace exists within, then how can it be fed? Peace is fed through the different fines and exchange goods that are produced during the peace ceremonies. Imagine a society with no such thing as punishment for stealing. In other words it is all right to take another person's property without asking. We would be in a mess!

When a fine is paid for a wrong-doing, psychologically this influences other members of the society to continue to uphold the perception that wrong-doing will result in heavy fines and bring a bad reputation to the family and the person doing the wrong. People will then continue to refrain from doing what is not right. Although this is not always true, it occurs in most cases of serious crime on North Pentecost. For example, killing another person will almost always end in 'holo'- the traditional way of compensating for the life of the person you have killed.

## Peace has body

Again, if peace exists within, then how can it have structure externally? The way to respond is to ask the question, 'What can you see in the society which is a sign of peace?' If peace prevails, then one can observe that peace exists in certain forms other than an actual physical structure. There is harmony, togetherness, respect, love, and so on. Mr Uloi Wanga summarized his definition of peace by saying that peace is basically the goodness within oneself—the virtues of respect, dedication and patience. Once you can achieve the virtue of peace, you find these three other virtues that will come into existence with you life.

## The peace process

### The tools for peace

We have mentioned briefly in the definition that peace exists within oneself and is expressed externally by certain traditional practices within the North Pentecost society. The items that are used within the social practices are pigs, pigs' tusks, traditional mats, chicken, food such as Yam (*Damu*) and Taro (*Bweta*), Kava (*Malogu*) and money. All of these items are man-made. Pigs and chickens are kept as domestic animals. Pigs—that is, male pigs—are usually kept for their tusks. Tam and Taro are planted as cash crops. There are also other materials that are used for the peace process such as the Palm leaf—as in Vanuatu's National Flag (the Raumwele leaf) and a particular fern leaf (Buroburoni). We will cover these things in more detail when we get to the specific events that involve the use of these things.

### Pigs (boe livo)

Pigs, in Pentecost and in the province of which Pentecost is part (ie P*enama*), are kept basically for pig-killing ceremonies which we will discuss in detail later. The value is in the body of the pig and most importantly in the tusk. Pigs' tusks are valuable in the commercial market too, but they have more value in the society. The pig's canine tooth is left to grow long and bends to form a circle, or more of a spiral. The longer the canine tooth, the more value it has, both traditionally and commercially.

### Traditional Mats (bwana/bari)

Traditional mats come in two forms—the big ones are called *bwana* and the small ones are called *bari*. These mats are woven from Pandanus leaves and are either traditionally dyed red with some special patterns or they are not dyed but retain the natural white-ish colour. The red mats are the most highly valued; the value is also measured according to the patterns burnt on the mat, how the mat was woven (there are special patterns of weaving) and the age of the mat. These traditional mats are used in the same way that money is used in western society today. They are used in marriage, death, custom dances, paying fines, buying goods, and so forth.

### Chicken (Toa)

Chickens, like pigs, are kept as domestic animals but they are not fenced in and are left roaming in the villages. Chickens are used, apart from meat, for *gonata*, the initial ceremonial stage that qualifies an individual for the pig-killing ceremony. During a *gonata*, an individual has to kill up to a hundred different kinds of male chicken. The differentiation between the chickens is made according to the different colours of each chicken feather.

*Kava (*malogu*)*

This is a Pentecost traditional drink that is now being commercialised. *malogu* is a traditional plant that is cultivated with other crops. When ready, the plant is uprooted, and the roots are cut up into smaller pieces and washed. These pieces are then crushed using stone (carved coral from the sea); the juice is then extracted and mixed with water, filtered and drunk. When consumed, it causes intoxication.

**Historical information**

In the past, in Pentecost (as in almost every society), there have been tribal wars. Pentecost has been through some very bad wars; most of them are not recorded but have been passed down through oral traditional from generation to generation. People have been killing each other for a long time. Fights were in the form of battles and guerrilla warfare. The killings were for survival, land, fame, women, and even for consuming food as cannibalism was very popular then. The major weapons during these times were spears, bows and arrows, battle sticks known as *Irubwi* (a similar type is known as *bwatibweta* commonly used today for killing pigs in ceremonies), and poison. Poison arrows known as *hui maita* were commonly used with witch craft. The arrowheads were made of human bones that, once they get through your skin, kill you instantly without you knowing who shot you, even if you saw that person.

Life on Pentecost was not as peaceful as it is today. People lived in fear and only the fittest would survive. There are legends about people like Toloa who lived in Aute area who killed many people and even burnt his wife to death. Bata lived in Anwalu area and killed many people and hid their bodies in secret places where you can still access the bones of these people. After he became a very high chief, he was a major advocate and instrument for peace; his footsteps are being followed today. Bata is approximately four generations away from the present generation. Thus, in terms of our history, these are very recent events that took place around a hundred years ago.

This killing era was evident in the manner of some of the traditional ceremonies that indicate a war-like environment. Two of the more common ones are the death ceremony and the marriage ceremony.

In the death ceremony, there was no burial as it is commonly done today because there wasn't time for proper burial. The body of the dead was thrown on the burial site and people coming to cry for the dead brought their pieces of rock and threw them into a big pile on top of the dead body. It was done in this way because enemies could attack them at anytime and there was not time to bury the dead. People wailed for a very short time and left at

131

once. These types of graves are called *bwaru*, meaning 'to stone or to throw rock onto another thing' and are found all over Pentecost.

The process of traditional marriage is very simple and quick compared to the current traditional marriage being practiced today. The current process takes longer and marriage is either arranged or the couples find each other; they know each other before they are married. With traditional marriage, the bride did not know whom she was to be married to, nor when she was to be married until the moment she was taken away. Once the bride price was paid, a special ritual was performed with the bride sitting in green coconut leaf, and the father committed her daughter to be there forever until death. The bride's family left once this ritual was performed.

Other evidence of the warring era is a type of food preparation that is no longer practiced today because it is not needed. It is referred to as *gaganiavanan bwalana* meaning 'war food'. Foods such as yam or taro or meat are prepared and wrapped and cooked quickly by heat and steam.

Why is it different today? Tribal wars diminished as people began to get to know each other; by and large, it was a combination of factors that allowed for the peace process to prevail. There was the chiefly ruling system, the introduction of the church through missionaries, and the colonisation of Pentecost. The creating of peace through the different rituals and ceremonies within the culture today also influenced the peace process.

## The past chiefly ruling system

Traditionally, a chief-to-be was selected by the current chief from among the young men based on the skills to be able to lead, to make decisions and to be able to protect his people. The selected young man is given pigs with tusks to kill in a pig-killing ceremony until he reaches a particular stage of the process. This varies from one area of Pentecost to another.

Within each village there was only one chief. Everything in the village belonged to him such as the *ara gogona* which were the sacred taboo gardens and the pigs. He practiced polygamy and may have had up to ten or more wives. He was in charge of all the decision-making that went on in the village. He had workers and messengers who would at times act as his soldiers. These were the young and mature men of the village.

The chief was in charge of the food supplies and making sure that all the families or people in his village were well fed, either through land division for gardens or through his own garden. He was in charge of paying for any fines imposed upon any member of his people, and he punished his people for wrong-doing. He acted as a consultant; he handled all the personal issues of his people and negotiated with chiefs of the different villages.

How did the system promote peace within the society? There was only one leader; there were no other chiefs who reacted against his decision or created conflict. The system encouraged and promoted communalism and togetherness. An activity to be done such as working or planting in the garden was shared between the members of the community. Women and girls were given tasks such as cleaning, collecting and preparing meals at the Nakamal. The males did more of the hard and heavy tasks, but they all worked as groups of men and women. The Nakamal was like the main community centre for getting people together. This was where the chief spent most of his time during the day giving out orders for the work of the day.

The chief's many wives were not really his wives. He used his polygamy system to prevent the young from creating adultery problems in other villages or areas. Most of the children conceived by the wives were not the chief's children. Any issue such as adultery committed in another village caused by one of his people was his problem and he handled the situation mostly by paying fines to the chief of the other village. The chief was responsible for keeping and restoring peace within his community.

**The church and peace**

The church played an important role in the peace process of North Pentecost. Pentecost was one of the only places in the Pacific, and especially in Melanesia, where the first missionaries to the island were welcomed and not driven away or killed. One example is Bishop Patteson who first landed on Pentecost in the mid-1800s and spoke the native language to the people. The people were amazed at what he had to say and were about to take revenge when the chief stopped them, saying, 'Don't touch him, he is a man of *Tagaro* (God)'.

Historically there was a peaceful encounter between the People of North Pentecost and the church partly because people had already believed that there was a superior being who could see or hear anything every person did. Whatever you did or said, the supreme being heard everything. He was referred to as *Tagaro*; his other name was *Bwalanmwalalai*. According to the old myths of the area, there were angels that had been visiting a number of places on North Pentecost. Some of the areas that were visited according to the myths were *Alanglengi* and *Abonarigi*. These angels were said to be sent from above to the earth by the supreme God. So it was then that people knew of a superior being in existence.

The church was introduced to North Pentecost in 1863 by a man called Louis Tariwale. He was from North Pentecost, from a village called Abwatvenue. The story began when his uncle Borotarere sent Louis to get him an axe. The axe he was sent for was an iron axe that had only just been introduced to Pentecost and very few people had them; stone axes were still in use. On his journey to get the axe, he was taken to New Zealand and was taught about the church. In 1863, he arrived back on North Pentecost and he introduced the church and its basic teachings. He first talked about the church with the three great chiefs of North Pentecost at that time—Pita, Bata and Boro. The people accepted the church because they believed their god was the *Tagaro* or *Bwalanmwalalai* whom they had believed in and who was now being properly explained to them by Tariwale.

What was the role of the church in the peace process of North Pentecost? Simply put, the church's principles influenced the process of peace. Since people were ready to believe in what Louis Tariwale brought to them about the church, they readily followed the teaching of Jesus Christ and his principles of better living. We shall cover the principles and teachings of the church in more detail in the biblical part of the paper below.

### Vatun Tamwata

The church has had dramatic effects on the peace process. Highly respected chiefs of North Pentecost such as Boro, Pita and Bata and other significant chiefs of that time, were responsible for another significant phase in history. When they accepted the message of the church introduced by Louis Tariwale, they felt they had to do something about all the past deaths caused by tribal wars, so they had a big ceremony that represented a peace process for people that were killed. They then began the 'Vatun Tamwata' building within their areas.

Vatun Tamwata means 'peace rocks'. Vatun Tamwata now exist all over North Pentecost and all of them are like a dais belonging to a particular chief. It is in the shape of rocks built to form two similar platforms of less than one meter high and these rock platforms are positioned in such a way that you have to walk in between them to get into the village. In some areas they mark borders between villages. The purpose of these rock platforms is to remind people that they must enter the village in peace. If you come with weapons, you must leave your weapons at these rocks before entering the village. Similarly, if you are angry, you have to make sure that your anger is not taken with you into the village.

This peace process was and is still upheld by very heavy fines when someone breaks the rules. The fines are usually pigs with fully grown tusks. These Vatun Tamwata are incorporated today into the chiefly system of North Pentecost. Only a chief who gets to a certain rank can have his Vatun Tamwata built.

### The colonisation peace activities

Despite the chiefly system of promoting peace and the church's principles of peace, there were still many cases of conflict arising from those people who would not respect the taboos, and who would kill people or domestic animals such as pigs, and did not want to pay fines. These issues became so serious that another measure was taken.

Britain and France colonised the republic of Vanuatu, then known as the New Hebrides. It was during this colonization process that certain peace initiatives were introduced to the island of Pentecost. Because of the problems arising on Pentecost, officials known as 'Government Posts' were introduced to the island. These posts were taken up by Europeans. They were in large part responsible for promoting peace within the area through imposing heavy fines when a wrong was done, or depending on the seriousness of the crime or trouble, the government representative could order police to come and take the person committing the crime to prison. Prisons were established in Santo, Malekula and Port Vila.

Since these government people were outsiders, they were highly respected and heeded. People were afraid of them as they had the power to send someone to prison or punish them. A lot of North Pentecost people were sent to prison at this time for killing other people. For example, a man called Livu killed another man and was taken away from the village to serve his sentence in Malekula from 1969-1972. Peace prevailed through fear of these government posts. They had the power that had before then belonged to the chiefs.

*Walter Lini and peace pre-independence*
Father Walter Lini, known as the 'Father of Independence' was the first Prime Minister of Vanuatu after its independence in 1980. He came from North Pentecost, and emphasised the idea of peace through respect. His famous saying, 'respect is honourable' was related to the understanding of peace within the hearts of individuals as defined by Uloi Wanga. One of the main reasons why Lini was such a key figure in the process that led to independence in Vanuatu is that he emphasized the fact that the power to maintain peace and stability within the islands of Vanuatu must be returned to the chiefs as before, and not be with the Europeans. He claimed that chiefs have more capacity to help their people than the 'Government Posts', because the chiefs know their environment and people very well.

**Traditional reconciliation and peace-keeping ceremonies**

The pig-killing ceremony is part of the process of becoming a chief within our society. The traditional process of selecting a chief varied from the current process of selecting a chief. The chiefly pattern today is more in the form of an egalitarian and democratic pattern, that is, everyone today has a right to become a chief depending on interest, wealth, wisdom and family support. There is no exception.

Within the society, there are several leaders who are responsible for particular aspects of life within the society. For instance, there is the chief of the Nasara, the chief of the Nakamal, the chief of the gardens, etc. Furthermore, aside from the duty he is given within the society, each leader stands as the representative of his clan. These leaders of different aspects of the society, work and feast together in order to maintain peace and unity in the society.

To become a chief, one has to kill a number of roosters in a *Gonata* ceremony. *Gonata* is the initial stage that qualifies an individual for the pig-killing ceremony. It is referred to as the first stage of the pig-killing ceremony (see the section above on 'chickens'). In the pig-killing ceremony a person has to kill ten pigs to become a chief. This is the second stage that qualifies an individual to become a chief. The differentiation between the various pigs is made according to the length of the tusks, beginning with the shortest tusk and progressing to the fully developed tusks which are in the shape of a spiral. Each time one of the pigs is killed a new title is given. When the tenth pig is killed the last and highest title is given which now qualifies the person to be a high chief. A chief-to-be is selected by the current chief from the young men, according to his skills to be able to lead, to make decisions, and to be able to uphold peace and protect his people. The system is a type of communalism.

With the system in place today, under the influence of colonial cultures, nothing in the village such as the taboo gardens and pigs any longer belongs to the chief; everything belongs to individual political parties. Also, the chief no longer practices polygamy and is no longer the only decision-maker in the society. Everyone has equal rights to talk and vote and make decisions. The chief no longer has his own workers who may at times act as his soldiers or messengers.

How does the current cultural situation promote peace within the society, keeping in mind the definition of peace that we have mentioned earlier, namely that peace exists within oneself and is expressed externally by certain traditional events which have particular value. Those values are contained within the pig-killing ceremony. This phenomenon of peace that existed within the society depended on having someone who had authority and power to establish peace and uphold it. Today this position of power is costly for an individual to acquire, and so be able to establish honour and respect for his role of maintainer of peace. Let me now consider some specific matters relating to traditional cultural peace.

*Rambe: Rambe* is a traditional name indicating trees or stones that have special power such as *Bwenbwena, Garisanvulu, Bwalbwale, Seseadomwae, Gaviga, and Garabihu.* These are the names of the trees that have special value and power. There are also stones that have special power such as *Vat Sarobihu.* All these trees or stones are believed to be given by *Tagaro* (the traditional name for god) to be linked with the chief to give the chief power to uphold and maintain peace in the society.

*The shedding of pig's blood:* The killing of a pig is done for a variety of reasons: in order to make peace, to reconcile people who are in dispute, to establish a person's standing in the community, to install a new leader, or to mark a special time in the life of a person, a family, a community, a church, an island or the nation. These are the special occasions or events related to the North Pentecost traditional concept of pig-killing; in particular bloodshed is a means of making peace and reconciling people who are in dispute.

In the pig-killing ceremony, the pig is tied to the foot of the namele tree and is killed with a *bwatibweta,* which is a traditional club for killing pigs, used against the pig's forehead. The blood of the pig is soft and runs freely. This blood of the pig becomes the sacrificial blood that is believed to wash away the sins of the transgressors who had acted against one of the requirements of the chief. The bloodshed marks the establishment of peace with the chief and with the people of the society. In the same way it reconciles people who are in dispute within the society so that a person or party can re-establish their good standing in the community.

*The pig's tusks:* The difference between the various types of pig killed at the foot of the Namele tree for the making of peace is determined by their tusks. The length of the tusks represents the value of the live pigs that are brought by the individual transgressors to establish peace.

*Poegani:* A *Poegani* is a pig with a short tusk just pressing out from the jaw about 1-2cm long. It is the first pig killed at the foot of the Namele tree in the pig-killing ceremony. This same type of pig, alive rather than dead, is used for peace-making by a person who has transgressed against any of the chief's requirements.

*Poe* means 'pig' and *gani* means 'to eat'. A transgressor who committed sin for the first time establishes peace with *Poegani* to re-establish his good standing in the community. The sin of the transgressor has been swallowed up by *Poegani* and been forgotten, so that now there is peace.

*Tavsiri:* A *tavsiri* is a tusk about 3–7cm long. Here the tusk is in the process of growing into a higher value; it is sharp and dangerous and can possibly cause a person harm. The one who establishes peace using such a pig is said to be in a very dangerous situation. *Tavsiri* means 'don't count the past, or the dreaded incident will be raw again'. The word *tav* means 'we' and 'siri' means 'to wash away'. Therefore establishing peace with *tavsiri* means we are washing away the transgressions and now there is peace.

*Boehere:* A *boehere* is a tusk that grows in a curve and sleeps alongside the skin in the hairy cheek of the pig. *Boe* (or *poe*) means 'pig' and 'here' means 'to blow'. Establishing peace with such a pig traditionally means the transgressions have been blown away and forgotten so there is peace again.

*Boebibia:* The tusk is now curving and sticking right through the cheek of the pig, but not yet touching the jaw. *Bibia* means 'to hide'. Therefore, establishing peace with such a pig means the transgressions are hidden, just as the end of the tusk is hidden in the cheek. The transgression will no longer be counted or seen as a sin, but it will be forgiven.

*Livoala:* A *livoala* is a pig with a full, rounded tusk. *Livoala* simply means the tusk has reached the end of the growth of the first spiral. Usually at this stage the *livoala* dies. An individual who continues over and over to commit a crime has similarly reached the final stage of establishing peace through the use of such a pig. After *livoala* there is no further form of peace-making for an individual, and only death can establish peace again.

With these traditional stages of establishing peace within the society, it is the chief who takes the initiative and gives leadership in the ceremony. He is a sort of traditional priest who, when anyone within the society has committed a crime, has the duty of bringing the pigs to the front of the *nakamal* and into a special area called *tanbona* which is the traditional public altar. Here the chief offers the sacrifice publicly, with the confession of wrong-doing being made publicly to the people, and also to god (*Tagaro*), on behalf of the transgressor who is asking for forgiveness and cleansing. It is believed that the wrong-doer is forgiven both on earth and also in the world to come, the spirit world called *Abanoi*.

*Mateana– the death ceremony:* When I interviewed another significant figure of North Pentecost, *Talai Lava* (Christopher Tosiro), he defined death according to the traditional concept as 'the most precious phase of establishing an everlasting peace in the life of an individual'.

What does Tosiro mean by this definition? In order to answer this question, we will look in detail at the understanding of the traditional death ceremony of North Pentecost, and explore how the dead person may qualify for an everlasting peace in *abanoi* which is understood as the spirit world where the dead man lives forever.

First of all, according to the traditional beliefs of North Pentecost, and also more generally, death is the one certainty which no-one can deny or hope to escape, so the experience of loss and grief when someone dies is common to all people, whatever their cultural background or social status. But the rituals performed at the death ceremony are different in different cultures and societies. Although death is a precious phase of entry into everlasting peace, it is a crisis for the living relatives who remain. When a member of the immediate family dies, the bereaved members are too confused and upset to carry on their daily routine and the life of the whole household becomes disorganized. So there is a need for comfort in terms of peace-making. We will be looking at two aspects of the death ceremony: 'ordinary death', and 'the *holo'* or traditional way of compensating for one's life after being killed.

*Ordinary death:* Traditionally when someone dies there is a lot of mourning where people express their reactions to the death, especially the immediate family and very close relatives, but also the extended families and the people of the community where the dead person lived. Immediately when he breathes his last, the *sinsini* (traditional gong) is beaten. There are different types of beating depending on the status of the dead person. This *sinsini* is beaten to inform the people that there has been a death. The body is bathed, and if the dead person is a man his beard is shaved. After that he is dressed with all the best clothes that can be afforded and is taken to the *Nakamal*.

People come and pay their last respects and mourn over the dead body, especially the grieving family who have lost their beloved. People who come each bring with them a traditional mat in order to wrap the dead body for the burial. After all the families of the dead man have arrived, the body is wrapped in a special traditional way. After this has been done a ritual is performed in order to comfort the grieving family so that they will live peacefully afterwards, and also to clear the way for the dead person to advance into the spirit world called *abanoi* so that the spirit of the dead man may be accepted there and he may live peacefully forever.

The body is then taken to the church for the funeral service. After the funeral service the body is transported to the burial ground and is buried. After the burial the immediate families continue to mourn for at least ten days which means there is quietness and silence within the society; during this time no work will be done and everyone remains in the *Nakamal*. The mourning is marked by outward signs, for example men grow beards, family members refrain from washing, women put ash on their foreheads and others stop combing their hair.

With the older traditional process there was no burial as there is commonly today. The body of the dead person was thrown onto a burial site and people came to cry for the death. People cried for only a very short time and then left at once. This practice was followed in times when there was a war-like environment. (See the earlier section of this paper.) It was done in this way because enemies could attack at any time and there was no time to bury the body. Graves of this type are called 'Bwar' meaning 'to stone or throw rocks'.

How was the concept of peace related to the traditional death ceremony? There were specific events that happened during the time of mourning that promoted peace.

*Poen bwatigoro (the sinner's pig):* A *poen batigoro* is a pig that is killed by the bereaved family members. The significance of the pig-killing by the bereaved is in the shedding of blood. The blood of the pig runs freely and is believed to wash away all the sins committed by the dead person in this mortal world so that he or she is then accepted into *abanoi* (the spirit world), to live peacefully there forever. It is also believed that if there is no forgiveness of sins, the spirit of the dead person will roam around the earth as a *vuiatmate* (evil spirit).

*Mwahalu:* The word *mwahalu* is derived from the word *mwahaluga* which means 'to bring to completion'. It is a special ceremony performed before the burial of the dead person in order to bring to completion the final traditional tributes; it is seen as an outward sign of comfort to the grieving family that they may live peacefully afterwards. The *mwahalu* is usually done to the father and the son of the immediate family of the dead person by the dead person's clan. This usually involves a pig with a rounded tusk.

*Mandue:* *Mandue* is a death souvenir that is given to remind one of the dead person. It is usually a pig with a rounded tusk. The *mandue* is offered within the same tribe, ie from brother to brother or between uncle and nephew. The person stands at the front of the line and gives the other the *mandue*. The recipient inherits the status of the dead person and it is his responsibility then to maintain peace and unity within the clan.

*The 'holo' peace process:* The word *holo* is derived from the word *gamali* or 'house', meaning to give shelter or coverage or protection in order to sustain life. The *holo* peace process is to compensate for the life of a person after the person has been killed by an opponent. To perform this process is the responsibility of the chief, his tribe, and more importantly the clan and the immediate family of the opponent. It will need at least ten pigs and many traditional mats to compensate for another person's life so that peace may prevail, and so that the life of the clan and the immediate family of the opponent can be protected from revenge.

## The biblical concept of peace

*The source of peace*
David, a man after God's own heart, prayed: 'The eyes of all look to you and you give them their food at the proper time. You open your hand and satisfy the desires of every living thing.' (Psalm 145:15–16)

Job, a man who had lost everything, replied to the Lord: 'I know that you can do all things, no plan of yours can be thwarted'. You asked, 'Who is this that obscures my counsel without knowledge?' Surely I spoke of things I did not understand, things too wonderful for me to know. You said, 'Listen now and I will speak; I will question you, and you shall answer me. My ears had heard of you but now my eyes have seen you. Therefore I despise myself and repent in dust and ashes.' (Job 42:1–6)

Commenting on the Psalms and Job, EG White wrote:

> Nature and revelation alike testify to God's love. Our father in heaven is the source of life, of wisdom and of joy. Look at the wonderful and beautiful things of nature. Think of their marvelous adaptation to the needs and happiness, not only of human beings, but of all living creatures. The sunshine and the rain that gladden and refresh the earth, the hills and seas and plains, all speak to us of the creator's love. It is God who supplies the daily needs of all his creatures.'[1]

God is the source of everything in the heavens and in the earth. Although the world is under a curse, nature itself testifies messages of hope and comfort that God is love. The colourful flowers perfuming the air and the lovely birds with their happy songs testify God's care and love and his desire to make his people happy.[2]

Because God is love, he perfectly made humans holy and happy in his own image and made the world to live in. There was no corruption, not even

---

1. See White, *Finding Peace Within* (Inspiration Books East, INC USA), 9.
2. *Ibid*, 9.

a shadow of curse; it was the transgression of God's law of love that has brought war and death. '. . . Cursed is the ground because of you, through painful toil, you will eat of it all the days of your life'(Gen 3:17b).

God reveals himself as the source of everything and is testified through nature and revelation. In this sense, God is the source of peace.

### The problem: our need for peace

Humankind was originally made in the likeness of God. He was perfect in his being and in harmony with God. He lived a pure and holy life. But through disobedience, he turned away from his proper nature and was made captive by Satan for the purpose of filling the earth with woe and desolation. Before he had fallen short of the glory of God, he was in joyful communion with God.[3]

After sinning he no longer found holiness with God. He was far away from the presence of God. He no longer enjoyed the company of the holy beings. Could he be permitted to enter the kingdom of God to share joyful communion with him? Could he share the companionship of holy beings? It is impossible for those who are wicked and whose hearts are evil and cannot be changed. There is a need to make peace with God, to full in the gap which sin has made. But who is able to make the clean out of the unclean, the holy out of the unholy? No-one! Humans can only do that by the indwelling power of the Holy Spirit within the sinners to bring new life in all its fullness. That power to change all people from sin to holiness comes only from above, from Jesus Christ whose grace brings life to all souls and restores them to God. The following scripture confirms this: 'I tell you that truth, no one can see the kingdom of God unless he is born again' (John 3:7), and 'Salvation is found in no one else, for there is no other name under heaven given to men by which we must be saved' (Acts 4:12).

Humans needs to make peace with God in order to be saved, in order to be permitted to enter the kingdom; that he may share joyful communion with God; that he may share the companionship of the holy beings; that he may have eternal life; that he may fulfil the purpose of creation as God's own image and steward of all creation.

### Peace in the Old Testament

#### a) The Historical Development of Peace Among the Israelites

The Old Testament is full of the language of peace. The Pentateuch focuses on the sacrificial lamb as a means of making peace with God. The people offered animal sacrifices in which the pouring out of animal blood was required to re-establish peace with God. Peace in the Old Testament is the

---

3.  *Ibid*, 16.

result of a process required by the demands of God.[4] TD Alexander explains:

> Peace is not simply an empty wish, it is a result of a process that, in this instance, exacts the high cost of life. Peace is not confined to present circumstance but is part of a larger perspective on life and the world, pointing towards the demands which a holy and righteous God makes on his followers.[5]

I am convinced that peace in the Old Testament is not an empty wish but the result of a process. I would describe it as a phenomenon that cannot be sensed, yet it can be sensed. For example, God is a mysterious God, yet we can see him through nature and revelation. Peace hasn't a body or a sense either, it is only a word, yet there are forms, methods, and processes of making peace in the Old Testament that one can touch, see, feel, smell or hear. Take for instance the following scriptures:

> Make an altar of earth for me and sacrifice on it your burnt offerings, your sheep and your goats and your cattle. Whenever I cause my name to be honoured, I will come to you and bless you. (Ex 20:24, 24:5, 29:28, 32: 6, Numbers 6:7, 15:29)

> For the life of a creature is in the blood and I have given them to you to make atonements for yourselves, it is the blood that makes atonement for one's life. (Lev 17:11; 3:4; 6:7; 9:10, 17, 19, 22, 23)

Peace-making was done continually by the people in order to make peace with God. The blood of the animal sacrifice was shed to establish peace. However, the process of peace-making was not perfect. The demands of a holy and righteous God had not been satisfied, because of sin.[6]

b) *The prediction about the prince of peace*
The people had no peace among themselves or with God despite the provision of sacrificial animals. Yet God is a God of love, a gracious God,

---

4. TD Alexander and others, *New Dictionary of Biblical Theology*, (London: Intervarsity Press), 682
5. *Ibid*, 682
6. *Ibid*, 682

who with his great love and mercy for the fallen world, had taken the initiative to save his people. Isaiah predicts the coming of a redeemer as the climax of Israel's history and the solution to their present difficulties (see in particular Isa 9 and 11).

This raises a question: why grace for peace? It is a reasonable enough question to ask. The cosmos, and creatures living in it are God's own. All have their functions and purposes for his mysterious plan. Specifically speaking, God made humankind in his own image for a purpose. To fulfil that purpose he permitted his only beloved son to bring peace. Isaiah confirms: 'For to us a child is born, to us a son is given and the government will be on his shoulders, and he will be called wonderful counsellor, mighty God, everlasting father, prince of peace.'(Isa 9:6)

*Peace in the New Testament : the solution*
a) *Why Jesus came*
We discovered earlier that according to the Old Testament, sin is the source of corruption in God's created order. It sweeps away the holiness of life that originated from God. It is the most devastating influence in the cosmos. Billy Graham explains:

> We have seen that the most terrible, the most devastating fact of the universe is sin. The cause of all trouble, the root of all sorrow, the death of every human lies in this one small word—sin. It has robbed the human of his nobility. It has caused him to fall into the devil's trap.[7]

For ages men had been lost in spiritual darkness and were seeking the way out from the locked door to which there is no key. Who has the key to unlock the door? Who can redeem them? God is a God of love, as the bible teaches us. Because of his love for the fallen world, God wanted to do something for humankind. He wanted to save humankind and free him from the cause of sin. His life was perverted, but God promised hope that some day a redeemer would come. Sin had come through one man, Adam as Paul states in his letter to the Romans: 'Therefore, sin first entered the world through one man Adam, and death through sin, and in this way death came to all men' (Romans 5:12).

But God our loving father began to teach his people that by substitution, he would again make peace between the world and himself. 'We all sheep have gone astray, each of us has turned to his own way, and the Lord has laid on him the iniquity of us all' (Isa 53:6).

---

7.    Billy Graham, *Peace With God* (London: Words Work Ltd), 73.

And so it is not the human who approaches God for peace, but it is God's own will to make peace with all humankind, so that they may be taken back to the position they had before they fell from grace. God fulfilled his promise. He revealed himself in the form of a servant to restore the fallen world and make peace with us. Jesus Christ took our flesh and blood that he might die for us. Jesus was born into the world and clothed himself with our human nature. As it testifies in the New Testament: 'Since the children have flesh and blood, he too shared in their humanity so that by his death he might destroy him who holds the power of death' (Heb 2:14). And again, 'But you know that he appeared so that he might take away our sins'(1 John 3:5). And further, 'The son of man did not come to be served, but to serve, and to give his life as a ransom for many' (Matt 20:28). And, 'No-one has ever seen the Father, but the one and only son, who is at the father's side, he has made him known'(John 1:18).

And so the concept of peace in the Old Testament is extended in the New Testament. Jesus, the Son of Man came and made manifest the Father as the source of everything in the heavens and upon the earth.[8]

DA Carson explains, 'Through the birth of the Messiah, God extends his favour to the people who have done nothing to deserve it, and he graciously grants them peace. Peace expresses the nature of salvation, the restoration of good relationships between God and sinful people and the consequent reception of his blessings.'[9]

In describing his own earthly ministry, Jesus says, 'The spirit of the Lord is upon me because he has anointed me to preach good news to the poor, he has sent me to proclaim freedom to prisoners, recovery of sight for the blind, and to release the oppressed' (Luke 4:11).

Jesus' earthly mission gave evidence of his divine, anointing love, mercy and compassion, revealed in every act of his life. Even though people rejected him, he regarded them with pity and care. He suffered death for the goodness of his people, so that peace may be restored. 'He was pierced for our transgression, he was crushed for our iniquities, the punishment that brought us peace was upon him' (Is.53:5).

It was for the burden of sin that God permitted his son to die, that peace may be restored in the relationship between God and sinful people.

*b) The concept of peace in St Paul*
The apostle Paul sees Jesus as the one who brings peace by his life and teaching, his death and resurrection.

---

8.   *Ibid,* 74
9.   DA Carson & Others, *New Bible Commentary* (London: IVP Press, 1984).

'All this is from God, who reconciled us to himself through Christ and gave us the ministry of reconciliation: God was reconciling the world to himself in Christ, not counting men's sin against them . . . God made him who had no sin to be sin for us, so that in him we might become the righteousness of God.' (2 Cor 5:18–21; see also Romans 5:8–11; Col 1:20–22; Ephesians 2:14–17)

According to Paul, God has taken the initiative to reconcile all people to himself through Christ, even his enemies. Through his death and resurrection, God has saved people from sin and death and hell, and Satan's power has fallen. In the opening greetings of his letter, Paul wished grace and peace to his readers, as from God our Father and from the Lord Jesus Christ, who is the source of all the blessings we receive and God's greatest gift to us which we only truly experience through the Gospel.[10]

The concept of peace in the Pauline letters is clear: it is not humans who approach God to make peace, but God who reaches out to humanity. TD Alexander explains: 'First God desires peace with humanity to the point of acting to bring it about, secondly is the work of Christ upon the Cross; in particular his death has established peaceful relations between God and humanity, and made possible peaceful relations between those who believe in him'.[11]

### c) *The conditions*

God revealed himself through the person of Jesus Christ to make peace with all humankind. However, in his ministry there are requirements in order to make this peace with God effective. The requirements are under three headings: conversion, faith, and regeneration.

#### i) *conversion*

Jesus in his ministry demanded confession from people in order to be at peace with God and restore relationships with sinful people. 'I tell you the truth, in the same way there will be more rejoicing in heaven over one sinner who repents than over ninety-nine righteous persons who do not need to repent' (Luke 15:7); 'Repent for the Kingdom of God is near'(Matt 4:7; Luke 13:2–3).

God was speaking through Jesus. He called upon people to acknowledge their guilt and turn from their ungodliness, in other words, to make peace with God. In the sinner's confession, God himself rejoices and God's people share in his rejoicing.

---

10. *New Dictionary of Biblical Theology* (London: InterVarsity Press), 683
11. *Ibid*, 683

## ii) Faith

Jesus also demanded faith in order to make peace with God. Only through faith in Jesus Christ is there salvation; only through faith in Jesus Christ can we acquire peace. The bible teaches us that faith is the only approach to God. Faith is a channel through which God's grace to us is received and peace restored. This is not from ourselves but by the help of the Holy Spirit. 'And without faith, it is impossible to please God, because anyone that comes to him must believe that he exists and that he rewards those who earnestly seek him' (Heb 11:6; John 14:11; Acts 16:31; John 1:12; Acts 13:39; Romans 4:5, 5:1, 10:17; Heb 10:10-39; Ephesians 2:8).

## iii) Regeneration

Regeneration means to be born again, to turn away from our sinful nature and step forward as the new person God wants us to be. Jesus demanded regeneration in order to make peace with him and restore the relationship. 'I tell you the truth; no one can enter the kingdom of God unless he is born again' (John 3:7).

Jesus here demands regeneration as the beginning of life. However nothing can be done to obtain new birth in order to make peace with God; it happens only through the work of the Holy Spirit. 'Yet to all who received him, to those who believed in his name he gave the right to become children of God; children born not of natural descent nor of human decision or will, but born of God'(John 1:12, 13).

Billy Graham explains: 'It is the infusion of divine life into the human soul. It is the implantation or impartation of divine nature into human souls whereby we become the children of God. We receive the breath of God. Christ through the Holy Spirit takes up residence in or hearts and we are attached to God for eternity.'[12]

In summarising the ideas of the scholars I have read, I would say that the concept of peace works in this way: A human person is a dependent being, depending entirely upon God's spiritual power for new birth in order that peace relations may be restored between humankind and God here on earth and at the end of time, and that a person may be able to overcome all temptations of the cosmos. 'So everyone born of God overcomes the world' (1 John 5:4). 'Now the God of peace . . . make you perfect in every good work to do his will, working in you that which is well pleasing in his sight' (Heb 13:20, 21).

Therefore, the moment we repent of sin and turn by faith to Jesus Christ we are born again and a peaceful relationship is restored between God and humankind.

---

12. Billy Graham, *Peace with God,* (London: Worlds Work Ltd), 124

### Traditional peace in the light of scripture

There are many things that people still do not understand. There are many mysteries. There are many problems that puzzle us. But underneath it all is that inward relaxation and peace that will lead to confident living.

We have found that there are many positive insights about the traditional concept of peace when compared with the biblical concept of peace. The aspects of traditional peace reflect what Christ offers in his ministry. Because Christ is the Lord of all life, everything in the life of an individual, family, church, or the community, must reflect the Gospel of Christ. We have seen this too with traditional peace. Christ is the imitator of God's peace through the Holy Spirit.

The traditional peace, *tamata*, was described as a living phenomenon that externally is expressed through certain values; these traditional values are a means of providing for a good life, and establishing harmony, togetherness, happiness and so forth within the society when something goes wrong. This is directly related to the new life in Christ, through the power of the Holy Spirit. Paul in his letter to the Galatians says, 'The fruit if the spirit is, love, joy, peace, patience, kindness, goodness, faithfulness' (Galatians 5:22) .

It is important for us to discern what is good and what is bad about traditional culture, to discern what needs changing and what to keep of the values and heritage of our traditional peace. We can do this by discerning what is in line with the will of God. The whole of our traditional peace process in this sense is confirmed to be in the likeness of Christ as a means of redemption.

Many Christians have in the past been too negative towards culture. We forgot that Christ is the Lord of all life since God calls for salvation in him. I affirm the fact that our traditional cultural practice of peace reflects that of our Creator. The apostle Paul made the same judgment about the culture of the people of Athens: 'For as I walked around and looked carefully at your objects of worship, I even found an altar with this inscription, "To the unknown God". Now what you worship as something unknown I am going to proclaim to you' (Acts 17:33).

Since the arrival of Christians, the traditional concept of peace has been Christianised. Since Christianity is a universal religion, it adapts itself to the local practices of traditional peace. Such adaptation must be in the light of the gospel of Jesus Christ in order for the gospel to be revealed. Christianity engages in cross-cultural communication with traditional peace to reveal the reality of the unknown God, and to claim that he is the Lord of all and demands total allegiance.

148

There are features of traditional peace that are compatible with the Lordship of Christ, and need to be preserved and there are features which need to be transformed. Messengers of the Gospel need to develop deep understanding of the traditional peace and a genuine appreciation of it before making any judgments. There is no tension between the traditional peace and the biblical peace but we must see the traditional peace in the light of the Scriptures. Christ came to fulfill the traditional peace as the Lord of all life. 'Do not think that I have come to abolish the law or the prophets, I have come not to abolish them but to fulfill them.' (Matt 5:17; Gal 3:24). Jesus is seen as the one who directs all people in our culture towards attaining peace.

*Combination of the traditional and the biblical peace*
The combination affirms that Christ is the initiator and the source of peace both culturally and biblically, as one person with two natures (Matt 5:17; Gal 3:24). No one can deny or oppose this combination as a reflection of faith in God as the source of everything. If we neglect the combination of the traditional and the biblical peace, then we are denying Christ's love. For Christ came to redeem both the physical and spiritual needs of people within their respective cultures, when they come to accept Christ as their Lord and Saviour. 'For God so loved the world that he gave his own and only son . . .' (John 3:16) Bishop Selwyn of the Melanesian Mission wrote, 'Melanesia ought to retain what is good in its culture in conjunction with the new teaching and new life in Christ. We must not make difficulties in the way cultural people receive Christianity.'

Peace can be experienced only when we receive divine pardon, only when we have been reconciled to God, only when we have harmony within ourselves, with our fellow human being, and especially with God. 'There is no peace', says my God, 'for the wicked' (Isa 57:21). But through the blood of the cross, Christ has made peace with God for us, he is himself our peace. Although Christ died two thousand years ago, we believe that if by faith we accept him, then we have peace with God, so in that sense, as Christians, we maintain the invisible continuation of peace through faith with God when we accept him. When he enters our hearts, we are freed from our sins and so we have confidence to know that we can stand before God in the hour of our death with this same feeling of peace and security.

There is no reason to neglect the traditional peace in the light of scripture. The traditional peace process is the visible confirmation of the God-given nature of our culture. We reflect the invisible reality of the continuity of peace through faith in God when we accept him internally from within the heart. 'Since the creation of the world God's invisible qualities—his eternal power and divine nature- have been clearly seen,

149

being understood from what has been made, so that people are without excuse' (Romans 1:20). In that sense, traditional peace values express the invisible peace externally.

The traditional peace process is a means of attaining life within the society. If it is a means of attaining life, then it automatically comes from God. 'I have come that they may have life, and have it to the full' (John 10:10). If it does not give life, then we should neglect the traditional peace in the light of the scripture. Culturally, there is still a tendency to allow our traditional form of peace to influence our conceptions of God. Peace is achieved by a moral approach in which Jesus himself is a great moral leader who in all that he did in the flesh until his death on the cross was the model of our moral concept of peace.

It is with a combination of both the traditional and the biblical peace that we dismiss all anxieties from our minds. We should be discerning what we do not have in the traditional peace and protect what we do have, when seen in conjunction with the will of God. The root or the focal point of this peace is the peace of Jesus and we need not be surprised that it rests on Jesus being the centre of our lives. It is the peace based on the traditional theological definition of peace as calm, quiet and undisturbed that puts all things in correct perspective through his Spirit at the centre of our lives. God gave us the means to come to grips with something that we can taste, feed, or smell as a visible demonstration of an invisible reality.

*Relating the traditional practices to the biblical concept of peace*
As we have seen, the bible has much to say about peace and reconciliation, but it is mainly concerned with restoring the relationship between humankind and God, rather than between two human disputers. It also recognises the importance of maintaining peace on earth between people, both inwardly and outwardly. The Old Testament law provided for compensation or restoration when one man had stolen from another or had wronged him in other ways, and the teaching of Jesus in the New Testament also encouraged this (eg in the story of Zacchaeus in Luke 19:8–9). However this was not always possible; even the Old Testament principles of 'an eye for an eye and a tooth for a tooth' (Ex 21:24) must be seen, not as encouraging the wronged party to seek revenge or compensation, but as imposing an absolute limit on the amount of compensation that could be required, so that peaceful relations could be restored. If I have committed adultery with the wife of another man, the principle must not be understood as requiring me to allow him to do the same to my wife. The consistent teaching of the bible, in both the Old Testament and the New Testament, is that we should forgive those who have done wrong to us, rather than seeking revenge or compensation. (See for example Gen 50:17–21; Matt 19:21)

What, then, should be the attitude of the Christian church to the traditional ceremonies of peace and reconciliation? First, we must encourage the role of the chief and accept his authority in settling disputes between individuals, families, tribes or clans. If he decides that there should be compensation in the form of an animal sacrifice or other gifts, then we should accept and support his decision. Every Christian, whether a priest or a pastor or a chief or any other believer, has a responsibility to maintain peace and restore peace in situations where there is none (Matt 5:9).

However it would be difficult, in view of the teaching of the scripture, for the church to have any involvement in pig-killing ceremonies if they are seen as bringing about reconciliation between humankind and God, or as atoning for the sins a person has committed. There are at least three important reasons why the church cannot support involvement in such ceremonies:

a) The bible clearly teaches that the pig is an unclean animal and had never been acceptable to God as a sacrifice for sin. (See Lev chapters 1–10). This also applies to dogs, camels, rabbits, lions and some other animals.

b) The New Testament teaches that animal sacrifices are no longer needed and now have no effect. Christ himself was the 'Lamb of God', the perfect and final sacrifice for sin. Now that he has died for us, to offer any other sacrifice would means that we are saying the sacrifice Christ made was not good enough to atone for all our sins and reconcile us to God. We must help people to understand their need to be reconciled to God and urge them to accept the sacrifice of Christ on their behalf. (2 Cor 5:18–21). But this must involve a work of God in the soul of the person, so that he is 'born again' (John 3:7). There is no ceremony or sacrifice or external payment that can bring about reconciliation of a person with God—not even baptism, confirmation or ordination.

c) Once a person has died no ceremony or sacrifice or prayers can make any difference to his eternal destination. The only way a person can secure eternal peace is to accept Christ as his Lord and Saviour during his lifetime on this earth. Having people offer sacrifices and pray for him after he has died will achieve nothing. Christians should pray for the bereaved relatives who remain, but should not take part in any ceremony or type of mourning that is seen as an attempt to ensure eternal peace for the dead person—it is too late for that.

**Conclusion**

Some of the traditional ceremonies can still have an important place in the life of a Christian community. The chief should be respected as a peace-maker and mediator in disputes involving members of his tribe or clan, but he should not be seen as taking the place of Christ who is now the *only* mediator between God and humanity (1 Tim 2:5l; Heb 8:6 and Heb 9:15) and our Great High Priest (Heb chapters 8 and 9). The Church and individual Christians should not participate in any ceremony that involves the worship of, or prayer to, any other god, or which supports values that are contrary to biblical revelation.

**Bibliography**

TD Alexander, Brain's Roosner, *New Dictionary of Biblical Theology* (London: Inter varsity Press 2000).

Billy Graham, *Peace with God* (London: Fletcher & Son Ltd, 1972).

EG White, *Finding Peace Within* (Washington: Inspiration Books East Inc. 1989).

David Hunt, *Peace Prosperity and the Coming Holocaust* (New York: Harvest House Publishers 1983)

Kathleen Lonsdale, *Is Peace Possible* (London: Fletcher & Son Ltd. 1957).

Edward Leroy Long, JR, *Peace Thinking in a Warring World* (New York: The Westminster Press 1983).

DA Carson, RT France, Ja Motyer, G.J Wenham *New Bible Commentary* (London: Inter-varsity Press, 2000).

Fr Stanley Ure, Lecturer *Gospel and Culture*, Talua Ministry Training Centre, 2004.

# Respect for the *Nakamal* as a Model for the Church Within the Culture of the Bathot People

## Amanrantes John Fred

### Introduction

In this paper, I attempt to explain how my ancestors on the island of Malekula treated the *Nakamal* in their tradition, and to suggest that this may provide a helpful symbol for the life of the Christian Church. My intention is to encourage individual members and leaders of the church to maintain holiness and respect within their lives and in the church.

In section one of my project, I will explore how the *Nakamal* was respected by my forefathers and how they made holiness part of their lives. Section two is about the Chief's (*Meleun*) life-style in the *Nakamal*, his responsibility and his behaviour. I will follow this with special reflection on biblical and theological perspectives, and finally I will offer a conclusion.

### The *Nakamal*

#### Definition of Nakamal

*Nakamal* is one of the most widely used names today in Vanuatu and has especially become common in Bislama speech. There are two places to which people today apply the term *Nakamal* — one is the meeting place and the other is the kava bar.

#### (i) Meeting Place

The village meeting place is called the *Nakamal*; it is a place where decisions are made, disputes are settled, community activities are held and traditional artefacts are displayed.

#### (ii) Kava Bar

Sometimes people call a Kava Bar, a *Nakamal* perhaps because the Kava Bar is used as a meeting place where usually men (rarely women) go to in the evenings to drink kava and to enjoy fellowship.

Referring to the article by Ps Johnny Naual when he interviewed David Blue of Pentecost in Fiji May 1995, Naual wrote, '*Nakamal* is derived from the root word Kamel from the dialect of Central Pentecost; *Kamel* means "shade"—either of a tree or a cave or a house; *Nakamal* is to hide under the shade'.[1]

In Vanuatu, we have different views of the *Nakamal*. In my culture in Malekula, the *Nakamal* is a meeting place, not for ordinary people but only for those who have received certain ranks of authority. Only ranked members of the tribal community can be members of the *Nakamal.*

In the Southern part of Malekula, the *Nakamal* is called *amel* which means 'shade of a house' and implies holiness. This word *amel* is widely used by *Bathot*[2] speakers. When we talk about *amel* we mean a holy place or a house that contains holy things such as carvings, and people with certain ranks live there. It is a place for men alone, not for women or children.

Mansif Bong, a high-ranking man from the village of Farun in the southern part of Malekula stated that, '*amel* is *amel*, which means that we cannot express its value; it is more than we can say. It is very holy.'[3]. Alang Welamb[4] explained, '*amel* is our golden treasure', and Abraham[5] stated that, '*amel* is our schooling place, the only place where we learn from our high-ranked people about how to live and survive within our environment.'

*Origin of the Nakamal*

Our forefathers believed that the *Nakamal* was founded by the instruction of a woman. The story was repeated from generation to generation and even today the story is still told. This is the story:

> Once upon a time there was a woman who had two sons.
> They lived together having a good relationship until one
> day, she told her two sons to build a special house apart
> from their home. So the two boys built the house; when
> they had finished, the woman gave these instructions to her
> two sons:

---

1. Randall, Prior, editor, *Gospel and Culture in Vanuatu 2: Contemporary Local Perspectives* (Melbourne: Gospel and Culture in Vanuatu Books, 2001), 52-58
2. Bathot is our tribe's native language
3. Mansif Bong, Farun Village South Malekula 2003
4. Alang Welamb, a custom name of my father from Bonvor South Malekula 2003
5. Abraham, from Bonvor South Malekula 2003

'Kill me inside this house, and by the shedding of my blood the boundary of this house will be the most holy and devoted place; this house is to be called *amel*.

After you have killed me and the house becomes *amel*, it is a rule that all women are to be excluded. You are not allowed to eat with women when you spend time in the *Nakamal*. If you do anything wrong, you are to be excluded from the *Nakamal* until you kill a pig as part of your purification, and then you can be accepted back into the *Nakamal* again. If anyone wants to be part of this *Nakamal*, he must first kill a pig.'

So the boys did what their mother instructed them to do and that is why the *Nakamal* is treated respectfully within my culture. The woman's instructions are still observed within the *Nakamal* to this day.'

*The value of Nakamal*
First, when people begin to build a *Nakamal*, women can help in doing some cleaning up, building the house and some other things. When everything is completed and ready to be used, the high-ranking men bring pigs and kill them within the boundary of the house, and by the shedding of the pig's blood, the house is set apart to become holy, and women are never allowed to enter the place again.

Only the specially ranked men who have killed the appropriate number of pigs required by the value of *Nakamal* are permitted to use it. It is a highly respected place, a place where the men meet to talk about developments, to handle disputes, to maintain peace and to encourage each other. The laws are established there, and these men make sure that people always keep the laws.

If any problem is raised within the community between a man and a woman, then this problem is to be settled outside the *Nakamal*, and the meeting will involve the man and the woman together with the Meleun (Chief). After reconciliation has taken place, if the man wants to go back to the *Nakamal*, he must first make some sacrifices which are part of his purification to re-enter the *Nakamal*. Should there be any problems such as adultery, fornication etc; these will be settled outside the *Nakamal* because the *Nakamal* is treated as holy.

The following are some of the activities which take place in the *Nakamal*:

i) Receiving important visitors: When a visitor arrives in the community, he is taken to the *Nakamal* and treated respectfully in the sense that he is to live, eat and talk with the high-ranking people; he is not to live with the women in the community. This is the way we show respect to the visitor.

ii) High-ranking people: High-ranking people mostly live in the *Nakamal* where they are treated with respect. They live there often to maintain their status, or not to mix with ordinary people. Sometimes they may visit their families in their communities but they spend most of the time living in the *Nakamal*.

iii) Holiness, peace and reconciliation: The *Nakamal* is a place where the men exercise holiness, peace and righteousness. People who enter the *Nakamal* always try to live a holy life. To live a holy life is not the same in my culture as it is in the western world. For example, our ancestors believed that murder is not a serious sin because the people kill people for a purpose. To live righteously means the people are to get rid of sexual immorality, adultery and fornication because they believed these activities make them unclean. Peace is always found in the *Nakamal*, and those who live there are very wise and give advice when someone has committed sin or tries to hide their sin.

iv) Celebration: The *Nakamal* is a place of celebration, dancing, and ceremonial activities (eg circumcision, namangki[6]). These celebrations are held inside the *Nakamal* boundary. It is a happy place where people share relationships together and participate in the *Nakamal* activities.

The *Nakamal* is our ancestors' schooling place, a place where the men taught the young people about their future destiny. In Ps Johnny Naual's article he wrote, 'People gathered in the *Nakamal* for various purposes. It is the place for settling disputes, where order and justice are operative (ie a decision-making body). It is a place where admittance, repentance, apologies and reconciliation are experienced; it is the place where forgiveness is established through the shedding of the blood of a pig'.[7]

The *Nakamal* activities unite people at different levels of family and tribe, and build relationships in the community.

*Things people do to be part of the Nakamal*
The instruction of the *Nakamal* is that if a person wants to be part of it, he must kill a couple of pigs that are appropriate to the value of the *Nakamal*. There are many 'stages' in being accepted into a *Nakamal* beginning with

---

6.  A name given to a ceremony of pig killing to achieve a certain rank. For further reading see AD Bernard, *Malekula: A Vanishing People in the NH*

7.  Randall, Prior, editor, *Gospel and Culture in Vanuatu 2: Contemporary Local Perspectives* (Melbourne: Gospel and Culture in Vanuatu Books, 2001), 54

*nalawan*.[8] We don't have time to discuss the rites of the Nalawan but 1 would like to mention three important stages people must pass through in order to become members.

i) *Amel nagorian*: *Amel nagorian* means you do something to be part of something. For example, a young male person must kill a pig and then be circumcised to be part of the *Nakamal*.

This is the first step in allowing a person to enter the *Nakamal*. When a boy is circumcised he is to perform certain ceremonies to enter in the *Nakamal*. He is to bring two pigs in; one pig is to allow him to enter the *Nakamal* as a declaration of his membership and the other pig is for the people who live in the *Nakamal* to eat as a declaration of acceptance that the young boy may eat with them and become part of the learning activities within the *Nakamal*.

ii) *Nailhor nalawan*: This is the second step. When a young boy reaches this stage, he now comes to learn many new things. This stage requires the offering of three to five pigs from the boy for him to be allowed to become part of the carving system and to perform *Nakamal* activities.

iii) *Amel bebalis* and *amel kaum*. These two stages are the most holy ones. For a person to enter these stages, he needs ten to fourteen pigs. Those who reach this last stage can be recognised in other *Nakamal*s throughout the Small Nambas[9] area. They now become the most respected holy men.

## How the Nakamal is respected

The *Nakamal* is a very respected and respectful place, a place where people are regarded as most holy. The way the members of the *Nakamal* live, act and behave towards the *Nakamal* is very strict with rules applied in the *Nakamal* and its surroundings. For example:

- The *Nakamal* is regarded as a quiet place. When people come close to the *Nakamal* they must talk and walk quietly.
- People are not to climb trees that are near and within the *Nakamal* surroundings.
- If anyone is caught committing adultery or if a woman says some evil words against a man such as swearing, that man is to be suspended from the *Nakamal* and the problems are to be solved outside the

---

8. *Nakamal* is a name given to a ceremony displayed in the *Nakamal* when a boy is circumcised and kills pigs to be a member
9. 'Small Nambas' is a name use to describe a group of people who use one language called, *Bathot*. These people live in different villages in Malekula, from Dickson Reef, South Malekula, Bonvor, Tisman and Unua. See Deacon, BA, *Malekula: A Vanishing People in the New Hebrides*.

*Nakamal*. As indicated above, this will only involve the man and the woman with the Meleun (Chief)

In the case of adultery, the male partner, before he can enter the *Nakamal*, must first kill a pig and burn it near the gateway to the *Nakamal*. It is part of his purification that allows him to enter the *Nakamal* again.

If a wife wants to talk with her husband who is in the *Nakamal*, she will make a signal by beating a gong which is intended to give a particular message to her husband who hears it. When those in the *Nakamal* hear the sound, they will send the husband home since women are prohibited from coming into the *Nakamal* and its surroundings.

We have three methods of sacrificial purification which are required in the case of disrespectful acts: to burn a pig near the gateway; to bury a pig in the middle of the road to the *Nakamal*; to tie a chicken to the tree as a confession and substitute for life.

There are two consequences which can apply to a person who has offended: if a person's sacrifice is rejected then he must be excluded from the *Nakamal* and he is sentenced to death; if accepted then his life is saved from death.

My ancestors regarded the *Nakamal* as the most holy place and that attitude led to holiness becoming part of their lives within their environment. I praise my forefathers for living a holy life-style in the *Nakamal*. This way of holiness associated with the *Nakamal* had already given light into their darkness and prepared them for a new future.

I do not accept everything about the *Nakamal*. For example, I do not accept their traditional belief that murder is not sin. It is also true to say that the *Nakamal* is exclusive; it applies only to some people and it is expensive for people to be part of its membership.

## The *meleun* (chief)

### Definition of meleun
*Meleun* is the name given to a high-ranking person who has proceeded through the different stages in life to receive his high-ranking name. It is one of the highest names recognised in Vanuatu societies. A *meleun* is a person who exercises his authority (similar to the authority of the Moderator in the Presbyterian Church); he is blessed by his possessions and treated with respect by everyone. A *meleun* is someone who always maintains his status and ability with his people and he is based mainly in the *Nakamal*.

*The status and ranks one needs to achieve to become a meleun*

There are many stages that a person needs to go through to achieve the status of a *meleun*. In fact, *meleun* is not the last step, but I chose *meleun* because it has become the common rank today among my people in the southern part of Malekula. People also use the term *meleun* today to describe honourable people such as a church pastor or a moderator.

In our culture we have about fifteen to twenty stages altogether but in this paper, there isn't enough time to talk about them.[10] The stages need different numbers of pigs, which total about one hundred altogether. Therefore, those who achieve the rank of *meleun* are those who are very rich.

A person who is prepared to achieve the *meleun* name, must first arrange to organise the ceremony called 'Namangki'. Those who are invited participate in the dance, beginning in the afternoon through to the following morning. In the morning everyone stands in silence to watch the performance of how to honour a new *meleun*. One of those who have reached the stage of *meleun* is to dance in honour and make a declaration of a new *meleun*. After the performance of honour and declaration the high-ranking man gives the name of *meleun* to that person. This is followed by pig killing and the pig is then distributed to the invited guests and to the one who danced.

This is a very big feast witnessed by people from different societies and recognised throughout different *Nakamals*. These are some but not all of the many activities associated with the Namangki ceremony.

*The meleun's responsibilities*

A *meleun* is a person who achieves rank in the carving system and has certain privileges and responsibilities. He makes carvings that are suitable to his rank and can sell them to different *Nakamals*. No-one else is permitted to make the same carving, especially those who haven't reached that stage. The *meleun* alone can perform the dancing ceremony to give the name of *meleun* to another person who is preparing to achieve it. A *meleun* is a person who organizes events because he is recognised to have status in all societies; therefore he meets with different *meleuns* from different *Nakamals* and discusses the events such as Namangki ceremonies. The *meleun* is the one to give speeches in ceremonies, to settles disputes, to arranges marriages and to help pay for the bride price. He is a leader with authority; therefore every decision by him must be respected in the society.

---

10. Further reading see *Malekula: A Vanishing People in the New Hebrides*, 375

*How the meleun uses Nakamal*

The *meleun* uses the *Nakamal* as his normal place of living and schooling. He teaches people special styles of carving, encourages people in the way to live and how to relate to each other. Children who are newly circumcised learn from the *meleun*. Every act of apology or reconciliation must be supervised by the *meleun*; nothing can take place outside of his sovereignty because the *Nakamal* is governed by his authority.

The *meleun* makes sure that the *Nakamal* always maintains its respect among his people by keeping order and justice. He makes sure that those who come to the *Nakamal* are members and will be ready to welcome others who have decided to become part of the *Nakamal* especially young boys who are ready for circumcision and membership of the *Nakamal*.

## Biblical perspectives

Now let me look at some biblical perspectives and identify some of the things similar to the *Nakamal* in the bible.

### Abraham

God called Abram and promised that everyone will be blessed through him (Gen 12:1–3). There is only one nation through which we can get this blessing. Abram's descendants are very special; those who are among his descendants are blessed through him. It is 'a holy *Nakamal*' established by Abram and requires circumcision (Gen 17:11–14).

### The holy mountain (Mount Sinai)

Moses led the people of Israel across the desert to Sinai, the holy mountain. There the Lord appeared to him. The mountain is called 'holy' because the Israelites believed that God was there. In the story of the burning bush, we see an image of 'the *Nakamal*', a holy place, that Moses tries to enter by himself. But God urges Moses: 'Take off your sandals for this is holy ground'. This act displayed on the holy ground is a promise of God's dwelling in the midst of his people. God wants people to live a holy life so that God's presence will be with them (Ex 3:2-6). In Exodus19:1-24 the people of Israel set up camp at the foot of Mount Sinai and Moses went up the mountain to meet with God. Moses was the only one whom God appointed to come into his presence (see also Exodus 24:1–8).

The people were organised into a special social structure of authority and responsibility. The role of leadership was given to Moses while other parts of the drama were to be played by Aaron, Nadab, Abihu, the seventy elders of Israel, the young men and the people. The meeting was the sealing of an agreement between God and the people of Israel at the foot of Mount Sinai the holy mountain.

## The tabernacle

God instructed Moses to build a tabernacle (Ex 25–26). A curtain was to divide the tabernacle into two, the ordinary holy place and the most holy place. The ordinary holy place represented God's royal guest chamber where his people came to find his presence (Ex 23:3). The Tabernacle was divided into three (3) rooms. The first one was the courtyard where the altar is; the second one is where the people are allowed to come in and sacrifice their offerings, and the final one is the holy place which is available for only the priest to go on behalf of his people. The Israelites camped around the tabernacle and it symbolised the Lord's presence and his dwelling in the midst of his people.

God's presence on Mt Sinai now transfers to the tent. God lives in the midst of his people. God is holy. God says, 'I am the Lord your God. Consecrate yourselves and be holy' (Leviticus. 11:44). This holiness must become part of their lives and God is now in the centre of their living. 'All who serve me must respect my holiness' (Leviticus 10:3); that is what God commands.

## The priest in the Old Testament

The priest in the Old Testament had to carry out responsibilities inside the tabernacle and outside the tabernacle. The high priests were anointed for special service; they were anointed as rulers to indicate their status within their communities. The priests were made sacred or holy by God for the work they did in the tabernacle.

This set them apart from the rest of the community (Num 8:14; Deut 10:8). God gave them special privileges such as access to the sanctuary, and made them subject to special regulations in their cultic duties. We know that sacrifices were also offered by the high priest, but in the early days sacrifices were offered at times by men who were not priests. Moses instructed some young people to offer sacrifices (Judge 13:16–23). The kings also offered sacrifices, for example Saul (1 Samuel 13:9–10), David (2 Samuel 6:13), Solomon (2 Kings 3:4, 15:8, 62–64; 9:25), and also Ahaz (2 Kings 16:12-15). These sacrifices were offered personally by them without permission from a priest. Later, however, we find that Uzziah is punished with leprosy when he enters the holy temple to burn incense at the altar (2 Chronicles 26:18). Uzziah is forbidden from undertaking the duties associated with the temple.

The tabernacle is a special place sanctified by God's presence; it becomes a holy place when we consider the original meaning of the term of 'holiness' in the bible, that is to say, a place which is separated for special purposes. Holiness does not mean goodness but separate-ness. Exodus 19:16-25 describes how the Israelites experienced God's holiness. God was present in the thunder and lightning and the Israelites were warned that if anyone tried to look, they may die. God was thought of as a holy God and whoever approached him needed to be without spot or stain; they needed to be perfect (Num 19:11–13). Therefore priests were set apart as representatives in the temple to offer sacrifices on behalf of their people.

## Sacrifice

The children of Israel agreed to do whatever God commanded them to do (Gen ch 24). For the sealing of the covenant relationship at the foot of Mt Sinai, new sacrifices were required to make sure that the covenant relationship was maintained. Moses appointed and delegated responsibility to the priest. The priest offered sacrifice on behalf of himself and his people.

Leviticus 9:8–23 tells us about how the priest offered sacrifices. At first the priest offered a burnt offering for himself. Then he offered a sin offering for his people. The priest, in acting on behalf of God's people, in order for him to represent them to God, first had to deal with his own sin. Sacrifice symbolized a movement from forgiveness to rededication and renewed fellowship as part of the covenant renewal.

The Israelites became powerful and attractive in their ways of living and that gained the attention of Ruth, a woman who desired to be part of Israel's holiness. She was not an Israelite and had not experienced that holiness, but she chose to leave her culture and her god and be part of Israel's *Nakamal*. (Ruth 1:16)

God wants to gather all people to come to him and be part of his *Nakamal*. God says that 'all nations shall come and see my glory' (Isa 66:18ff). Christians believe that Jesus comes as 'king of Israel' but also welcomes any other nation to be part of his *Nakamal*.

## Christ fulfils the tabernacle

In claiming that Christ fulfils the tabernacle we can point out a few ways in which some of the specifics of the tabernacle and its symbolism come into sharper focus in Christ. I think the idea of creation is important for understanding the tabernacle. The tabernacle represents God's presence on earth, just as the coming of Christ does. Also the tabernacle represents a new creation which comes into clearer focus in Christ. He who was in the beginning comes now 'to tabernacle with his people'. He is the man of heaven, come to live among his people; in other words Christ is himself holy and the sacred ground in whom the glory of God resides. With the spread of the gospel, God's glory can now be seen in a new way. Christ himself is the

162

high priest, the mediator of God's grace who offered himself as a sacrifice (Heb 10:1ff)

## We are the temple of God

Between the first and second coming of Christ, there is another stage. Christ the new temple has ascended to the Father, but his presence however has not left his people, for he has sent his Spirit to abide with us. This is what Paul means in his description of the Church in 1 Corinthians 3:16–17, 'Don't you know that you yourselves are God's temple and that God's Spirit lives in you? If anyone destroys God's temple God will destroy him. For God's temple is sacred and you are that temple'.

This is not just a way of saying that the church is special to God. Paul is saying that the church now has become God's dwelling place. Paul continues the thought in 1 Corinthians 6:19 'Don't you know that your body is a temple of the Holy Spirit who is in you, which you have received from God? You are not your own.'

God's glory can now be seen in new temples everywhere, that is where men and women repent and come to know God. God's sacred space is no longer restricted to a building in one part of the world. It means that this temple is now within us. It is embodied not only in his son as it was during his lifetime, but by the work of the Holy Spirit, God's sacred space has spread over all the earth, and now human lives become God's holy dwelling.

The Samaritan woman argued about the place of worship. She said, 'My Samaritan ancestors worshipped God on this mountain, but you Jews say that Jerusalem is the place where we should worship God' (John 4:19–23). Jesus began to talk to her about the new temple, that the time will come when people will no longer worship on the mountain or in Jerusalem, but through the power of the Holy Spirit people will worship the Father as he really is, and that is the true worship.

Therefore, we can say that the New Testament indicates for us that Jesus Christ fulfils the symbolism of the temple, and so do Christians, because they are in Christ and have also become the dwelling place of God.

## Comparisons between the traditional Nakamal and the Bible

- Sin sacrifices were offered in order for a person to enter the *Nakamal*; sin sacrifices were offered in the Old Testament so that a person may come into God's presence. ___
- Meleuns were in charge of the *Nakamal*; priests were in charge of the tabernacle.
- People respected the *Nakamal* as the most holy place and they themselves live a holy life-style; God is holy and where He dwells is holy; therefore Jesus is holy and those who believe in him are holy.

### Theological perspectives

*Christ the high-ranking man*

A couple of pigs are to be killed to achieve certain ranks, but there is a high-ranking man who goes through different stages and received his high-ranking name, which is above all names. It is Christ the Lord who did not go into the *Nakamal* made by human hands which was a copy of the real one, but he went into the heavenly reality (Heb 9:24).

The pig ceremonies performed in the *Nakamal* are intended to maintain holiness and to achieve rank. But they cannot make the members' hearts perfect, as the writer of Hebrew says, 'This is the symbol which points to the present time' (Heb 9:9).

Our *Nakamals* are the copy of the heavenly original (Heb 9:23). Christ did not use pigs to achieve his high-ranking name. Paul describes Christ's greatness as walking in the path of obedience and humility all the way to death to achieve his title. 'For this reason God raised him to the highest place above and gave him the name that is greater than any other name'(Phil 2:9ff). In honour of this great high-ranking name, all cultures, *Nakamals*, nations, people and languages look upon him and bow before him (Rev 7:9–12)

Due to his high-ranking name, Jesus established a *Nakamal* (Church) and gave an invitation to different cultures, nations, people and languages to come and be part of his *Nakamal* (Matt 11:28). It is not expensive but merely demands our acceptance (Luke 14:25–33). He also commissioned us to be witnesses of his new *Nakamal*. He appointed some to be Meleun and teachers in order to build up the body of this *Nakamal* (Eph 4:4ff).

In my culture, people think of high positions mostly in terms of performances to achieve a high- ranking name. But Jesus turns the structures of my culture upside down. He says, 'The greatest in the kingdom of heaven is the one who humbles himself and becomes like this child' (Matt 18:14). God's *Nakamal* has a better corner-stone (Jesus Christ). It has a better foundation, built by the prophets, apostles and the scriptures. It is made of better materials, believers from every age and every ethnical background, joined together in one household as one people and inhabited by the one Spirit.

When my forefathers became Christians, they began to look through the bright light of the church and discovered that the *Nakamal* is a shadow. They removed their respect from the *Nakamal* to the Church, and regarded the Church as the most holy place where God dwells. Rules of the *Nakamal* are now applied to the church, for example, the church is now regarded as a quiet place; when people approach the church, they walk quietly so as not to interrupt people worshipping. It is very interesting to watch how women

164

enter the church; they walk with knees bent to where they are to be seated. It is cultural respect towards the church.

Pulpits are regarded as the most holy place. Only ordained people are allowed to go up and preach in pulpits, but it is not allowed for ordinary people and women. Respect for the church became reflected in their dressing system so that men wore white shirts and black trousers while women wore white dresses. Day by day they tried to live a holy life-style, as previously exercised in the *Nakamal* and now in the church.

*Holiness must always be maintained within the church*
Jesus was angry when he saw people mistreating the temple. He made a whip and drove out all who were buying and selling. He quoted the words written by Isaiah and Jeremiah, 'My house shall be call the house of prayer' (Isa 56:7, Jer 7:11).

The church is a place of worship, a place to give God praise and acknowledge that he alone is worthy. It is a place of connecting with God. The church may be described as the place where heaven and earth meet. This is why we go to church on Sunday mornings. It is a holy time, like the Sabbath. It is the only day in seven set apart for worship. It is a holy space in the sense that church buildings are set apart from common use and are dedicated to the worship of God. I do not mean that church buildings are important, I only mean that there is something different, something set apart; something holy about Christians meeting together at an appointed time and space each week.

Many people don't always feel like going to church. Sometimes they think it is boring, sometime they just want a break. At times like this they just read some passages and encourage themselves. Maybe they have reasons why they do not really like going to church. My argument is that the church is not a place where other programmes should take place. It is not a place to go to be noticed by others. It is not a place to meet people. It is not even a place where we listen to sermons, but it is the place where heaven and earth meets. It is where the saints of God meet together in worship every Sunday morning. We go to church because it is the appointed manner by which we enter into God's time and space. Going to church is a testimony of the heavenly reality. As redeemed people we participate in a heavenly reality. Christ has now established the true church within us, because Christians are in Christ and have also become the dwelling place of God.

God is holy, therefore all who serve him must be holy (1 Peter 1:16). The holy life-style of the church should now be practiced by individual Christians, so that God's glory can be seen in their new heart, in the reflection of their lives. Whenever men and women come to know God and gather together to worship, God's sacred space is no longer restricted to a building in a place. This sacred space is spread all over the world. Wherever two or three are together in the name of the Lord, he is there (Matt 18:20).

## Conclusion

A proper understanding of *Nakamal* theology motivates us to live in order to please God. It does this simply by reminding us of how God is, and who we are in relation to him. The understanding of *Nakamal* helps shape our mind to reflect more the way God wants us to think. It is the Christian community that inherits the promises of God. The holiness which God' presence gives to people must be maintained within their community lives so that all people around them may come to see and experience this holiness.

Today we are the church of God and this church of God should act as the special chosen people of God. This church should act differently as its people live among non-believers. Peter encouraged his readers to live as God's chosen people, as aliens and strangers on earth whose citizenship is in heaven; therefore they are to be separated from the corruption of the world (1 Peter 1:9–11). As leaders of the church; we should regard our responsibility seriously because we are in the midst of thousands of eyes. Eyes are watching, and there is much to be done; therefore we need to take seriously the opportunity given to us and we need to fulfil our leadership destiny.

May our life and example be like a light which shines so that it may lead others to become members of the church. The church must always exercise discipline within her people. For without discipline there is no different between the church and the world. Sins are excluded from God's kingdom and are not allowed in the community of God's people. Our holy living is a reflection and prediction of a heavenly reality.

## Bibliography

Deacon, BA, *et al*, *Malekula: A Vanishing People in the New Hebrides* (Netherlands: Sterhout NB, 1970).

Grudem, W, *Systematic Theology: An Introduction to Biblical Doctrine* (London: Inter-varsity Press, 1984).

Prior, R, *Gospel and Culture Vanuatu 2: Contemporary Local Perspectives* (Melbourne: Gospel and Culture in Vanuatu Books, 2001).

Storm, M, *Days are Coming: Exploring Biblical Patterns* (London: Hodder and Stoughton Ltd, 1989).

## Personal Interviews

Alang A Bonvor, South Malekula, 28 December 2002.
Ambong L Bonvor, South Malekula, 28 December 2002.

Ps Jonathan Vanua, Middle Bush Malekula, 5 January 2003.
Mansif L Farun, South Malekula, 23 December 2002.
Rev David Maher Burwood PC, NSW Australia, 12 June 2003.
Wolet Melgen, Middle Bush Malekula, 07 January 2003.

# Sacrifice in North Pentecost:
# Relating the Gospel to
# Traditional Melanesian Belief

## Emmanuel Tanihi

### Introduction

This research paper will examine the beliefs associated with traditional sacrifices among the people of North Pentecost. On the basis of this, I will then try to present a Melanesian Christian theology of sacrifice in the context of North Pentecost. This does not mean changing the gospel of Christ and the meaning of the cross; nor does it mean doing away with the Christian tradition and adopting Melanesian culture. Rather, it will involve asking how we in North Pentecost might understand the cross of Christ in relation to our traditional sacrifices. What this paper is concerned about is the possibility and desirability of combining both traditions; of taking aspects of our traditional culture that are compatible with Christianity and integrating them into the local Christian Church.

This is an issue that I believe the church must consider very seriously in order to speak to Melanesians effectively today. Our theological reflection should involve the principle that, as Christians we should uphold the Christian gospel as the new meaning of our traditional sacrifices; at the same time, we must consider whether it is possible to combine them together and be true to God.

### Traditional belief in spirits

Belief in the spirits is the most distinctive feature of traditional belief in the Pacific Islands. The Melanesians have a one-world view with the spirit world being part of this physical world and that everything that happens in the physical world is due to the influence of the spirit world. Hence the heart of the religion of the Melanesians is their concept that the supernatural embraces the physical and includes the whole range of beliefs and practices. There is no sense of a spiritual world above and a material world below, but in Melanesian understanding the two worlds are interconnected, although of course there are important differences between material and spiritual things.

### Spirits connected with objects

In the cultures of northern Vanuatu, the spirits are often connected with objects. For example, in Santo the spirits are associated with stones, caves, rivers, hills and shrines. There is a spirit connected to Mount Tavuamasana which covers the mountain with clouds to prevent people from climbing it. In other islands such as Malekula, Ambae, Banks and Maewo, the spirits are also connected with various stones and special shrines. But there are also certain differences. For example, in Maewo the spirits are connected with rivers and it is believed that there is a supernatural spirit in all the rivers of Maewo. If a person goes fishing in a river too often, the people believe that the spirit of the water will curse her/him with sickness. In Ambae, people believe that the Maharo Lake has its spirit known as Kelevu. In Malekula, the oak trees, strong bamboos and red leaves for baking are some of the objects connected with the spirits. In the Banks group of islands, stones, the namele (a tree with large palm-like leaves), banyan trees and shrines are said to embody the presence of spirits.

According to North Pentecost belief, the god *Tagaro* has created all the shrines and has given the powers of the spirits to humans as their possession. The spirits are connected with stones, caves, trees and water. These objects are not to be destroyed by people because these are the secret places where *Tagaro* lives. People search for *Tagaro* in these places. If people violate these places they will become sick, and sometimes even die. Therefore the people respect such places.

The differences in the way spirits connect with objects in the cultures of the northern islands of Vanuatu may be due to differences in the cultural background, environmental setting, or historical traditions. The differences also contribute to aspects of their traditional religion. For example, all the vantage points of these islands are believed to have association with spirits. It is believed that when a person dies their spirit returns back to these places. On Ambae the special place is the last point in the south of the island which is called 'Devils Rock', referring to a big stone standing in the sea. On Maewo, the special place is the long point reaching into the sea on the southern tip, called 'Hinoin Vui'. On Malekula the special place is the point on Okai, referring to a big stone standing out in the sea; it is believed that the spirits of the dead have to pass through it. On the islands in the Banks group, especially on Gaua, the big lake is called Letes; the spirits of the dead return back to this lake, and this is known as 'Werisris' meaning 'Spirit-changing'. On Pentecost it is believed that the last point in the south is a stone called 'Vatagele' where the spirit receives back the person when they die.

The religious practices on Pentecost include the making of traditional sand drawings in various circular patterns where the inside circle symbolises a pool where, after death, a man jumps inside in order to be transformed. The understanding of the people of Pentecost is that all the vantage points of the islands contain spiritual beings in them, indicated by a namele tree on the rock or on the ground. A sea snake which lives in the sea is also connected with the spirits. These objects represent the god *Tagaro* who is present in this spiritual world and rules over it.

## The North Pentecost understanding of spirits

Believing in spirits for North Pentecost people is traditionally very important. That is because in every aspect of life, guidance is sought from the spirits. It is believed that there is no separation between spirits and the lives of human beings. As on other islands in the north, so also on North Pentecost it is believed that spirits are connected with certain stones and places. The stones and places have a spiritual or 'vui' content to them. Such stones are called *rabe* (pronounced 'rah-bay', meaning 'sacred') and with those *rabe* stones traditional baptisms[1] were performed. These *rabe* stones are believed to have come down from the sky as well as from the sea on what is called *matatiora*, which is one particular type *of rabe* stone.

On North Pentecost there are different *rabe* stones for different things. There is one for rain, one for sunshine, one for earthquakes, and another for thunder. It is believed that these stones have no power of their own, but the power is the property of *Tagaro*. In other words, the stones are sacred only because of the power of *Tagaro* communicated through them. This is very real to people because they have experienced the power in these stones to bring rain, sunshine, earthquakes or thunder.

In practice, whenever the owner of a *rabe* stone wants rain, sunshine or an earthquake, he takes the stone that is believed to be associated with one of these; the important thing is then to pray to *Tagaro*. If it is for rain, then after the prayer (which is not the formal type of prayer which Christians know and practice today but rather a distinctive form of prayer), the stone will be put into water. For however many days the stone remains in the water, this is the number of days of rain.

---

1.  I have used the term 'traditional baptism' to refer to a ceremony which could be given other names. This is mainly because the word used in our tribal language for this ceremony is also used as a translation of the Christian Baptismal ceremony; and also because (as we shall see later) it can involve the pouring of coconut juice over the head of the participant. It seems to bear some similarities to what other writers, writing about traditional ceremonies on other islands, have called 'initiation' or 'grading' ceremonies. Because the ceremonies differ from village to village, it is not possible to establish a clearly-defined term for each one, and so I have chosen to use the term 'traditional baptism'.

In the same way, it is common for people to seek guidance for various aspects of life from a spirit; that spirit has the power to lead and direct what will happen, but the power to do so always comes from *Tagaro*.

In traditional understanding, the spirits are connected with the nine different beings regarded as the first beings that lived on North Pentecost and known by the present-day people as *Tavalarau*. This name means 'the opposite side of life'. In other words, human beings live in this world and these spirit-beings lived on the 'opposite side' of this world, which we cannot see. These *Tavalarau* were created by *Tagaro* as his original servants or representatives to carry out his purposes, but legend has it that they were either inadequate or disobedient. Therefore, *Tagaro* changed them to spirits, and decided to create human beings to serve him instead. This explains the creation of the spirits and human beings.

The names of the original nine spirit-beings and their descriptions are as follows:

*Muganioro*: The *Muganioro* did not do the work that *Tagaro* asked them to do. Therefore *Tagaro* sent them out to live among rubbish and eat what was left in the rubbish after human consumption.

*Varirigi*: The *Varirigi* are very short and strong. The main task given to them by *Tagaro* was gardening but they could not do this work. Therefore *Tagaro* dismissed them.

*Atmatdule*: It is believed that these were the first angels to live in the sky, but they did not obey *Tagaro*, and so he threw them down to hang among the trees of Pentecost as evil spirits.

*Vatu* (stones): At one time all the stones are believed to have been able to talk and move. Their chief was called *Vatulo*, meaning, 'calling other stones together to discuss'. In any matter they discussed their ruler Vatagele would give the last answer, but *Tagaro* said 'not yet', meaning that he was not yet satisfied with his creation.

*Danu* (spring water): Once upon a time the springs were also talking and moving. The one who ruled over them all was *Danu Lavoa,* but *Tagaro* said they also were not yet the representatives he was seeking.

*Mae* Spirit: *Tagaro* devised for them various duties to do but they did not do them. Instead they spent all their days beating bamboo and dancing custom dances. Again *Tagaro* said 'not yet', meaning that he had not yet created the type of being he was looking for.

*Manu* (birds) *Tagaro* created *Manuware-batai* (a type of small bird) and *Batigo* (kingfishers) to reveal his message but they could not. Therefore he handed over the responsibilities to *Birivia* (a small black bird with a long tail and a red dotted head) to reveal his message to the creatures, and these birds continue to serve him today.

*Sarivanua*: These spirits have long hair and white skin, and are also interested in custom dances. *Tagaro* instructed them to serve his world but they did not do it. Instead, every day they danced, and they still dance instead of representing *Tagaro*.

*Lailainago* (ghost): The *lailainago* can change its appearance to that of a man or a woman. Therefore *Tagaro* withdrew it and sent it to live in the trunk of a tree called *Igoha* (a red wood tree).

The inadequacy and disobedience of these nine spirit-beings led to the final creation of human beings who *Tagaro* also made, and he saw that these humans could be his representatives in all his creation. *Tagaro* also saw that humans could do everything that he wanted done. Nevertheless, the other nine types of being remained in the 'opposite world' as unseen spirits, except for the stones, the springs and the birds who were allowed to remain in this world. It is believed that the spirits 'on the other side' can reveal hidden secrets to people through dreams.

### *Tagaro*: the supreme spirit

According to the people of North Pentecost, *Tagaro* is believed to be the supreme spirit or god. *Tagaro* is referred to as the creator of all that exists in the world. As far as the people of North Pentecost are concerned, 'the world' traditionally is the island of Pentecost itself. *Tagaro* created everything on Pentecost for the people's benefit. He created yams, taro and bananas as food; he created fowls and pigs for meat and feasting; he provided herbs, or healing medicines, in certain trees and leaves; he also gave the people their spirit-life after death.

*Tagaro* is also referred to as *I Togo*, meaning 'who is, and who was in the creation', or in other words, 'the one who was there before creation came into being'. No-one knows exactly where *Tagaro* lives, but it is believed that he is not separated from humans and is present wherever people live.

Having created the world, *Tagaro* is also believed to play an important role in the life of the people, and that is where they believe spirits are at work. For example, the primary function of *Vui* (the spirit of *Tagaro*) was to blow into the mind of (or indwell) humans to influence their behaviour. Therefore in every aspect of a human's life, guidance is always sought from *Tagaro*. If a person wants to become a chief or a wise man, he must consult *Tagaro* for guidance. In everything concerning the livelihood of humans *Tagaro* must always make the final decision.

*Defining the godhead of Tagaro*

The North Pentecost people believe that traditionally *Tagaro* is three persons. There is *Tagaro* himself, his son and his spirit. The name of the son is 'Tosese', which means 'revealer of truth', and the third person is *Vui*, which is the spirit himself. The unity of these three divine beings is called by the name *Sagaire*, which means 'clothed in one', or 'three in one'; it has the same meaning as the Christian term 'Trinity'. The name *Tagaro* also means everlasting or eternal. This is how the people of North Pentecost have understood the three persons of *Tagaro*.

*What is Tanaroa?*

*Tanaroa* as it is understood on North Pentecost implies 'essence of being'. Another word for it is *Rorono*, which in English can be translated as 'power'. *Tanaroa* or *Rorono* refers to the essence of the very being of *Tagaro* and implies power of such high intensity that man cannot stand in its way. It was handed down from *Tagaro* to our ancestors, and through them to the people of today, so everyone shares in the *Tanaroa*. For example, suppose an old man sends a young man to get him some water. The young man later comes back pretending that the hollow bamboo tube he holds is full of water. He leaves the bamboo inside the old man's house. When the old man takes the bamboo to pour water for his cooking, he finds out that there is no water inside the bamboo. The young man has tricked him. The notion of *tanaroa* is represented in the words the old man then uses to the young man, namely, 'You cannot do anything right for the whole of your life'. These words are regarded as *tanaroa*, meaning powerful. The words will remain with the young man and will continue to influence him for the rest of his life. It is a form of curse.

In the Bible, *tanaroa* is evident in many situations which reveal the power of God; for example, it was by the *tanaroa* (power) of God that Jesus rose from the dead.

*Prayer and worship*

In North Pentecost there was no elaborate pattern of worship traditionally. It is believed that the main object of worship is the spirit of *Tagaro*. Prayers are offered directly to *Tagaro* the supreme spirit, and the emphasis is placed on *Tagaro* himself. For North Pentecost people *Tagaro* is the only god to whom the whole focus in worship is directed. The worship or prayers are presented through patterns of chanting, talking and acting, with all of these things directed towards *Tagaro* as the one to be worshipped.

There are places of prayer traditionally called *Tanontataroi*. These are shrines where *Tagaro* is worshipped, but there is no regular attendance at these shrines for worship or prayer. To speak to *Tagaro*, prayers were

173

traditionally offered only at certain times, such as times of danger and times of need, as well as before going to war with another tribe. The prayer for going to war would be something like this: *'Taga Tagaro, Taga Tagaro, Taga Tagaro, Gamen lagoi atunana. Gov gogonai kamai i gov gita goro kamai vui ia birimatam sagaire.'*

If the prayer goes with drinking kava, (as one tribal chief named Molgaviga said to me) it could be like this, *'Taga Tagaro, Namen min mangu malogu nai sieri, Gov sieri (4 times). Nav sieri la gabain matam sagaire.'*

These prayers ask for the guidance, help and power of *Tagaro*, that he might be with them and lead them to win the battle. A sign will be given to the people to direct them whether or not to go to battle. (See section ii below on *muani*, signs.)

North Pentecost people approach the holy place for prayers very early in the morning before sunrise and again in the evening before sunset. These are the main times. It is believed that through prayer one can really feel the presence of *Tagaro*. This practice of prayer helps to explain why a new-born baby wakes up in the very early morning. It is believed that this is the right time to offer prayer because that is when the presence of *Tagaro* is there for all nature or living creatures to praise *Tagaro* in their own languages in the silence of the morning and again in the cool of the evening.

Another connection with this belief about times of prayer is in the act of one friend visiting another. When someone wants to visit a friend, the visit is normally done in the early morning or in the evening because at those times the friend is most likely to be at home. In the same way, the people of North Pentecost believe they should visit the places of prayer to worship and offer sacrifices to *Tagaro* early in the morning or in the evening because those are the times they will relate most closely to *Tagaro*.

There are traditionally two special types of prayer offered to *Tagaro*: a prayer that *Tagaro*, through his help and guidance will enable them to kill another person in tribal warfare, and a prayer for wisdom and knowledge.

For the second of these prayers, the man should go with one stone and the head of a pig called a *tavsiri*. Its tusks are like the youngest shoot of navara (a young coconut). Near the shrine the man offers a tavsiri as a sacrifice to *Tagaro* and then prays like this: *'Matai sao be gon van maia, namen laia. Nan tugu boena gin tavrisi. Nan voha goro lolmatana gin vatu.'* It means: 'Your knowledge, *Tagaro*; reveal it to me, let me have it through the head of this pig I am offering as my sacrifice. Give to me your wisdom.' After this, the man remains standing with his eyes firmly closed in order to experience the presence of *Tagaro* all around. Later, after he returns to his home, the man will be a very wise man.

174

We have seen that there are two special times when prayer is offered to *Tagaro*, early in the morning and before sunset. The quietness experienced early in the morning proves to the people of North Pentecost that all creation is now praying. They believe that before they pass urine in the morning they must pray. This is because early in the morning is a good time for asking *Tagaro* to provide their daily needs. Other creatures too ask *Tagaro* for their needs. This is done in the house rather than in the shrines.

The type of morning prayer in the house for seeking wisdom from *Tagaro* would be:

'*Taga Tagaro, Taga Tagaro, Taga Tagaro. Nam doron be namen matai saoga va gabain matam sagaire.*' This prayer means: 'God *Tagaro*, I want to be wise. Give me your wisdom. Praise to your all-seeing trinity.'

Such a prayer is accompanied by the experience of *muani*. *Muani* is a local Pentecost term to indicate silent meditation or prayer with a certain action of the hands. The two hands are folded and during the prayer, a sign will normally be given in the right or left hand of the person praying. When this takes place in prayer we then refer to it as *muani*. A possible English translation would be 'divination' or 'special guidance'. If there is a sign in the right hand, it is understood as favourable, but if the signal is on the left hand it means bad luck. For example, in the context of a prayer about going to war with another tribe, a sign in the right hand would mean that they can go to war, and in the left hand, that they should not go to war.

The prayer about going to war with *muani* (hand actions) would be something like this: '*Tagaro, Tagaro, Tagaro*; we are about to go to war. Confirm, strengthen, sanctify and take care of us. Praise to your all-seeing trinity.'

However, the act of *muani* is not performed by everybody; there are special people, especially women, whose particular gift or task is to use *muani* to find out from *Tagaro* the response to a particular prayer. The reason why women were specially gifted to use *muani* is that after she was created, the first woman used the *muani* to find out what would happen to her next. The answer she received from *Tagaro* was 'marriage and children'. That is why, in the language of Pentecost, mothers are called *mua*, a word which derives from *muani*.

There are prayers used with *muani* for a range of purposes. Another example is the prayers that are offered to *Tagaro* for a good harvest. Such prayers come in various forms of chanting and repetition. Here is one of the chants for a good harvest of taro (a root vegetable): '*Taga Tagaro! Taga Tagaro! Taga Tagaro bwet matere, yan matere (3 times). Bwet matere lagabain matam saguire.*' This means: 'Good harvest of taro from fertile ground; *Tagaro* will provide it.' This is consistent with the belief that

175

*Tagaro* has put life into the earth and causes these plants to grow and to bring good harvests.

In the case of sickness, *muani* is offered for healing or recovery. If the sickness was because of a violation of one of the shrines, then the man who owns the ground where the shrine is, prays with *muani* for the recovery. In some cases herbs are also given to the sick, and prayers of *muani* are offered to *Tagaro* asking him to grant healing through the herbs. The following is an example of muani for a sick child: *'Lang lang mataburi, atmate mataburi (2 times) La gabain matam sagaire.'* [Then blow four times on the sick child.] This Muani means: 'Rubbish wind of sickness, by the help of *Tagaro* come out of this child.' After the *muani*, the child is expected to become well again.

### Sacrifice: comparing sacrifice in different islands of North Vanuatu

The forms of sacrifice practised across the cultures of northern Vanuatu involved the use of a wide range of different objects. Nevertheless, across the differences, there were similarities. For example, they all had reconciliation sacrifices which were for the purpose of restoring peace between the people, and they all had sacrifices that the people made to their respective gods in order for the gods to provide their needs. Sacrifices were often performed as public ceremonies but sometimes they were held as secret ceremonies in the local shrines. The following is a comparison of some of the sacrifices around the islands of northern Vanuatu.

On the island of Mota Lava in the Banks group, a reconciliation sacrifice is called *Nahalgoi*. The objects sacrificed are pigs, kava and traditional shell money. It is the chief who performs the sacrifice on behalf of those who are to be reconciled. During the ceremony the sacrificed objects are exchanged and an offering made to their god *Quat*. For example, in kava-drinking to reconcile enemies, a first drop of kava must be allowed to fall to the ground. It is believed that this is for *Quat*. Therefore *Quat* is present when there is a sacrifice made to restore peace.

In South Santo (for example, in the Malatao area), sacrifice is called *Maibolobolo*. The objects sacrificed are foods like yam and taro. Again it is the chief who performs the sacrifice on behalf of his people to restore peace and solve any problems or troubles. The foods are then shared between the two groups who perform the ceremony.

In Malekula (around the south coast), sacrifice is called *Harerfanai*. The offerings to their god *Haifutrabasi* are burnt sacrifices in the form of pigs. This is to restore the violated relationship between the people and *Haifutrabasi*.

We have seen so far that sacrifice has an important place in the life of the community, especially in the maintaining of peace. Such traditional sacrifices involve peace-making, not only between human tribes, families or individuals, they may involve offerings to the gods to heal a violated relationship with them. We will make this distinction clearer in considering the concept of traditional sacrifice in the particular context of North Pentecost.

*Sacrifice on North Pentecost: Boe Tugutugu*

*Boe tugutugu* is a North Pentecost word that can be translated into English as 'sacrifice'. Now that we have seen how people on other islands offer sacrifices to their supreme god, we come to answer the question of how the North Pentecost people offer sacrifices to *Tagaro*. I have already set out above some important elements of worship relating to sacrifice, and I will elaborate these in more detail below, relating them to what we call *Boe tgutugu* or sacrifice.

On North Pentecost the objects of sacrifice to the god *Tagaro* are not burned or killed, but are kept alive.[2] The most common object for the people to sacrifice is a pig. The following explains how a pig sacrifice is offered to *Tagaro* during a traditional baptism.[3] If a man or woman wants to live to an old age, they must go through the process of a traditional baptism. The offering made to *Tagaro* is a pig. This is referred to as *Maduguboena*, which means a person's offering to *Tagaro* made in order to open the way of traditional baptism. The offering is not made directly to *Tagaro*, but to the man who knows the sacred place which is to be used. This man, called the processor, would offer a prayer to let *Tagaro* know that the pig is being offered to him as a sacrifice. The pig no longer belongs to the processor, but to *Tagaro* (see further explanation below).

There are five main traditional types of sacrifice on North Pentecost:

1. *Violating the peace of society*: This sacrificial ceremony is used to reconcile one person to another. If someone has done something that the

---

2.  There may also be sacrificial offerings to *Tagaro* using a dead pig, but only if the dead pig has died naturally. A pig that has died naturally is considered still to be alive to the god *Tagaro* because no hand of a human killed it. If the pig is killed by someone, then the head of the pig cannot be offered as a sacrifice. It is believed that only a live pig (that is, one that is 'alive' to *Tagaro*) can be offered for sacrificial purposes.

3.  See the footnote above explaining the use of the term 'traditional baptism'.

society regards as violating the peace, then they have to *Tuguboe*, that is, make a peace offering in the form of red mats or pigs to the chief whose peace has been violated. The sacrifice is made to the chief because the people believe that the chief is the representative of *Tagaro* among his people. It is the chief who holds absolute authority in the maintaining of peace. By the chief walking three times around the one who makes *Boetugutugu* (the peace offering), the burden of wrongdoing is lifted. In other words, the chief sets the person free from the sin as he circles around, and peace is restored again. The chief acts on behalf of *Tagaro*; it is really *Tagaro* who maintains the peace in such a situation.

2. *Living to an old age.* There is also a North Pentecost version of the sacrificial ceremony for people who want to live to an old age through the process of traditional baptism. The following is the method of traditional baptism for a woman. If a young woman wants to live to an old age, she brings a pig as her offering to *Tagaro*. This offering is not made to *Tagaro* directly, but to the man who knows the sacred place or has been introduced to it by the processor. The owner then takes the young woman to the holy place of traditional baptism and he offers a prayer in chant to *Tagaro*. The chant would be something like this: '*Huri vavin ata behe, ven huhuri, ven huhuri. Surai suri sage. Surai na ura te boe, ven huhuri, ven huhuri.*'

This chant means that *Tagaro* is informed by the man about the young woman who has offered a pig as a sacrifice. Then *Tagaro* is asked that the man may perform the traditional baptism on her behalf through the sacrifice of the pig the woman has given him. Symbolically, the pig is sacrificed to *Tagaro*, but the pig is actually with the man.

After the prayers of chanting, the man who acts on behalf of *Tagaro* then breaks a very young green coconut and pours its juice on the head of the woman. The empty coconut shell is then placed on the shrine stone as an additional offering to *Tagaro* so that he may give life to the woman and enable her to live to a great age.

A similar ceremony of sacrifice is also carried out for a young boy in determining his future as a chief. The same ceremony of baptism takes place, but with different chanting: '*Maemae, maemae! Bilam boe ma horago, Bilam tanaranana ma horago, uvi uvi, ulolo, uvi sagaire.*'

In this chant *Tagaro* is informed about the boy's pig so that through his pig he will become a chief, and *Tagaro* will delegate authority to him as a future leader. After the chanting there is traditional baptism to find out whether or not *Tagaro* will accept him as a chief. At this ceremony a sign will be given which will determine the future of the boy. The possible signs are:

- If a hawk is seen flying above, or a snake is seen on the stone where the baptism is performed, then it means that the boy will be a great chief.
- If a dove flies or sings, it means that the boy will be a wise man.
- If a bird called 'verumemea' flies or sings then it means that the boy will not be a great man because he will not live long, but will be killed.

These signs are believed to be revealed by *Tagaro* as the answer to the boy's request. Later, after returning to his village, the boy will spend time in retreat. This is the time of prayer where he asks *Tagaro* for guidance in his life in order to become a great chief.

*3. Violation of holy places:* This is a private sacrificial ceremony where an offering is made by a man to *Tagaro* after he has violated a place regarded as holy or taboo. The sacrifice is in the form of a young shoot of coconut, called *navara*. Because the man has violated a holy place (for example by cutting down a big tree or making a lot of noise), it is believed that he has made *Tagaro* angry. Therefore spirits representing *Tagaro* will harm the man by making him sick or stealing his pigs. The idea of the sacrifice is to restore the man's relationship with Tarago. He takes the young coconut shoot and offers it to *Tagaro* in the particular place which has been violated. *Tagaro* then receives the young coconut. The offering of the shoot of a coconut symbolises and begins the new life in which there is peace again.

A similar ceremony is performed in order to help the sick to recover, or to find a pig which has been lost.

As we consider these different types of sacrificial ceremony, we come to recognise that North Pentecost people traditionally placed more emphasis on the one supreme spirit than on ghosts (spirits of dead ancestors). Even the other lesser spirits mentioned earlier did not have sacrifices made to them. This is not so in the traditional religious practices found in some other parts of Vanuatu where the focus is more on the lesser spirits. It is clear that the North Pentecost people had great respect for *Tagaro*. Their sacrifices and worship were offered only to him. It was believed that during all these ceremonies, somehow the spirit of *Tagaro* passed through the sacrificial elements. Inwardly, all sacrifices are offered directly to *Tagaro* but outwardly the offering is not made to *Tagaro* directly, but to the man who performs the sacrificial ceremony.

*4. Bolololi or pig-killing:*The pig is the animal to which the people of Vanuatu turn when it comes to festive events or ceremonies of peacemaking, marriage, death, etc. On the various islands of Vanuatu the practice of pig-

179

killing by the chief may be done for a variety of reasons, for example in order to make peace, to reconcile people who are in dispute, to establish a person's good standing in the community, to install a new leader, or to mark a special time in the life of a family, a community, a church or the nation.

In Pentecost, especially in the north, pig-killing is practised for two main reasons:

a) in order for a man to become a chief. Without the killing of a pig there would be no chiefs in North Pentecost.

b) in order to make peace [see below under (5)].

The following describes the pig-killing ceremony on North Pentecost and its connection to sacrifice.

The ceremony begins with dancing by men and women to the music of a tam-tam (native drum) to show the happiness of the man who is performing the pig-killing ceremony. Several times during the ceremony the man sings *ieu* which signifies how happy he is with the ceremony. When people are ready to bring their pigs to the man several people clap hands as a sign to run inside the *nasara* (which is the special place set aside for such ceremonies) and offer the pigs. The pigs are then fastened to a namele tree ready to be killed. Usually, there are ten pigs. However, before the man kills the pigs he must paint his face and body with a red stain known as *ulmemea.* This symbolises the blood of the pig. The man is then ready to kill all the pigs. The pigs are killed using a *nal-nal* (traditional club) against the pig's forehead, and the blood of the pigs flows to the ground at the foot of the namele tree.

The meaning of the pig-killing at the foot of the namele tree is that the blood of the pig both on the ground and on the namele tree represents the making of sacrificial peace, and the man who has killed the pigs is the chief. It also indicates that the chief is the mediator of *Tagaro* and therefore a sacred man, the one from whom the people will seek peace and forgiveness. All people are under his rule; he holds absolute authority over his people.

The pig-killing ceremonies were started long ago for the purpose of saving the lives of people who were being killed in battles with other tribes. The pig-killing ceremony created peace and brought an end to the war. The *nasara* (the place where the pig-killing took place) is regarded as a holy place where the people can find peace and refuge. For example, if one man wants to fight his enemy, then the moment his enemy runs and stands inside the *nasara* there can be no more fighting; the man is standing in the holy place of peace. The *nasara* is the place where the blood of pigs is shed for the purpose of preserving peace. (Compare in the bible, in Hebrews 9:22 'Sin demanded sacrifice by the shedding of blood').

On North Pentecost it is believed that in ancient times peace was owned by a woman. This is consistent with the fact that it was the women who had a peace-making character; they fed the pigs, cared for the house, did weaving, kept silence, opposed war and prepared food. All of these are works of peace. However, when the woman 'muami'-ed (prayed for a sign regarding what was to come), she was instructed to marry a man. The woman then decided to hand over peace to her husband. The legend is that the woman handed over a walking stick of peace to her husband when he was killing a pig. The walking stick is called *garabihu*. Therefore, whenever there is a pig-killing ceremony on North Pentecost it is likely that it is a peace-making ceremony. The man who is killing the pigs then becomes a chief who has the responsibility for making and keeping the peace among his people, so that they will at all times live in peace toward each other.

The peace-making role of the chief is connected with three holy places:

a) The *nasara* (the place where the chief performs the pig-killing ceremony)

b) The chief's *gaibalbala* (stones together with a namele tree which are placed or planted outside a part of the *nasara*)

c) The chief's Nakamal (the house where he gathers the people together)

The people regard these places as if walking into them means that you are walking inside peace. If you perform immoral deeds you are violating the peace. If you want to be safe from your enemies, you can run and stand inside one of these places. This refers back to what we said at first: the chief is the representative of *Tagaro* and owns peace on *Tagaro*'s behalf.

*5. Sacrifice as reconciliation:* The reconciliation sacrifice was used on North Pentecost to re-establish friendly relations between people who had become enemies because of immoral deeds. People first practised reconciliation by exchanging gifts. Later this was changed to the ceremony of peace sacrifice known as *boetugutugu*. The reconciliation involved pigs and mats which were offered to re-establish peace, as well as to spare the man's life in order to maintain unity in the community.

Sacrifice as reconciliation is highly valued and taken very seriously, in that people on both sides really confess and surrender themselves with their gifts as the peace offerings are exchanged. Nevertheless, the peace is made directly between the two people involved. The exchange of offerings is made to signify the restoration of joy, peace and a good relationship. The ceremony involves the shaking of hands to indicate that the wrong-doings are forgotten by the people and forgiven by the unseen *Tagaro*. In other words, the people who witness the ceremony also release the sins of the two people by saying that their sins are no longer to be spoken of because they are now reconciled before the face of the people. After the reconciliation ceremony there is usually feasting to show that there is real joy and peace in the hearts of the people. In this way the sacrificial pattern provides security for the social aspect of the life of the people.

### Reflection on traditional sacrifice today

When we look at the effect of Christianity on our traditional sacrifices, we see that in many ways Christianity has destroyed some important basic elements of faith that could have strengthened the Christian church today. This calls for reflection on the kind of approach that was taken by the church in the early days of missionary expansion, and for the investigation of a new understanding of Christianity that will be meaningful today in the cultural setting of North Pentecost. [This will be developed further below.]

However there have been some missionaries with more accepting views for the expansion of the Christian church; for example, Bishop George Augustus Selwyn who was the founder of the Anglican mission, said: 'The church was to be planted among them in a way suitable to their customs and culture, as it had once been planted among the English'.

That means he realised that Melanesians already had an understanding of worship, and therefore Melanesians should adopt the Church of God and fit it into their cultural context. In other words, he did not come to destroy the basic belief of the Melanesians.

On North Pentecost, in the early days as we have discovered already, the people of the past knew about worship and sacrifice before the arrival of the first Christian missionaries. They believed in and relied on their god *Tagaro* to give them whatever they needed, and so they offered sacrifices to him. In other words, the spirit of *Tagaro* was already active in North Pentecost.

In our time, when we reflect upon and evaluate the importance of the god *Tagaro* in the history of North Pentecost, it is possible to see that the traditional worship of *Tagaro* can be used to open the gate of Christianity to the people. This is because through their traditional worship they already knew how to worship the God of today. The worship and sacrifice to *Tagaro* can lead to worship and sacrifice to our God today, whereas without believing in *Tagaro*, North Pentecost people would find it difficult to believe in any god. The result of the church combining Christian teaching with the traditional beliefs is seen in the rapid expansion of the church in some areas. The early traditional sacrifices have changed very quickly into the modern 'traditional sacrifice' which has become contextualised by the people of North Pentecost.

However there is the challenging question of the relationship between the gospel and the culture, and it leads us to seek further answers. The question is: How do we proclaim the message so that it becomes contextualised, or in terms of John 1:14, so that it becomes 'incarnate in the flesh' of the culture?

We need to consider this question in relation to the context of North Pentecost culture.

When French Marists founded a small mission on Pentecost in 1898, the Anglican missionary priest Edgel W. Hendry was inclined to welcome their presence because he felt that it was good to bring Christianity to the natives. Hendry interviewed a North Pentecost chief concerning 'Incarnational Mission'. That is, he sought ways to identify his mission with North Pentecost culture and custom. The conversation between the chief and Edgel Hendry went like this:

> Chief: I have a Nakamal where I gather my people together.
>
> Edgel: The Nakamal is similar to a church house where people gather together to worship God.
>
> Chief: The sign of peace is a namele tree standing in front of my Nakamal.
>
> Edgel: Very similar to Christianity, with a cross in the church house reflecting the peace we can have through Jesus Christ.
>
> Chief: I have a holy stone inside my Nakamal.
>
> Edgel: It is the same with the altar inside the church house reflecting the presence of God.
>
> Chief: I call my people to gather inside the Nakamal through the tam-tam (drum).
>
> Edgel: Very similar to the bell calling the people to the church house.

The conversation continued and finally the chief said:

Chief: I offer my sacrifice to *Tagaro*. He is my god. *Tagaro* is god the father, *Tosese* is *Tagaro*'s revealer, and *Vui* is the spirit of *Tagaro*. The unity of all is called *Sagaire*.

The missionary responded: My God took away the sins of the world through his begotten son Jesus Christ who died on the cross and rose again after death and ascended to heaven, leaving his Spirit upon all the people on earth.

As a result of this conversation the chief adopted the church into North Pentecost as if it were his child. We could say that the words from Edgel W Hendry to the chief are an incarnation in the flesh of Christianity into the culture of North Pentecost. That meant that during the expansion of Christianity the knowledge and understanding of worship was not something entirely new.

On the other hand, we see a contrast in that the modern 'traditional sacrifices' replaced the early practices and gave new directions in how to live and relate as friends rather than people killing and eating each other. We also see how the modern sacrifice can fit inside the traditional concept of sacrifice, combining both beliefs into one.

As G Miller said: 'Long before the coming of the Spanish explorers Quiros and Torres in 1606 or the coming of Captain James Cook in 1774, the New Hebridean people knew about the High God. As far back as tradition goes they speak of the High God whom the ancestors reverenced and to whom they made sacrifices.' These words by Miller actually refer to the people of the southern islands of Vanuatu, but we can equally apply them also to the northern islands.

### Further personal views of the effect of Christianity on the traditional beliefs and sacrifices on North Pentecost

Christianity first entered Pentecost in 1876, introduced by a local man Luis Tariliu. In 1875 he went to Norfolk Island to school. However his main reason for going to Norfolk island was to get an axe for his father. At Norfolk, he was converted and baptised. In 1876 he returned to North Pentecost and established a first school in his own village Abatvenue. From here Christianity spread to other parts of North Pentecost and gradually down to South Pentecost.

Christianity, in entering Pentecost, taught people about God, his son Jesus who became man, died and rose again, and the Holy Spirit. The missionaries trained some local people to be missionaries also, and made it their task to bring about belief in the Christian God. They focussed their evangelism on the principle that Christianity not only conquered heathenism as such, but also censured the beliefs and sacrificial practices of the people.

The attitudes of the early and local missionaries were negative in regard to the whole system of religious belief and the sacrificial practices of the islanders. Their basic teaching was that the religious beliefs of the islanders were false and must be replaced by the true religion, which is Christianity. For example, David Tambe says: 'The island of Raga is still with its custom' (ie its traditional culture and religion; 'Raga' is an old name for Pentecost island). There were two groups of people on the island, he proclaimed, one group that belongs to Jesus and the other group that belongs to Satan.

The missionaries made a complete change in the way of life. One of the obvious examples is the school itself where men and women attend the same school. This was traditionally forbidden. As ES Armstrong was right in saying, 'Getting girls and boys together in school is an immense step forward at Araga' on North Pentecost.

Apparently early missionaries who came into contact with this new field of mission took it for granted that the islanders' beliefs were bad and must therefore be replaced with so-called Christian truth. They regarded the traditional beliefs as Satanically inspired, and they must therefore be eradicated. They said that my people were sons of Satan and our sacrifices were Satanic practices. They also taught that our religion was pure superstition and had no truth in it. They regarded the traditional beliefs and sacrifices of the islanders as a stumbling block to the reception of the Christian faith in the true God.

This attitude was also found in the church in New Testament times where Jewish Christians insisted that before a Gentile could become a Christian he had to first of all keep all the Jewish laws and must also be circumcised (Acts 15:1–21; Gal 2:1). St Paul made a very strong attack on them saying that there is no need to paralyse the Gentiles with all the Jewish tradition, for what is important is the worship of the risen Christ. Christ fits no formula, therefore Jewish (or European) traditional practices and forms of worship are not the only context through which to receive Christ.

Similarly, this is what Christianity did in the islands: it tried to fit everyone into the European Christian formula at the cost of destroying many of the traditional concepts which were healthier than some of the western Christian teachings, or could have helped facilitate the acceptance of the Christian gospel.

Traditional concepts are not false beliefs, but rather true ones, because Christian teaching grows out from them. They are founded on preparing people to worship the unseen creator-god who is superior to all other gods. I agree with what Codrington said: 'The urban Oxford scholar implanted in the continuing tradition of the (Anglican) mission the idea that no religion was wholly false, and that heathen belief should be always approached with sympathy and respect'.

Unfortunately, in North Pentecost most missionaries to the islands of Vanuatu approached our ancestors, not with sympathy and respect, but with force and threatening. For example, history records that on North Pentecost at Aute Parish the Roman Catholic church was planted forcibly by a man called Dory. He spread his teachings with a gun in his hand to make people follow his Christian teaching. This is not the right way. The right approach is what Codrington advocated.

Therefore, as far as Pentecost people are concerned, their whole system of belief and sacrificial conception about God is reality in itself, and not a superstition as the missionaries described it.

## Biblical reflection

*The origin of sacrifice in the Bible*
In the Bible there is much talk about sacrifices made to God. We find at the beginning of Bible history that Cain and Abel appear to have been the first to offer sacrifices to God (Gen 4:3–5). Cain sacrificed the fruits of the soil as his offering to the Lord. Abel brought fat portions from his first-born sheep and he sacrificed it to the Lord. The Lord looked with favour on the sacrifice by Abel but did not look with favour on Cain's sacrifice.

*The Passover sacrifice*
The Collins Dictionary defines Passover as an eight-day Jewish festival commemorating the sparing of the Israelites in Egypt. In other words, the Israelites who were slaves in Egypt were rescued from their slavery, and that is what this festival of Passover sacrifice celebrates. Christians believe that the Passover sacrifice was fulfilled with the death of Jesus Christ, our 'Passover sacrifice'. As one writer states: 'The Passover is undoubtedly the best known of all the Jewish festivals. This is due in part to its prominence in the remarkable events surrounding the Israelite exodus from Egypt, and in part to the association of the death of Jesus Christ with the killing of the Passover sacrifice as reflected in the famous words of Paul: 'For Christ, our Passover, has been sacrificed' (1 Cor 5:7).

*The Levitical sacrifice system*
In the Bible there are some main approaches to sacrifice that we will do well to understand. First, there is a burnt offering. The burnt offering is the most important sacrifice because only male animals are required to be offered and they must be completely burnt (Leviticus 1–7). The burnt offering deals with the sins of the people removed by God through the blood of the animals. The understanding is that the death of the sacrificial animal whose blood was shed substitutes for the sin of the man who offers the animal to the priest to be sacrificed. 'The laying on of hands (Lev 1:4) identifies the substitute, whose death (v 5) takes place instead of the sinner and results in acceptance (vv 3–4), represented by the pleasing odour (v 9)'.

There is also the purification offering or sin offering relating to forgiveness of sin. It does not apply to a specific sin, but to a person's impurity. Therefore the sacrifice is known as purification, meaning that out of impurity one can be purified through the purification offering to God. 'Impurity can result from physical conditions for which a person is not responsible (eg in Lev 12, childbirth).' The materials are different depending on who is making the offering. A priest offered a bull; the congregation a young bull; a ruler a male goat; an individual a female goat or sheep; the poor a dove or pigeon.

The third type of offering is the reparation offering, or guilt offering. This sacrifice is used to reconcile the sinner to God. 'When a person commits a violation and sins unintentionally in regard to any of the Lord's holy things, he is to bring to the Lord as a penalty a ram from the flock, one without defect and of the proper value in silver according to the sacrificial shekel' (Lev 5:15).

All these passages and more in the Bible explain to us how the people of Israel approached God to offer sacrifices in order that God would regard them as his holy people. The purposes and meanings of the sacrifices are all different, but we can see in these sacrifices the ideas of communion, petition and expiation.

## A theological view

The concept of sacrifice and reconciliation in the Bible is the fulfilment of the covenant relationship with God. God wants his people to know him as their God and to follow his commands and to worship him. This requires a committed relationship to God, and his people develop this through their sacrificial worship.

In the past, in the time of our ancestors of North Pentecost, the concept of sacrifice and reconciliation was similar to that of the Old Testament. God *Tagaro* created everything for the benefit of his people, and he wants his people to know him as *'Tagaro i togo'*, the creator-god. They will also obey what he wants them to do (for example, observe holy places) and worship him, and rely on him for their needs.

Our task is to find ways of combining this belief with Christianity in order to strengthen both the church and the culture. Here are some of the aspects of the North Pentecost culture that are compatible with Christianity, and which I think we can adopt to strengthen the Christian people of North Pentecost.

### Worship

The book of psalms is a book of prayer and praise in which the people offer their worship to God through music like stringed instruments and flutes, under the direction of people like King David who danced to the Lord. To combine the true worship in the book of psalms with the culture of the people of North Pentecost, people are to pray to and praise God with their traditional instruments like bamboos (flutes), fange (rattles), tamtams (drums) and bubus (conch shells). In this way they can relate to the psalm 'I will praise you with the harp for your faithfulness, O my God. I will sing praise to you with the lyre, O Holy One of Israel' (Ps 71:22 NIV).

Also, for some special services like Christmas, the procession can be led by dancers to express our praise that we are coming before God who has become man to us. This is consistent with the psalmist's instruction, 'Let them praise his name with dancing and make music to him with tambourine and harp' (Ps 149:3).

*Giving*

God is a giving God. He sent his son Jesus Christ to die for the sin of the world. Therefore he requires his sons and daughters to give freely to him and to others. Paul's teaching to us is very clear, that 'each man should give what he has decided in his heart to give, not reluctantly or under compulsion, for God loves a cheerful giver' (2 Cor 9:7). He says that one can become rich and generous by the blessings of God as the fruit of his/her generosity, and this generosity will result in thanksgiving to God (2 Cor 9:11). He also urges that people should offer their bodies as living sacrifices, holy and acceptable to God (Rom 12:1).

Giving an offering to *Tagaro* is similar to giving an offering to God or a neighbour. But to combine the Biblical teaching on giving with the culture of the people of Pentecost, I think the first fruits of every garden should be offered as a sacrifice to God. The chief can give some land to the church for a church garden as his offering to God. The people should offer their pigs and fowls to the work of the church, and they should also offer the shells and fish from the sea for the Lord's glory.

This type of contribution can combine and strengthen both the idea of traditional giving and the idea of Christian giving, since if the traditional giving is weak then also will be the Christian giving. But let us strengthen both, and use the giving for the glory of God in our worship and sacrifices. Moses instructed the Israelites to 'give generously to him (Yahweh) and do so without a grudging heart, then because of this the Lord your God will bless you in all your work and everything you put your hand to' (Deut. 15:10)

*Hymns or songs*

We must also adapt the hymns and songs to fit the cultural situation of the people of God. As David said, 'He put a new song in my mouth, a hymn of praise to our God. Many will see and fear and put their trust in the Lord' (Ps 40:3).

Therefore, as the people of North Pentecost, we should have new songs to sing to the Lord. Today we are familiar with the tunes from America and England. They are our new songs that we sing to praise God. But what about the tunes of our own culture? I think they can also be used for our new songs. That is, we should compose Christian songs using our traditional tunes that are easy for us to sing. They can be our new songs to the Lord in our own context. In support of this I would quote Psalm 96 which says 'Sing to the Lord a new song; sing to the Lord all the earth. Sing to the Lord, praise his name, praise his salvation day after day' (Ps 95: 1–2). Therefore let us use songs and tunes that are familiar in our own culture to proclaim that Christ has provided our salvation. If David used the context of his life to praise God, we too are to use the method of our own context to praise our God.

## Sacrifices

'God revealed himself to us through his only begotten son born into the world. He came to establish a new life and a new way of worship to save us and provide salvation or eternal life.' Jesus Christ is the climax of God's dealing with sin, shown in his words on the cross 'It is finished' (John 19:30).

Jesus' life and his death are focussed in the concept of sacrifice and reconciliation as the fulfillment of all Old Testament sacrifices according to God's divine plan to save people. Isaiah says: 'Yet it was the will of the Lord to crush him with pain and make his life an offering for sin' (Isa 53:10).

And so Paul says: 'Jesus Died as a sin offering to end all sin offerings' (Rom 8:3 and 2 Cor. 5:21), and 'He is the lamb of God who finally removed the sin of the world' (John 1:29 and 1 Cor 5:7).

Hebrews also concludes that 'where there is forgiveness of these, there is no longer any sacrifice for sin' (Heb 10:18 NRSV). That means that there is no longer any sacrifice needed for sin. Christ died for every kind of sin; the sins of the past, present and future. 'Therefore, with the death of Christ the old things have completely passed away and the new has come' (2 Cor 5:17).

Therefore, past, present and future sins are to be confessed through the man Jesus Christ. 'He is the atoning sacrifice for our sins and not only for ours but also for the sins of the whole world' (1 John 2:2). Through his sacrificial death all sins may be forgiven. 'For if we confess our sins, he is faithful and just and will forgive us our sins and purify us from all unrighteousness' (1 John 1:9).

'It was only when Jesus offered himself on the cross, however, that the potential for encountering God through sacrificial worship was fully realised. The mysterious ripping apart of the temple's veil as Jesus breathed his last decisively demonstrated that sacrifice had fully opened the way into

God's very presence.' This is based on the account of Jesus' death on the cross (Matt 27:51).

In relation to this Biblical teaching about sacrifice, how can we compare or combine it with our North Pentecost context as our task requires us to do?

First, let us note that the Gospel combines the Israelite sacrificial system with its fulfillment in Christ: 'The entire Israelite sacrificial system comes together in Jesus in such a way that he does not merely fulfil individual sacrifices like the Passover or the sin offering, but reveals the true meaning of sacrifice as something greater than the sum of the parts'. The true meaning is in Jesus' sacrifice rather than that of bulls, goats or sheep that were used as sacrifices. It is no longer the blood of these animals but now the blood of Christ that takes away sins.

Secondly, we should realise that in some ways the concept of North Pentecost traditional sacrifice is also compatible with Christianity. For example, in my interview with Chief Willie Gere, I asked, 'What is custom?' He responded by saying, 'Custom is prayer'. However, traditional prayer is compatible if we can find some of the advantages of it and combine it with the concept of Christian prayer. This applies also to the methods of traditional sacrifice. Here are some of my views:

- Traditionally the right time to offer prayer to *Tagaro* is very early in the morning when the pigeons are cooing before the sunrise. Therefore as Christians we too should wake up very early to pray to God for our needs. For example, at Talua Ministry Training Centre, the bell rings at this time, and it is the time for the students to meditate and pray. This does not mean other times are not good; and this does not apply to public worship but to our own private relationship with God through our communication in prayer. We should express how great God is and bring our needs before him, relying on him to give us what we need for that day. Hannah prayed in faith that God would give her a son: 'Early the next morning they arose and worshipped before the Lord' (1 Sam 1:19); and David, wrote: 'In the morning I lay my requests before you and wait in expectation' (Ps 5:3).

- As mentioned earlier, in the language of North Pentecost sacrifice is called 'boe tugutugu'. The chief is the representative of *Tagaro* to maintain peace, therefore he is also the representative of our God Yahweh to the people. In North Pentecost the chiefs are the main people who deal with problems regarding sins, in order to ensure that peace is restored. There is compatibility here in the sense that the priest and the chief could work together in dealing with these problems. For example, after the chief has made the sacrifice of the peace offering in the Nakamal, the priest could also hear the confession of the penitent wrongdoers inside the church house. The

190

pastor's prayers and counselling should be given as well as the chief's immediate practical solution to the matter. This can be seen as fulfilling the *boe tugutugu*, in that 'Christ is the mediator of the new covenant that those who are called may receive the promised eternal inheritance, now that he has died as a ransom to set them free from their sins committed under the first covenant' (Heb 9:15).

- In relation to 'traditional baptism', my view is that there should be no more traditional baptism, but rather only Christian baptism. If we were to adopt some basic elements from the traditional baptism I think it is necessary only to sing its traditional song. The means the North Pentecost people can sing this traditional song while leading someone to be baptised in the church. Furthermore, it can be emphasised that, according to tribal cultural belief, traditional baptism leads man to live longer in this material world, while Christian baptism leads to the inheritance of eternal life. In Mark's gospel we read: 'Whoever believes and is baptised will be saved, but whoever does not believe will be condemned' (Mk 16:16). Here 'believes' refers to believing in God to inherit eternal life rather than believing in *Tagaro* in order to live longer in this world. Peter also emphasises that 'this water symbolises baptism that now saves you also—not the removal of dirt from the body but the pledge of good conscience toward God. It saves you by the resurrection of Jesus Christ' (1 Pet 3:21). Christian baptism is a symbol of salvation in that it depicts Christ's death, burial and resurrection and our identification with him in the experience of new life (see Rom 6:4).

- For the traditional sacrifice relating to pig-killing, the blood of pigs flows as a symbol of the peace that the chief exercises in such a place. Jesus Christ has already fulfilled this by his death on the cross to take away the sin of the world. However, in the North Pentecost context the pig-killing is for the chief, so that he can forgive his people and maintain peace between them. Nevertheless, 'God has provided for our salvation. The blood of Jesus shed on the cross is enough. Jesus is the 'number one pig' for us and he has died once and for all'. Here the words 'number one pig' mean that Jesus is the one supreme sacrifice for our sin. The compatibility here is seen in that the *nasara* or Nakamal symbolise the court of the chief, and the church house symbolises the court of God. To some extent we can see the chief as having both a religious and secular role in the administration of justice, similar to the 'judges' in Old Testament times, while the priest or pastor fulfils a distinctively Christian role.

191

## The future outlook

There is a new look at sacrifice in relation to the Christian church in North Pentecost today.

First, is the Spirit of God (or *Vui*) as active in Pentecost Island today as it was (according to our assumptions) before Christianity came? We know from the stories of our ancestors that *Tagaro* was active among them. When they prayed to *Tagaro* he gave them what they wanted. They saw miracles within that moment when they offered prayers. Therefore, if they found the answers to their prayers immediately it means that the spirit at that time was active.

What about today? Of course, the missionaries came, saying that this spirit of our ancestors was not good and they destroyed some basic elements of the traditional worship and prayer life. They gave a new meaning to it, that we should believe in God (Yahweh) rather than in the other gods. At that time the spirit was active. We know some stories of our first pastors and priests who performed miracles witnessed by the people. This was due to their commitment to, relationship with, and faith that they had in Jesus Christ as Lord, which resulted in them being people through whom it was evident that the Spirit of God was working.

Today that same spirit is within us. Our desire is to fully commit ourselves to the service of God. We must fully accept that our lives are under Christ's lordship. We must have faith in God the Father, Son and Holy Spirit. We must not let ourselves get stale in our Christian lives. We must allow God's spirit to fill and control us. Paul says, 'the fruit of the Spirit is love, joy, peace, patience, kindness, goodness, faithfulness, gentleness and self control' (Gal 5: 22–23). We must have these in order to be active Christians enjoying spiritual growth.

I believe that the spirit which was brought by Christianity is not a new spirit to the people of Pentecost. The Spirit brought by Christianity rather gave a new and better understanding of the spirit worshipped by our ancestors. The Spirit came as a wind to give the truth that everyone should be born of the spirit which is God's Holy Spirit. As John mentions, 'The wind blows wherever it pleases. You hear the sound, but you cannot tell where it comes from or where it is going. So it is with everyone born of the spirit' (John 3:8). As Christians we should allow this Spirit to fill and control us in all that we do. That is, to follow God's command we must have the desire to pray. The life of Jesus within us will be clearly seen and we should be hungry for God's word.

If a Christian applies all these things, then that is the meaning of what Jesus was teaching Nicodemus about the Spirit and he/she is born again with the Spirit. Hence the spirit of the past is the Spirit of today. As John explained, 'Through him all things were made. Without him nothing was made that has been made. In him was life and the life was the light of men' (John 1:3-4). The Spirit of God existed before man. The same Spirit of God was hovering over the waters in Genesis 1:1,2; and the Spirit of God in the Old Testament is the same Spirit that today's Christians have.

There is an important truth to be emphasised here, in that whatever leads man to do the will of God is the Spirit that comes from God, but whatever does not lead man to do the will of God, that spirit is demonic. This is an essential concept and in the Bible there are some examples that relate to this. For example, the healing of the dead girl where Jesus says, 'My child, get up! Her spirit returned and at once she stood up' (Luke 8:5 NIV). This is evidence that the Spirit of God was working in the girl in accordance with the will of God the Son. For whatever shows the goodness of God to man, or in this case to a girl, that is the work of the Spirit of God.

In the account of Jesus' death, before he died he cried in a loud voice and gave up his spirit (see Matt 25:50). It is therefore apparent that the Spirit of God is another name for the life-giving breath of God. In the beginning, when God created Adam, he breathed in his nostrils the breath of life (Gen 2:7). The spirit in man is God-breathed life.

Traditionally, on North Pentecost when a man died his spirit returned back to *Tagaro* at *Vatagele* (a large stone at the southernmost point on Pentecost). Now Christianity has come with a new meaning and we can see that the idea of God breathing into man his life-giving spirit is compatible with our traditional belief that god breathed the seed of religion into our ancestors who therefore inhaled the spirit of god. Our life comes from God; and at any time we can call out like Jesus, 'Lord, I give you my spirit', because it was God who created and owns our life and our spirit.

The Spirit of God also inspires men today. In our daily prayers we call to God to lead us with his indwelling Holy Spirit. We believe as Christians that whatever we do should be under the inspiration and control of God's Holy Spirit. Without the Holy Spirit we cannot do anything that pleases God, and therefore we must allow God's Holy Spirit to lead us in all that we do.

Traditional sacrifice is understood by the people of North Pentecost as very similar to the sacrifices in the Bible. In considering the relevance of sacrifice to our modern civilisation we again need to ask whether the two concepts are compatible. For example, the name of our island was originally *Raga, Uretabe, Arato*, which are versions of the same name; but God revealed a new name to Captain James Cook who first saw it on the day when the Christian Church was celebrating the giving of the Holy Spirit, and so he gave it the name 'Pentecost Island'. And even 168 years before that, in 1606 the Spanish explorer de Quiros had landed on a nearby larger island

and name it *Espirito Santo*—the Land of the Holy Spirit'.[4] Therefore we regard Pentecost Island as the island of the Holy Spirit. It is holy ground, with its new name meaning that the Holy Spirit has come, not just on the land, but in showers of blessing to the island of Pentecost and all those who live there.

In the same way, the traditional sacrifice also gained a new meaning with the death of Jesus Christ as the perfect blood sacrifice to take away the sin of the world, and there are some concepts related to traditional sacrifice which are compatible with the new meaning, and which we can adopt into the Christian faith. The Gospel of John (John 1:1) speaks of the word which was with God from the beginning and is the same word which is with us today. We have seen the incarnation of Christ in the Bethlehem manger; but Christ was also born in the manger of North Pentecost.

In Bethlehem Christ grew, developed and changed. In North Pentecost also the 'body of Christ' is growing, developing and changing. Therefore in future, according to the situation of culture, government and Christianity, we must expect this process to continue. We see new sects bringing more changes and leading many Christians to go to and fro. In order for our island to be a holy ground as in Captain Cook's vision, we should adopt and maintain the desirable changes in the light of both the gospel and our traditional culture. This requires that priests or pastors should go out and teach the correct approach to the people who will otherwise be confused. I believe that through combining together what is compatible in the traditional culture and Christianity, Pentecost island can always be the island of the Holy Spirit—yesterday, today and forever.

I wish to stress that the views I have expressed here do not mean changing the gospel of Christ, but rather my desire is to strengthen the Christian Church of God in a way that North Pentecost people will understand and accept, for the benefit of believers of today and tomorrow.

## Conclusion

It is important to have a clear understanding of the purpose and meaning of sacrifices in our culture, and to analyse these in the light of their fulfilment by Christ's sacrifice. I am thankful for the deep joy which has come to me because God's Holy Spirit has inspired me to write about this. I hope that what I have written will not be seen as questioning or changing the Christian beliefs, but as strengthening the gospel and promoting its growth in our own culture.

---

4.　O'Byrne and Harcombe, *Vanuatu*, third edition (Melbourne: Lonley Planet Publications, 1999), 211.

I have tried to explain what traditional sacrifice is and what the Christian approach to it should be. God created us, including the people of North Pentecost in his own image, to express who he is in relation to his natural creation and in relation to mankind. We must be willing to reform our cultural beliefs in this changing society, but not to discard the things that are good and can benefit our society in the future. Let us retain the parts of our culture that are compatible with Christianity. Let us encourage one another to build and strengthen the church of God, not just by what we say with our mouths, but by offering ourselves as living sacrifices to the Lord, as Paul urges us to do in Romans 12:1.

Let us praise God that through his wonderful providence our ancestors have practised traditional sacrifice, but now they have been evangelised through the gospel of Jesus Christ. Let us continue to evangelise. Let us search for others in order to make both our culture and the Christian gospel relevant in all the ceremonies. We are spiritually the children of God. We are also by traditional descent the children of *Tagaro*. Let us be true to both of these relationships as the people of North Pentecost—the land of the Holy Spirit.

# Human Sacrifice in North Pentecost

## Colin Steve Sosori

### Introduction

The Old Testament has no general word for 'sacrifice' except the sparely used word *qorban* which means 'that which is brought near'. It appears once in the New Testament, in Mark 7:11 (*But you say that if anyone tells father or mother, 'Whatever support you might have had from me is Cor'ban, that is, an offering to God'* . . .). The other more frequently used words describe particular kinds of sacrifice and are derived either from the mode of sacrifice, such as 'zeba' (sacrifice) meaning that which is slain (*zebah*) and *ola* (burnt offering) meaning 'that which goes up', or *asam* (guilt offering), and hattat.[1]

In this article on sacrifice, I will base what I want to say on the particular mode of sacrifice referred to as *zeba* ('that which is slain'). But the level of sacrifice to which I will refer is more profound than the cultic sacrifice offered during the times of the Israelites in the Old Testament because I will be speaking of the sacrifice of human beings and not animals (goats). It will be closely associated with what Leon Morris says when mentioning the six stages of sacrifices, two of which are the killing of the animal by the worshipper and the manipulation of the blood of the victim (done by the priest).[2]

God has wonderfully made all the human races of the world and placed each tribe according to their cultural geographical setting. Each tribe had its own way of worshipping their god before Christianity came. We can say that these various cultural ways of worship are the shadow of what the Christian gospel came to fulfil. Particularly from the island of Pentecost where I come from, we have our own god which we believe is the supreme spirit and has the name *Tagaro*. His messengers function as mediators between this god *Tagaro* and the people. Some of the mediators are spirits who were called to make peace, to make the trees and the gardens fruitful, to make the seas abundant for fishing, to enable successful hunting; indeed every aspect of our ancestors' lives depended on these spirits. If you consult the appropriate spirit to perform for you whatever activity you want to do, then you use the process of sacrifice and offer right prayers to this spirit. When agreeing with your prayer the spirit answers immediately and does what you ask for. There are many sacrifices offered to the spirits and different forms of sacrifice are applied to different spirits.

---

1.  In 'Sacrifice and Offering', *New Bible Dictionary* (London: IVP, 2000), 1035-44.
2.  LL, Morris in 'Sacrifice', *New Dictionary of Theology* (London: IVP 1998), 608-609.

The days of our great grandparents were the days of war. The tribes fought against each other. Therefore each tribe performed their own sacrifices to their gods whom they believed would give them victory in a tribal war. The wars might continue for many months, or even years, but if the chief of one side decided to surrender, then he would choose one of the men (not a woman) from his tribe and kill him as a sacrifice offered both to *Tagaro* and to the god of the opposing tribe in order to restore the peace. This practice is known as *Ngarianbwaloana*. It is a common practice in reconciliation and the restoring of peace between two warring tribes.

**The definition of *Ngarianbwaloana***

It is the practice of the Raga people (Raga is the local name for the island of Pentecost) to use name-giving to designate the function and character of a person or event. The name *Ngarianbwaloana* represents the 'decoration of victory' when peace is restored after the death of a human being. After the death of the person, the victory has been won and the perfection of peace has now been restored between the two warring tribes. To celebrate this peace and restoration, the people decorate themselves with *Ngaria* which is the name given to a particular valuable flower. The word B*waloana* means 'battle' and refers to any form or practice of violation between people. By combining the two names we get *Ngarianbwaloana* which means 'decoration of victory'.

**The process of *Ngarianbwaloana***

To identify more clearly the process of *Ngarianbwaloana*, I have to designate two tribes 'A' and 'B'. If tribe B attacks tribe A's boundary and kills some women, and the chief of tribe A refuses to make war against tribe B in order to restore the peace, the chief of tribe A has to pick one man (normally man and not woman) and kill him. It is all about reconciliation and building peace. The chief must do this whether or not his tribe is stronger or weaker than the tribe B. It was said that the man who was to be killed as part of this *Ngarianbwaloana* would never know about his death. It was only by the choice of the chief that a person would come to know that they were to die on behalf of their tribe. In every community, when the chief goes to war with another tribe, there is always the thought that someone from one of the tribes will have to die, depending on which chief decides to bring the war to an end and whom he then chooses from among his people to die.

The sign of *Ngarianbwaloana* occurs when the other tribe does not retaliate after some of its members have been killed in battle. The chief speaks out to the opposing tribe as they remain silent and tells them that he will perform the human sacrifice. The man whom the chief chooses to die is brought into the middle ground between the two tribes with all eyes focused on him. The man submits himself to die and does not refuse or complain. The chief chooses another of his own tribe to do the killing by striking him on the head with a *Bwatibweta* (a strong hard wood with a round node on the end used for hammering). After the death of this man, both the tribes come together, contrite and repentant for having fought with each other. The men of both sides all pay their honour and respect to the man who has been sacrificed by picking up some stones and covering the man with them. The stones are piled upon the man in the form of an altar. Many stones represent the many people who would otherwise have died except for the sacrifice of this man who carries all of their deaths on himself. In other words, he 'bought' their life in tribal war through his own death, and paved the way for reconciliation, peace and freedom.

After the funeral ceremony, both tribes walk back together to commemorate the death of the man, following behind the chief of the tribe who has surrendered. Feasting is organised and dancing is performed; the people decorate themselves with *Ngaria* celebrating in their hearts that victory has been won. They all dance together and forget about the war that they have fought against each other. The sacrificial death of the man helps peace prevail and they trust that from now on there will no longer be any war between the two tribes.

## The basic elements that function for peace restoration in the *Ngarianbwaloana*

There are two basic elements in peace restoration between two tribes who have been at war. They are the death of a person and the shedding of blood.

### The death of a person

Death is one of the most important aspects of our human life culturally. It brings together families, neighbours and relatives from everywhere to witness the funeral ceremony. It is believed that there are three important ceremonies in human life into which all humans have to enter. They are birth, marriage and death. These important ceremonies have a very special place in our societies. Death in particular is a final ceremony which brings people together to think about the leadership that the dead person has given, so that the surviving members may follow in the same footprints which are left for us. The one who has died has borne the good fruit of life, and those who remain can imitate their example.

### The shedding of blood

Our basic concept of blood is identical to the Hebrew concept of blood in the sense that we believe that life and blood are one and the same (see Genesis 9:4–6). Therefore to have peace is to have pure blood, that is, blood that is not of hatred, cruelty, anger, sorrow, gossip and so on. The idea of peace that is centred in the blood is about a life that is coloured not by immorality but by purity of life. For instance, in the culture of North Pentecost blood has a profound meaning and is linked directly with the making of peace. A red rooster which has been fastened and is killed during a peace ceremony called *conato* ('fowl performance') designates the fact that peace can only be restored after the shedding of blood. The same idea applies in the practice of pay-back in the case of the murder of a person; the putting to death of one person in response to the murder of another is a practice in our culture called *matan mateana*. This practice is carried out when a member of one family clan murders someone from a different family clan. The family clan of the victim has the right to retaliate by murder as a pay-back, and the shedding of blood in this way is about the restoring of peace.

Although these practices in Hebrew culture and in the culture of North Pentecost are not identical in every way, both are concerned with the matter of making peace. However *Ngarianbwaloana* is different from *matan mateana* in the sense that in the former practice, the chief selects a man from among his own tribe to be sacrificed even though some of his own tribe have already died in battle; to think about the innocent death of one man and the shedding of his blood encourages them to continue to fight on longer as they understand that in tribal wars, one person is being put to death to save their own lives from death.

But both practices in our culture, *Ngarianbwaloana* and *matan mateana*, are about the shedding of blood as having a most important part to play in the restoring of peace.

## In remembrance of *Ngarianbwaloana*

In Northern Pentecost today, on all common sacred feasting occasions such as marriage, pig-killing and whatever other festivities, people decorate themselves with *Ngaria*, the flower plant that designates the decoration of victory. They celebrate and dance as a reminder of a victory that has been won, that is *Ngarianbwaloana*. The concept of decorating in a festival is derived from the idea of *Ngarianbwaloana*.

## The Christian perspectives of *Ngarianbwaloana*

The death of Christ is the centre of the Christian gospel and was viewed by our grandparents as a type of peace from which the *Ngarianbwaloana* is a prototype. The way we understand the biblical idea of Christ's death on the cross is in relation to the death practice of *Ngarianbwaloana* as a means of reconciliation and peace. When St Paul was writing to the church in Colossae, he says: *through him to reconcile to himself all things, whether things on earth or things in heaven, by making peace through his blood shed on the cross* (Colossians 1:20). When Christ died on the cross, he made peace between God and humanity and he restored harmony on earth, although the full realisation of this will come only when Christ returns (Romans 8:21).

However the story of human sacrifice for peace making seems to be much more profound than the common stories of cultic sacrifice, of give-and-take, of retaliation or pay-back, in that it is practical for the compensating of tribe B with human sacrifice and of making peace. In other words even if tribe B is stronger than tribe A who attacked tribe B, tribe B holds back its powers to avoid war by killing a man among its members. This story has great affinity with the Christian story of the crucifixion in which God, as almighty power, holds back his power and sends his Son, not to destroy humanity but to let his Son die on the cross to save the people who have rebelled against him.

Therefore the human misery of the battle period during our ancestors' days can be understood as symbolic of the human misery caused by sin that brought about a division between God and humanity as represented in the time of the Old Testament. How God deals with this rebellious people can be understood in the light of his covenant with them. They disobeyed him and refused his command as their God and creator because they were a sinful people. In order to bring back his people in unity with him, God initiated the new covenant with full assurance in Jesus Christ that neither humanity nor God will ever break, because unity with God is finally established through Jesus Christ. There will be no more sacrifice of animals because Christ has suffered once for all people (1 Peter 3:18).

## Conclusion

The new covenant in Jesus Christ will always endure not because we keep it, but because Jesus has kept and continues to keep it for us. The Father will not reject us for one important reason—he will not reject the Son. During the final entry of Jesus into Jerusalem on his way to his death on a cross, a large crowd spreads their cloaks on the road while others cut down branches of trees and spread them on the road, while he road on a donkey. Arousing their excitement, the crowds that went ahead of him and those that followed shouted out 'Hosanna to the Son of David! Blessed is he who comes in the name of the Lord! Hosanna in the highest!' Matthew 21:8–9). I understand that this celebration of the triumphant entry of Jesus into Jerusalem is beatified with the branches spread on the road while the riding of Jesus on a donkey identifies his joyful decoration of a death victory that he is going to accomplish in a very humble way. This celebration of the decoration of his death victory does not stop here but will continue after his death and resurrection.

The man who is the *Ngarianbwaloana* in traditional culture did not retaliate but was humble and accepted the offer to die on behalf of the two tribes at battle, in order to uphold peace. Many people might have died in the battle but the death of the one man prohibited and prevented it. In the same way, Jesus as the Son of God did not retaliate when he suffered (1 Peter 3:23), but accepted the offer to give his life as 'a ransom for many' (Matt 20:28; Mark 10:45) in order to reconcile us to God and to give us peace. The resurrection of Christ accomplishes the purpose of the restoration of peace; he reconciles us to God through his death and the shedding of his blood on the cross (Col 1:20).

In remembrance of the death victory that Christ has accomplished, the great multitude in heaven decorated and celebrated the death as victory with palm branches in their hands. 'And they cried out in a loud voice, saying 'Salvation belongs to our God who sits on the throne and to the Lamb . . . Praise and glory and wisdom and thanks and honour and power and strength be to our God for ever and ever, Amen' (Rev 7:9–12). The Hebrew understanding of the palm branches here is that they are used in celebration of victory (cf. the triumphant entry of Jesus into Jerusalem recorded in John 12:13). In this sense there is a close connection with the practice of *Ngaria*, the decoration of victory in North Pentecost.

This is one aspect of the culture of our ancestors which meant that they understood Christ as the ultimate focal point of peace maker and reconciler. Because of this they no longer continued the practice of *Ngarianbwaloana*; they believed that Christ's death as the Son of God was unique, the very means of true peace and reconciliation in the midst of their tribal warfare.

# The Ownership of Land in East Santo:
# A Biblical Reflection

## Gideon Paul

### Introduction

This paper is a Biblical reflection on the ownership of land and the issues of land affecting my people on the East coast of Santo. I am a member of a Church which has been greatly affected by land problems so much that families, communities and churches have divided and churches and communities have not been able to develop.

Therefore I have a strong interest in this topic, and a desire to help my people to be aware of the serious problems and bad influences which land issues are creating in villages, communities and the nation as a whole.

### Locating the issue

*The cultural system of land inheritance*

Vanuatu has different cultures and customs in terms of land ownership, which are complicated, yet are widely shared and respected by the people. In the Eastern area of Santo our ancestors believed that land is given to them by someone superior who became known to them as *Ietaro* (God). To them land is not just something to give them food. Their understanding is that land is the basis on which people understand the world they live in, and land is the foundation of customs and cultures and life of people. Therefore the land of our ancestors is of great importance and cannot easily be given to someone else. The first occupants of a piece of land were the owners of that piece of land, and land inheritance today is proved by tracing the genealogy back to the first occupants.

Every tribe and clan of our area has a piece of land; no one can live without owning a piece of land. In our custom land belongs to the people and people belong to the land. Without land, the people cannot exist, and if there are no people, the land is useless. When someone is seen without a piece of land, that person must come from somewhere else and cannot be a real native of East Santo.

In terms of boundaries, our ancestors did not have land with recorded boundaries. Boundaries are marked by features of the land. For example, some places have rivers as their boundaries, some places have trees, or stones, or mountains; some have taboo places as their boundaries. These designated boundaries still exist today.

*Mentality of land and owner*

In an interview with Chief Joseph Segion, a Land Tribunal member on East Santo, he said our customary way of thinking about land is that land is a mother to us; it provides all our human needs. For example, it feeds us, gives us shelter, and provides us with a place of rest at the time of our death. It is also with land that people define their identity. However, our ancestors did allow others the use of their land, but they always retained the right of ownership.

The customary way of using land is totally different from the modern practice of using land. Each clan has a piece of land. The clan is headed by the first-born male in a family, but all the male members in that clan are part owners of their land, except for males that are born from the sister of the father. The clan does not usually distribute its land to individuals. Instead they all benefit from it, even any one outside their clan, in terms of gardening, hospitality, and economy such as keeping a piggery and poultry. The cultivation of land is essentially for making a garden to produce food in order to survive, not for commercial purposes such as crops of coconut, cocoa, coffee and cotton. The members of the clan move from place to place to make their gardens. After harvesting their crops from the first garden, they then move to another place to allow enough time for the used area to become fertile again.

Culturally our ancestors did not have a recorded land policy but a 'heart-written' policy, which worked so well in their time. It was through this policy that land was allowed to anyone outside the clan to cultivate, and yet is still rightfully belonged to the clan.

During that time the people did not have permanently located homes; they moved from place to place because of tribal wars. However, every-where they went they were welcomed and secure in every aspect of life, even when they lived as strangers in that place.

This does not mean that spending some years in a place will make them part owners of land. It means that land is free for anyone to use, yet is still in the hands of the owner when the others leave. All pieces of land are well known to the people in terms of ownership and land boundaries.

*Patriarchal and matriarchal system*

*Patriarchal:* Around the eastern areas of Santo, land is owned by men. Only men can transfer their land to their children, to the male children. A father can have four to five male children yet they all have the right of ownership which is controlled by the first-born male in the family.

In my interview with Chief Joseph Segion about land rights he said that women have no right in land ownership because when they are married the bride price ceremony has important implications. Because land is like a mother to a child, so land belongs to the people and the people belong to the land. When a woman is married, payment of the bride price means transferring her from her father's family to her husband's family. In this transfer, the woman, who was provided for by her father is now provided for by her husband.

However, arrangements are sometimes made between a girl's family and their son-in-laws for a low bride price in order for the husband to live with his father-in-law so that the wife can retain her share of ownership. This sometimes happens in our society but the girl's ownership of land remains under her brothers who are the rightful landowners.

Normally we do not own land through names or through friendship. We only own land through blood, and ownership continues through heredity. The following diagram may help to explain how land ownership works through three generations.

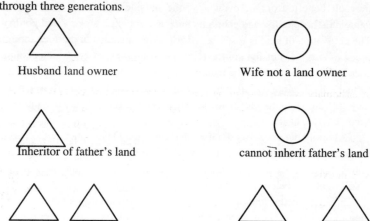

| | |
|---|---|
| Husband land owner | Wife not a land owner |
| Inheritor of father's land | cannot inherit father's land |
| Inheritor of grandfather's land | Have no right over grandfather's land |

In this diagram, children from the women have no right over the grandfather's land because their mother has been bought out from her right with the bride-price system. However in terms of family relationship they can still benefit from their grandfather's land but not claim ownership. They are under their uncles, who are the rightful landowners.

*Matriarchal:* The matriarchal system is not our customary practice of owning land. However, it can happen if necessary. For example land is owned by women only when a father has no son, therefore in this case his daughter directly inherits her father's land and no other close family has a right to dispute her right of ownership.

It can also happen when all male members of a family are dead, leaving a surviving female. So in this case she also has full right over her kinship's land. This does not mean that it will continue on with a matriarchal system of land ownership. Later in her marriage when she has a son, the son then is the inheritor of his grandfather's land.

The following diagram explains what I mean:

Husband land owner                                    Wife not land owner

Inheritor of father's land    Inheritor of the father's land    Inheritor of father's land

Have no right over grandfather's land        Inheritor of grandfather's land

A customary system of securing land so that members of a clan will benefit from their kin's land occurs by the system of arranged marriage between boys and girls. For example, a boy normally marries a girl from his father's line, which is his uncle's daughter. This is purposely for the coming generation that they can always benefit from their kin's land. This system is still in existence in this modern day; a parent selects his son's wife always from his own line. The main idea behind this customary system of marriage is to maintain the family relationships and to secure the land.

## The modern practice of land inheritance

In recent modern times the traditional system of using and owning land has not been maintained. People come up with new ideas of owning and using land and this leads to land disputes. It might be the change of civilisation or the development of an industrial economy in our country which has led to the adoption of new practices of land ownership and use. This change has become a common thing elsewhere in the Pacific, and this fact needs to be made known to the local people so that the valuable customary system of land inheritance does not completely disappear for future generations.

### Selling of lands to developers

The first sale of land to Europeans was during their arrival in mid-1800s. Europeans began to negotiate with local landowners who were ignorant of land values at that time. Some landowners 'sold' their land (or allowed their land to be used) in exchange for items with very little value. Europeans then developed the good coastal land with plantations of coconut, cocoa and coffee. These newcomers did not understand the East Santo land system as previously mentioned, namely that land is available for anyone to use but without them becoming the rightful owners of the land. With this mentality among the indigenous people, the practice of the registration of land under the British or French administrations did not mean anything to the traditional landowners.

The Europeans did not appreciate that on East Santo, land and man belong to each other. Fifty to sixty years later the areas of land which had been occupied by the Europeans were then prohibited to indigenous people, including even the resources of the sea. The local people also found out that the foreigners were now earning more money from their land, which was originally exchanged for items that had no value. This has prompted them to react against the foreigners.

In that same period the joint court began hearings for registration of land, at first on the main island of Efate. The issue became complicated because some of the occupied areas were not properly sold. However, the joint court began to hear cases involving land which had been used. The dark bush areas which were being surveyed ready to for use by foreigners were taken back by our indigenous cultural and political leaders (with the support of the New Hebrides National Party known today as the Vanuaaku Party), and were returned to the traditional owners.

The late Jimmy Moli Stevens was also one who worked on behalf of Santo natives to reclaim their land from foreigners. He was the spokesman for the people of Fanafo after recognising that the local people were losing large areas of land to foreigners. In early 1960 the Nagriamel movement was formed under the leadership of Stevens, to reclaim alienated land. The movement stood very strongly against the foreigners to prevent them from using dark bush areas. Stevens' idea was to allocate to his people the undeveloped areas along roadsides. The allocation of land on East Santo was in three places. One of their centres was near Natawa Bridge on the north side; another was where the Lorethiakarkar Primary School now is, and the final centre was at the village opposite where the family of the late former president of Sanma Province lives. They used the areas for gardening purposely to secure these areas from the foreigners.

In earlier times before independence in 1980, the New Hebrides as a whole stood together as one to fight in gaining back their land from the British and the French governments. However, this does not mean that the selling of land came to an end; it still continues on today. In more recent times, the selling of land is done by individual people to both foreigners and to local ni -Vanuatu people. Foreigners take out a lease as required by the

National Government. For a ni-Vanuatu there are problems because the selling of land does not follow a proper procedure either culturally or accordingly to Government requirements concerning land tenure.

The following are some of the common practices among the locals:

*Contribution to death ceremonies:* Mutual agreements are sometimes made between landowners and islanders about land, but there are times when an islander may contribute a significant amount towards a death ceremony, then later demand a plot of land in return for his contribution to the deceased family. When there is lack of money among the members of the deceased family, then a plot of land must be provided for the islander.

*Buying vehicles:* More and more people are selling their land on East Santo in order to buy vehicles. People want to own vehicles; instead of looking for other means of money they sell their land. Many hectares may be sold to someone for only a small amount of money, even just enough to put a deposit on a vehicle. Most of these vehicles do not last due to road accidents, or they are taken back by the bank because of a failure to keep up loan repayments. This may seem foolish but this is what is going on with some of our people.

*Exchange of land for vehicles:* A variation on the above practice is that some of our land owners ask wealthy people to buy them vehicles in exchange for a large plot of land. To the buyers this is a welcome chance for them to profit because, as business people, they know the value of land as a resource for them to produce more products to improve their business.

*Laziness:* Laziness is one of the main factors in selling land to foreigners and to islanders. Some people are too lazy to work but want more money in their pocket, and so they sell their land to get money. A good example can be seen at Palon village with a man by the name of Tacpai. He sold all his land in order to enjoy his life with friends drinking alcohol and buying vehicles. A few years later he was seen hanging around with no more vehicles, no more land for his future generation, nor even for himself. Some of the original plot of land has been sold more than once.

These are some of the practices concerning the sale of land which are occurring among some of our people on East Santo today. People no longer think of the future generation, but only of themselves. They sell land for their own interest. The valuable system of land inheritance, which was so important during the time of our ancestors is no longer in practice; instead new practices are occurring today which lead to land conflicts that greatly affect the health and development of communities as well as churches today.

## Core issues

### Disputes over land ownership

I have looked above at the cultural system of land inheritance, and also the modern practice of land inheritance. Now I want to explore more closely some of the core issues. As we have seen, land is like a mother who cares and provides for her children and that land is of great importance to our culture. Therefore land boundaries are well known to their people and freely used and respected by the owners. However, due to recent changes and the land disputes that have followed, we have lost touch with our ancestors' practice.

In the time of our ancestors the industrial economy of our country was not as important to our people as it is today. The population was small and there was more land available. All farming was subsistence farming and what the people grew was for their own consumption, and any leftovers went to feed pigs or chickens or was thrown away.

Dispute over land in Vanuatu today is no longer between Europeans and locals but between ni-Vanuatu themselves. These disputes over land are increasing because of population growth, increasing awareness of the value of land in our society today, and also because of certain economic development plans by the Government in our area.

Population growth on East Santo is very high compared to the time of our ancestors. Improved medical services provided in the country, and early marriages contribute to the population growth. People live much longer than in the past and young couples produce more children. But with the current rate of population growth, land is no longer shared within families in the way that was previously done. Each person or family wants to own a piece of land for themselves without their family's participation, and this leads to land disputes.

Disputes also arise when a member of a clan claims ownership from his uncles; culturally this is totally wrong. Usually if a boy wants to have access to his uncle's land he has to get permission form his uncle, but he has no right to claim ownership in the way that is happening in some areas on East Santo today.

Land boundaries are also one of the main causes of land disputes today in our society. Some places have rivers as their boundaries but after some years rivers may have changed their course. Some have trees, which for the next generation can be mistaken or confused with other trees. Stones can also be mistaken by younger generations. The Vanuatu courts often find it difficult to deal with these land issues, therefore many land dispute cases are referred back to local community chiefs and local dispute parties to deal with them. This has led to the foundation of Land Tribunals where power is given back to local chiefs to resolve issues about customary land, which is very familiar to them.

Boundaries are traditionally well known to their owners, but because of the population growth rate today and the awareness of the value of land and the potential of land for production, people have started to create new boundaries. For example, when a logging company is operating in an area, a landowner may sometimes move his boundary mark to include some valuable trees just outside his boundary. Naturally, when he moves his boundary, this creates a dispute between him and the other landowner next to him.

The customary names given by a father to his son can also cause dispute over land ownership, especially when a wrong name is given to a boy who belongs to another piece of land. This can cause problems when later generations try to trace their genealogy back and are misled due to the wrong given name by their earlier ancestors. This is one of the main factors in disputes over land ownership and it is difficult to deal with. The only way to avoid this issue is for right names to be given to boys who are rightful landowners of a piece of land.

Some of the first pieces of land which were occupied and developed by traders and missionaries are still in dispute today. The land might have been bought by some particular people who were supposed to become land-owners, but the later generations still claim ownership of the same piece of land. This might occur because some of the land was sold by the wrong people. This is what happened to the people of Siviri village where the chief of the place said, 'The land in question was not sold by the natives of Siviri who were the legal land owners but by Nasthalo a native of a neighbouring island who pretended to be the chief of Siviri'.[1] This is a clear example of how land in Vanuatu might be sold to Europeans by the wrong people. However, it could also happen that the land may be sold by the legal owners of the land, yet later on the original owners still claim ownership. This is happening sometimes in relation to a lease which is ready to be given by the church office for mission land, or by the land department for a trader's land. Land ownership is sometimes also disputed in order to stop a lease being given to the legal owners. This is what is happening to our society today on East Santo.

*Land rights*
There are many land disputes in our societies today because everybody wants to get land rights, such as uncles, grandsons/grand-daughters and

---

1.    This account appears in Howard van Trease: *The Politics of Land in Vanuatu*.

others through their given names, which is totally wrong according to our customary system of rights to land. It may sometimes happen that way when necessary. For example if there is no true blood-line left, in this case anyone of the clan can claim a right over that piece of land. According to our culture, land rights are from the father, and continue in heredity through the blood-line as has been discussed earlier.

It is not rightful for a boy to claim land rights from his uncle, or a son from the mother's side to claim land rights from his grandfather, or someone to claim land rights through a given name. But this is a reality among some people in our societies. As I have stated before, it is not wrong for all members of a family to have access on their kin's land, but they have to get permission from the ancestor who is the legal owner. Then normally permission will be granted as requested.

Land rights are not very easy to determine because of the complexity of issues which are involved. For example it may happen in some areas that when a child loses his father while he is still a baby and he alone is the life blood of a piece of land, and he grows up in someone's care, he may then give his carer a piece of his land. The given land must be handed over through a custom ceremony in which a pig is to be killed to seal their agreement as a customary land registration.

Concerning islanders who have bought land from East Santo landowners, they should know that how important it is that this customary system of land registration must be followed. Unfortunately however, much land has been given over to islanders without any proper customary land registration. The ceremony which takes place seals the agreement between those involved and shows the people concerned that something heavy and powerful has been done. It also makes the buyer of the land feel that they have the right to develop the piece of land they bought, though they will still be under the authority of traditional ownership in terms of respect.

According to article 71 of the constitution of Vanuatu, land always belongs to the landowner. Any islander who buys a plot of land before doing any project should consult the landowner regarding the project. He needs to have the approval of the landowner before he carries out any project on the land.

Land resources, such as trees for producing timber and minerals, will always belong to the traditional landowners, and the buyers are not to sell them. The buyer is only to cultivate the land to produce local products and sell them. The islanders are also required to respect the taboo places inside the piece of land they purchased; no destruction of taboo places is permitted by the buyers because these taboo places represent the identity of our people on East Santo. Wild animals, birds, fish of the rivers and sea including other sea resources are available to the buyers to eat and use but they are not permitted to sell them outside.

## The negative impact of land disputes upon society

### Family division

Land disputes are one of the main causes of family division in our society. The assumed lifestyle among our ancestors in which a family lived in unity is no longer practised today among some clans. This is because of the selfish attitude of some family members which led them to want to own more land by themselves, and excluding other family members.

Usually in the past a clan lived together in a particular and defined area of a village, whereas today this is no longer the case. The practise today is that some families live by themselves. Some others live with another clan or with their in-laws which is not the customary way of living.

Some people find it hard to leave their property and go to live in another area. This can lead to a break-down of relationships . . . one consequence is that there are many bush marriages (that is, illegal marriages which are not supported by the society or the church) in our societies today. When there is separation of people from their families, then there is also loss of support in terms of bride price and foods, and ceremonies.

### Community division

During the time of our ancestors people lived in unity as previously mentioned. Division among clans was not their present as it is today where communities divide a lot. People today no longer live in unity. New villages have been formed, and the establishment of people in mission areas by missionaries is no longer valued. Instead land issues have led to people leaving the mission areas and their original homes.

A good example is at Natawa village which was once populated, but later two clans left and went to Fanafo village and formed a new station, which is still called Natawa village. Another example is at Kole village where my own clan left the village and we formed a new village now called Lorum. These two examples were the result of land disputes, which led to the exodus and the formation of small villages.

Some people found it hard to leave their property and so stayed on, but do not take part in community events and have withdrawn their support from social activities.

### Church division

Land disputes have also resulted in the formation of small churches in communities. When two parties come to a disagreement concerning land issues this is represented in a division in their church involvements; one of the parties breaks away from the main line church, gets involved with and invites in another religious group. This then affects the main-line church, its yearly budget and other social activities in the community. According to the Parliamentary Bill concerning 'freedom of worship' in the country, it is impossible to chase any unwelcome religious group out of the village.

In the way explained above, people move from church to church just because of land problems. This then undermines the unity of the church, which was established by God through His son Jesus Christ, and it is a violation of the cross of Christ which unites all people. All Christian churches should know that we have different ways of worship, different ways of giving out sacraments, different working structures and different beliefs, but we all worship only one Christ who is the head of the Church. Therefore there is no basis or need to separate and hate each other. This separation and conflict are the consequences of land disputes.

## Biblical reflection

### Land in the Old Testament

In the Old Testament there are passages which teach us about land, especially in the early part of the Old Testament known as the Pentateuch which tells us how God was dealing with His people. One thing that comes out clearly is how land is linked with God and Israel; this is particularly clear when we read the accounts about the Exodus of Israel from Egypt. T Desmond Alexander and Brian S Rosner wrote, 'Throughout the history of Israel, it is clear that the relationship between God and His people is intricately linked to the land which has been given to them. Israel's involvement is always with the land and with Yahweh, never only with Yahweh as though to live only in intense obedience, never only with land as though simply to posses and manage.'[2]

It is a covenantal relationship between God and Israel in which land is the place where Israel must make their choices and live in obedience in order to maintain the covenant relationship. This is clearly stated in Deuteronomy chapter 4 and 30, where Israel's faithfulness and obedience allows the continuing occupation of the land given to them.

What happened in fact was that Israel's occupation and enjoyment of life with Yahweh in the land as fulfilment of the covenant promise failed as a result of disobedience (Jeremiah 25:1–11). However, Israel was always convinced that the father-son relationship established by God with His

---

2.   Alexander TD & Rosner BS, *New Dictionary of Biblical Theology*, page 625.

212

people was inviolable (Deut 9:26, 1 Kg 8: 52–53). They believed that although they lost the land, they were still the people of God who will still find blessing through obedience.

The gift of land promised to the patriarchs and given to the Israelites is more than an agricultural point; in fact it is a theological point. The relationship with God represented in the description of Eden, although broken, is restored through the Exodus event which was the beginning of God's act in preparation for the fulfillment of the promised covenant. The account of God dealing with the Israelites which leads to the chasing out of the Canaanites and entry to the land reveals to the world that God is the owner of creation; therefore land must not be used selfishly but must be well used and managed for the good of all who live in it.

The removal of the land from the heart of Israel's relationship with God was a preparation for the broadening of God's purpose in the world as predicted in Ezekiel 47:22–23 and Zechariah 2:11, namely that there will be nations who will share the inheritance from God that was previously reserved for Israel. Alexander and Rosner refer to this where they write, 'It was possible only because possession of the land held had previously been removed from the heart of Israel's relationship with God'.[3]

We have seen how the relationship between God, Israel and the land were linked together, that the land is a gift from God to Israel, which Israel is to care for and use. At the same time we can also see that land can cause problems to Israel especially when they forget their God who brought them out of Egypt to the promised land. Forgetting God leads to the misuse of land as their own property and not as a gift from God. For the Israelites, to continue enjoying God's blessing in the promised land is to remember God at all times. In that sense the cause of land disputes in Israel was the neglect of God as their creator and turning to other gods. Many people turned to idols for their protection and care, rather than to the God of the land.

*Divine ownership*
In the Old Testament the Israelites saw God as the owner of the whole earth including everything on it, both living and dead. Everything that a person, family, class, tribe or nation can possess comes as a gift from God. This includes not only the land but also wives and children (Ps 127:3–5, Prov 19:14, Job 1:2), all-material prosperity (Hosea 2:8, Jer 5:24–25, Ps 6:9–13, 1 Chron 29:14) and even the power to get it (Deut 8:18); these are all from God.

---

3.    *Ibid*, 626.

With this truth the Israelites knew they really owned nothing. The land they lived in they did not obtain by their own power but simply by God speaking and it happened (Genesis 1); therefore to Israel land is a gift.

Leviticus 25–27 tells us that God owns land and that nobody is allowed to sell it to another person. One cannot transfer the land to another tenant but it must be passed on to succeeding generations as required by God. For example, in the story of Naboth's vineyard in 1 Kings 21, when King Ahab of Samaria asked Naboth to sell to him his vineyard, Naboth replied, 'The Lord forbid that I should sell the inheritance of my father' (1 Kings 21:3).

For the Israelites, the land is to be used wisely and there must be a seven-year cycle of land use. God is the owner and they are the stewards. They do not own the land permanently. They know the land given was for agricultural provisions and to sell it means selling the lives of the inhabitants who are fed from the land.

*Land in the New Testament*
It is clear that the disobedience of the Israelites led to God's initiation of the new covenant in Christ. It was a long process of God dealing with His people through to its fulfilment in Jesus Christ. During his lifetime, Jesus also promised to the world a land (the Kingdom) which they would possess and into which entry is through him alone. (Matt 5:5, 25:34) As such, Jesus rescued God's people from darkness and brought them into light; we are part of this gift and promise and are yet on the journey to the promise land. In John 14:6 Jesus said, 'I am the way, the truth and the life; no one come to the father except by me'. Jesus is the only way to the land promised in the Old Testament.

Therefore, according to the New Testament message, God, through obedience to Jesus Christ, is now the only way for the Israelites to enter the promised land. To disobey the gospel message of Jesus Christ will result in the loss of salvation, which has been offered by God through Christ and who is the key to the promised land.

Taking Jesus now as the key to the promised land, in John 15 we see the same idea of a link between these same three (God, Israel, land) when Jesus says, 'If you remain in me and I in you, you will bear a great deal of fruit, for without me you can do nothing' (John 15:5).

Paul's understanding of the Church as the community of Jesus and the Gentiles is based on his reading of the Old Testament teaching on land. In Colossians 1:13–14, Paul speaks of the inheritance in Christ, so also 1 Peter 1:3–5. With this Biblical understanding of land in the Old and New Testament, I agree with Alexander and Rosner who argue that, 'The inheritance in Christ is no doubt different from the land received and lost by Israel, but it is greater not less, than the land'.[4]

With all these we are to know that we are accountable to God for our actions, especially concerning land use as it was for the Israelites in the Old Testament. Therefore as Christians, disputes between us as members of the church of Jesus Christ about land is wrong. The first allocation of land to each of our ancestors was, we believe, given to them by God for their survival and for our survival today. And so claiming other pieces of land is wrong because it has been allocated to someone else for their survival; to claim it means to steal someone else's land which has been given to them by God.

## Pastoral direction

As we looked at the biblical understanding of land we found that land is a pure gift from God to his people. It is given to us for the purposes as discussed. The areas of land which had been allocated to our ancestors are the areas where we are to claim temporary ownership. Claiming too many pieces of land is something contradicting the Biblical understanding of land, so also is transferring and selling land to another person, because land is required to be preserved for the succeeding generation and not to be sold off or disputed about between ourselves. However, this is exactly what is happening in the modern social life on East Santo. The important question is: what will the church do about it this situation in order to reduce or to stop the disputes?

The problem is that there is not enough biblical teaching about land among our people. The biblical views of land must be well taught to people so that people may know how to manage and use their land. As such, seminars and bible studies must be held in our communities for this purpose. However, the fact is that in several communities the chiefs and church leaders are the ones involved in land issues, which means therefore that they might find it difficult to teach and lead the people on this topic. As we continue to ignore the issue, the people continue to remain with the mentality that they are the owners of the land rather than just stewards of God's land; that attitude will continue to create problems in our societies.

The apostle Paul has given us good direction and instruction in his letters to the churches in Asia Minor. The letters contain his teaching about a range of situations in the church communities of his time. In our own time there are very many land problems but there is very little if any biblical teaching about this situation. I think some clear direction and teaching about

---

4 .   *Ibid*, 627.

land is what church leaders should provide today. They should not be involved in land issues but should be neutral and teach the Word of God about the situation. In this way people will recognise their failures and turn to live according to the will of God. As for the chiefs, they are to encourage people in the valuable way of land use that our ancestors practised in their lifetime, as has been discussed earlier.

To forget or to neglect God is also a factor in land disputes on East Santo today, leading to the misuse of God's creation. Land must always be used according to God's will, not against the will of God, as required for His people. Land must not be disputed between families, clans and tribes, because this is contrary to what is required by God. For God, land is to be well managed and shared by everyone who lives in it, as illustrated for example in Joshua 14–19.

My last suggestion is that, in order to avoid land issues, people should remain on the land which they have inherited from their ancestors and not interfere with any piece of land which has belonged to another person, because the land has been given to our ancestors by God. In order to reduce or avoid the land issues among our people, these proposals must be implemented.

## Conclusion

The common cause of the problems about land in our societies today is the wrong mentality of our people; people consider that they own the land, and do not recognise that it is God who has created and given the land for our use. We forget that we do not own the land permanently but we are only caring for God's property.

Forgetting God in our lives leads to selfishness about land, which then causes land disputes. We do not own the land, rather the land owns us. We come from land and survive from land, and in our death we return to the land.

### Bibliography

Alexander T D & Rosner B S, *New Dictionary of Biblical Theology* (London: InterVarsity Press, 2000

Brueggemann W, *The Land* (Philadelphia: Fortress Press, 1977).

Habel C N, *The Land is Mine* (Philadelphia: Fortress Press, 1995).

Van Trease H, *The politics of land in Vanuatu* (Fiji: University of the South Pacific, 1987).

Lini W, *Beyond Pandemonium, From the New Hebrides to Vanuatu* (Fiji: Asia Pacific Books, 1980).

Interview: Joseph Sigeon, at Kole Village, East Santo, July 2, 2003

# Kava Consumption as an Issue of Gospel and Culture

## Christopher Iawak

### Introduction

In this paper l would like to present the ongoing issue of Gospel and Culture in Vanuatu, in particular in relation to the use of kava. We believe that culture is given by God as a means by which people relate to each other and govern themselves so that they may be at peace and harmony in the society. There are many traditional cultural practices which the missionaries, when they first arrived, tried to abolish because they thought of them as evil.

Kava is one of the traditional drinks that is used throughout all Vanuatu. Only some of the islands regard kava as part of their traditional culture, such as Tanna, Pentecost and parts of the central islands of Vanuatu. I will be presenting this paper from the point of view which considers that kava is a highly valued part of our God-given culture.

The main purpose of this paper is to explore some valuable uses of kava and to see how its traditional use has been transformed so as to reduce its meaning and result in some bad effects in a person's life, in the family, in the community, in the nation and especially in the church. This misuse has made many people think and teach that kava is sinful.

When the gospel first arrived, it was accepted in different cultures in different islands. Since our cultures are not the same, we should respect one another and allow the people to receive the gospel within their culture while at the same time not ignoring the effects.

### Definition

Kava is a root crop that is grown in most parts of Vanuatu and some parts of the Pacific. It is a small plant with small round leaves and small branches. People use the juice that comes out from its stem when it is chewed or grounded by some special stone or machine to make it soft. It is then mixed with water and properly sieved so that it is ready to be used. When it is mixed with water, it gives the kava juice a muddy look.

### Origin of Kava

*Tanna's mythology*

Long ago before human consumption of kava, it was traditionally believed and taught that stones were the first to drink kava but not the kind of kava used today. They drank 'wild kava' (we called it Nakium in our language;

this refers to the spirits that existed before the creation of humans). The difference between wild kava and today's kava is that wild kava cannot be consumed by humans.

### The story of Kava's origin

Kava is said to have originated from women. The story goes like this.

One day a woman on the island of Tanna went to the river. She sat by the river bank peeling wild yam and slicing it into the pool to get it washed. As we know, women of the past wore grass skirts. Suddenly the woman felt something coming under her. A young kava plant germinated from the ground and was having sex with the woman. Later the woman nurtured the plant until it grew big and was then used as kava. That is why the Tannese women are not allowed to drink kava because it shows disrespect to eat something that has originated from them.

### The distribution of Kava

While stones continued to drink wild kava, one day two men decided to taste ordinary kava for the first time because it was similar to the wild kava. So they dug up a stem and drank half of it. After discovering that kava was better than wild kava, one of the men took the remaining half of the kava to his village and the men of the village drank it the next day. This is when humans started to consume kava. It was this man whose name was Kalpapen (a great chief of Tanna), who distributed kava all through the island of Tanna to be used by men. Today when you go up to the big hill of Tanna, (Tokosmera), you can find where this chief used to kneel down to get his kava ready to drink. It is there till today.

### The origin of sin

According to the people of Tanna, in the past people were living in what we called two ships or spheres of life. One was called 'Nimruken' and the other 'Kouiameta'. There was a great dispute between the two about power. One wanted to be greater than the other. There was a man called Iovanovan who belonged to one of the spheres. He initiated the problem. He said to one of the other men, 'You must remove that feather, if you do not want to, we will kill you'. (In Tanna the feather of a rooster is a sign of authority.) This resulted in a big war which led everything into chaos. That is the origin of the sin and disorder which still exists today, and Tannese people believe that this is what has caused the abuse of kava and other troubles today.

### Etymology (origin of the name 'Kava')

Different islands in Vanuatu may have different names for kava. In Tanna we called it 'Nik-Kawa'. There are two words that make up the name. The first three letters 'Nik' is a name that covers all plants (as 'tree' does for example in English). 'Kawa' means 'a drowsy state'. When you drink or chew the kava, your mouth becomes numb, your head feels thick and after a while you begin to get drowsy.

In some other islands there are different names: In Pentecost 'Malogu', in Malekula 'Namelek', in Santo 'Hae'.

## Use of Kava in the past

As I have said earlier kava has had an important role in traditional cultural ceremonies. Any ceremony without kava is regarded by the people as incomplete. I will not try to give a list of all the ceremonies where kava is essential because there is no issue or problem in relation to that. The problem is the attitude and behaviour of people (as the people of God) in relation to kava. I will concentrate on some areas where the use of kava is being transformed because of modern influences and economic development; it is these which have caused the problems today. To do this I need to explain the use of kava in the past and investigate any differences in its use today.

### Appropriate people who used Kava

When men started to consume kava it was only those who had gone through certain stages in life and rank who could drink. In the past only the Iaramara (chief) drank kava. There was also a special man who worked for the chief and his people, Tupunes, a holy person, who drank kava. Tannese people believed that when God created the world, he also gave some special stones by which they can learn about the will of God and his abundant blessing, especially in fruits. There are many fruits and each fruit has its special stone. These stones are kept in a taboo place where men are not allowed to enter, only the holy man Tupunes. During his time in the taboo place, he had to abstain from sex, and he ate certain food. He offered some rituals and after these he drank kava and offered prayer (damara). When all his work was done in the taboo place, there was a public declaration and dedication in the *nakamal* by the chief and then the people could use the fruit discovered by Tupunes.

### A theological perspective (typology)

In the OT it is only the high priest who enters the most holy place once a year for the sins of the people, on Yom Kippur (the Day of Atonement). Tupunes is a type of high priest who enters the taboo place on behalf of the chief and his people. The stones used by Tupunes are the stones in the priestly garments (Urim and Thummim—Ex 28:30—especially Thummim which symbolises the perfection of God that is demonstrated in fruits.)

## Who can drink kava?

The use of kava was strictly controlled. Women were not allowed to drink kava or even go near when kava is being prepared. Young people were utterly forbidden to drink it. The forbidding of kava indicates that the people of the past knew something of kava's effect and would not allow everyone to be affected. For example kava can cause young people to be lazy and not work; it can also cause a young person not to marry because kava is said to have originated from woman and it can become a substitute for a wife; kava causes weakness or ineffectiveness to the reproductive system and women do not want to marry such people. A person can be easily addicted to kava and so he is permitted to have his own garden but not to steal from others.

Traditionally kava was limited in its use to people who had gone through certain stages in life such as marriage, and were ready to start their home. When someone reached the appropriate stage, it was usually his uncle who gave him kava for the first time. Older people usually drink kava at sunset because it symbolizes the approaching end of their life.

## What happens when men drink kava?

Traditionally, when the first person drinks kava in the *nakamal* all noise in the community is lowered or even ceases. We say that there is a spirit in kava. In order for kava to do its work, you have to sit quietly and be sensitive about making any noise, so usually kava drinkers talk in whispers. Anyone found to be making noise in the community when kava is being drunk will pay a heavy fine to the chief. Kava drinking is to be respected and honoured.

## Place where kava is used in culture (Nakamal)

In my culture kava is not used anywhere one wishes to prepare and drink kava. The appropriate place is in the *nakamal*, located usually under a big banyan tree. In Pentecost island it is in big thatch houses. Women are not allowed to go past the *nakamal* when kava is being prepared and drunk.

## Functions of the Nakamal

The *nakamal* does not serve only as a place for drinking kava. People gather in the *nakamal* for various purposes. It is a place for setting disputes, where issues of order and justice in the community are decided, a place for decision-making. It is a place where repentance is experienced. It is a place where forgiveness is established through the shedding of blood of a pig and kava drinking. It is a place where men commune with their god through

Damara (Prayer) while kava drinking. The *nakamal* is a place of custom dancing and other celebrations such as marriage, circumcision and worship.

The *nakamal* unites people at the level of family and tribes. It affirms, sustains, builds relationships and provides reconciliation, hope, peace and love. This is the purpose of the existence of *nakamal*. It exists to affirm life, it has a unique role in building cooperate life.[1]

Kava is part of the function of the *nakamal*; it serves as a shield for all things that are done in the *nakamal*; kava drinking accompanies Damara (prayer), that all things may work well for the community and their gods are served and honoured. The *nakamal* is the right place where kava is to be used because only there does it fulfil its true traditional meaning and purpose for the community.

*Amount of kava*

I constantly appreciate what is involved in the way kava is prepared and the amount of kava used by each person in the *nakamal*. In my culture, kava is prepared usually by being chewed by young people while older people stand by and give them encouragement, teaching and historical accounts. This is the time when young people can gain a lot of wisdom from the older people. While the chewing of the kava is taking place, one person counts all the people in the *nakamal* who drink kava, putting out leaves according to the number. Each person in the *nakamal* has kava chewed for them and that is all for that night. Kava is drunk from a coconut shell.

Whenever the chief drinks his kava, he has to sit quietly, thinking of his work that needs to be done or that has been done. The motive for drinking kava at that time is not to get drunk but to relax, to settle down and that is the kind of kava drinking which brings about new ideas or thoughts. That is why one coconut shell of kava is always enough and is appreciated by the drinker.

**Use of kava today**

As we take a deeper look at the uses of kava today, we will try to compare this with its use in the past. We will look carefully at some changes in kava's use today and consider what I believe is its major effect on the family, community, nation and most of all on the church of God.

*People who use kava*

---

1. Prior, Randall *The Gospel and Culture in Vanuatu 2* (Melbourne: Gospel Vanuatu Books, 2001), 54.

221

Nowadays there is huge change, especially among men who drink kava. Kava is becoming a source of financial income for people and is no longer a ceremonial drink. This has led to the serious abuse of kava; it has lost its traditional meaning in our society. Today kava is drunk in any place, by any person, including women and young people. This is in conflict with the rules of the past. In the past kava drinking required the uncle's approval because he would ensure that a man had gone through certain ranks and stages into maturity. Today young people who have just left school or even are still at school use kava without the traditional approval. Modern secular education clearly does not guarantee that a student is wise. Today it is no longer the uncle who gives approval but the drinker gives their own approval according to their biological changes and educational levels; that is contrary to what was required in our culture. That is one of the big changes in the practice of kava drinking today. You will hear many people say 'Oh it is just food like any other food' but they forgot that they are denying their culture.

In kava bars (places where kava may be drunk), the manager's only aim is to make more money so it doesn't matter who his customer is, even a young boy or a woman, because if he stops them from drinking kava he is losing good customers. He is concerned about money making not caring about the person or the culture or the effect that the kava will have.

*From Nakamal to kava bar (red light): why a kava bar?*
Nowadays kava has become one of the most important contributing factors in our national economy as a source for income. Many local farmers can g row kava and they get a good income when exporting or when selling in kava bars. Since kava is part of our culture in the Southern islands, especially on the island of Tanna where kava is highly valued, it is becoming an issue where we can say that we are selling our custom and it is reducing the value of kava in traditional society.

There is something to note about the terms *nakamal* and kava bar (red light—kava bars are often marked by a red light outside). Sometimes people use the name *nakamal* to refer to a kava bar. This is quite wrong because it reduces the whole value and function of the *nakamal* as explained earlier. The *nakamal* is not a place for making money or even just for drinking kava as some think when they use the word *nakamal* to refer to any kava bar.

On the island of Tanna today, as well as on other islands, there are some kava bars. At times when someone does not have kava but has money, he can go to the kava bar and buy his own kava. The difference is that he does not have only one shell, he can have three or more shells which is just too much. With this approach to drinking kava, the motive for drinking has changed. The drinker is more self-centred and may want to get drunk, and to do so he needs more than one shell; the more he/she consumes, the greater the effect of the kava.

This does not mean that drinking kava in the *nakamal* is now totally abolished but it does mean that drinking just one coconut shell of kava in the *nakamal* today is not enough for many people, they have one coconut shell in the *nakamal* and more in the kava bar.

*The amount of kava used today*
As stated above the aim of the manager of the kava bar is to make money and so to achieve his aim he has to prepare a lot of kava. It used to be the practice for them to use a bucket but it is now too small for them so they use bigger containers. It has encouraged the practice of people drinking even more kava. (There are now some common words used to refer to a person who drinks a lot of kava, for example 'Pupel' or 'Tanker' which are degrading.)

In comparison to the past, this is big change.

There is a practice going on in Tanna today that I have observed after drinking kava in a *nakamal*. If you stand and watch carefully what happens in the kava bars, many of the same people who drink kava in the *nakamal* are also there in the kava bars. They drink more than they should and more than they did in the past. Many drinkers do not seem to be satisfied with one shell in the *nakamal*, they want more and more. The more they want and search for, the greater is the effect on their life, their family, the community and the church of God. It is a self centred attitude.

*Nakamal and kava bar 'utensils'*
In the *nakamal* especially in Tanna, each drinker has his own coconut shell which he has prepared for himself. Each person knows his own coconut shell and it cannot be used by others. In the kava bar however, drinkers drink from each any other's coconut shell because there are too many customers. The coconut shells are not properly washed and a drinker does not know exactly which person has drunk kava from the coconut shell they are using. This is unhealthy because this way of drinking from anyone's coconut shell can lead to rapid spread of all kinds of diseases.

## Effects caused by the changes in the use of kava

We can make a long list of what I strongly believe are the results of the very significant change in the use of kava.

*In family life*

The kava bar is becoming a meeting place for men and women especially in our two main towns. When a woman is addicted to kava, but has no money, the place she goes is to the kava bar where she is likely to become involved in prostitution. This applies not only to unmarried but also to married women. The result of all this is marital unfaithfulness and a person is often caught in such practices. A man will drink at the kava bar not only as a place for kava drinking but also as a place for meeting nice young women.

This problem also leads to unequal sharing of resources, power, time, knowledge, love and income. One of a married couple (normally the man) wants to keep everything for himself in order to support his drinking. The children then become the victims of such unequal sharing in the home where kava is abused; this is especially so when the parents become divorced. The children experience the mother's love and care but lack any attention and care from the father.

*In the church*

As these problems creep into the lives of families, they begin also to affect the church because it is Christians (including some church leaders) as well as non-Christians who are involved in kava-drinking. Most Christians today use the word 'church' to refer to a building but the real church is a community of people who believe in the Lord and are committed to their God. That is why I make the claim that when there is disruption of time, teaching, prayer and worship in the home, it has already weakened the church. For church leaders, kava drinking leads them to become slack in private bible study and prayer. Leaders are meant to be good examples, but because of the behaviour of some church leaders, many of the programmes that are carried out at night are not successful.

One of the principles of the church is generous giving. Most Christians find it hard to contribute to the church because they have very little money but when you look closely at what is going on in the 'red light' areas, you will find Christians spending up to 500 vatu or more every night on kava. Kava drinking means that people become weaker in their giving to the church.

Abuse of kava can also lead to apostasy. I say this because that is exactly what is happening today, and it happens without people realising it. When evening approaches, a Christian who is a kava drinker cannot sit quietly or concentrate; even church meetings at this time of day will not be carried out properly. The thought of drinking kava arises and they will be busy thinking about trying to find kava for the night. Even during the day time when men meet together, and especially on Sundays after worship, the first question some people ask is about kava. Many Christians today prefer to work for someone if they will provide kava.

## In relation to health

The active ingredient in kava is called Yagonne which is reduces the level of anxiety. This is a drug similar to Diazepam and Metazoans. For health reasons it is not ideal to routinely take a stress control measure. Where there is stress to be controlled, it needs to be addressed with care and supervision.

Kava is also used by many to lower their appetite. Again it is not a good way of managing weight problems or obesity. The nest way of managing weight problems is to consider dieting and exercising regularly.

Kava also gives rise to gastric ulcers or problems which produce stomach pain. This can be very painful and may produce a poisonous substance in the stomach because kava is a member of the pepper family. Constipation and further complications are common when people drink kava.

Kava can promote other substance abuse such as smoking and alcohol. It also promotes impotency in men and causes early aging. It can cause problems to kidneys and can precipitate liver diseases.

Contrary to common belief, kava also leads to population growth. It is becoming a substance which people use to help them enjoy their sexual activity and especially in kava bars and this is leading to increased incidence of pregnancies.

Kava wastes money and time; that is why the foreigners in Vanuatu prosper in their businesses while local people cannot prosper. Kava robs family of their time together and disrupts family life, time with one's children and wife. So problems arise in the home where kava is abused.

In an interview with Dr Christopher Tari, he concluded[2] 'Everything created by God is good but when we abuse something, that is when it produces physical, social and spiritual problems.'

## The benefits of kava

### Source of income for the PCV[3]

As 1 have said earlier, kava is becoming a source of income for local producers who sell their product locally or export it. It is also a source of income for the PCV. The PCV is a self-supporting church depending a lot on the money contributed by the local people (Christians) especially for her

---

2.  Interview with Dr. Christopher Tari: Northern District Hospital Santo 10 July 2003
3.  Presbyterian Church of Vanuatu (PCV)

administration and her staff. Kava has contributed greatly in one way or another in that support. This raises the question, 'If kava is sinful, as some think, should the church accept any money that is gained from kava selling or not'? Should Christians themselves be involved in kava planting?

During my field experience in the Presbytery of Santo in 2003, a presbytery meeting was held in Narango (Tokolau Session, South Santo) where the session clerk reported that the outgoing pastor's salary was subsidised by twenty-seven bags of kava.

The agreement was made by the pastor concerned and the session. The presbytery did not endorse the payment and it was not recorded. Outstanding salaries for pastors today is a big problem; during the pastor's induction the parish members make a promise before God to provide a salary for the pastor. To the presbytery members it may be a big problem if the payment is made partly with kava but to the session concerned, the burden of payment is lifted and they have fulfilled their promise. But is it from God or not?

*A theological perspective*

God is sovereign and Lord; he is in control. God can use things, even things that are foolish to humans, for the good of those who love him, who have been called according to his purpose (Romans 8:28). For example out of the deadly waters of the River Nile which was ready to swallow up all the sons if Israel (Ex 1:22) comes the deliverer of Israel, Moses (Ex 2:10). Paul the great persecutor of Christians becomes the one who greatly strengthens the early church. Crucifixion was meant to be a form of death for law breakers or criminals but out of the shameful cross of Jesus comes everlasting life for all people. That is why Paul says, 'For the message of the cross is foolishness to those who are perishing but to those who are being saved, it is the power of God' (1 Cor 1:18).

We must then be careful not to be too judgmental but we must search for God's wisdom in Christ who has comes to give life in its fullness, freeing us from being enslaved by man-made laws. With the twenty seven bags of kava, the outstanding salary was paid. While there is lack of employment in the country today we can be thankful to God that kava has played an important role economically in the nation, and in the church.

**A biblical perspective on kava**

*The creation*

First of all, when we refer to the biblical accounts of creation (Genesis 1–2), God the Creator concludes that all that he has made was 'very good'(v 31). All creation was ordered and fashioned by God perfectly without any forces rising to threaten God or man. Even darkness and light function to bless and to sustain life (Psalm 104:19–26; 127:2). The climax of God's work is the creation of man and woman (Psalm 8), created in God's Image (Gen 1.27), having inhaled the breath of life (Gen 2:7).

It implies God's imparting of part of his divine character to human life and that humanity has an absolutely unique relationship both to God (as his servant) and to other creatures (as their divinely appointed steward).

I wish this state of life would continue forever, but there is a problem and the problem is sin (Genesis 3). There are many questions to ask: Where does sin comes from? Where does Satan appear from in relation to God's good created order? Why did God introduce the command concerning the tree of good and evil (Gen 2:16) if the law stimulates or reveals sin?

Before God their Creator, selfish humanity yielded to Satan's temptation, wanting to be like God and adding to God's word, 'You must not touch it' (Gen 3:3$^b$), and finally breaking out into disobedience to God. Humanity did not find joy in obeying God's law. The problem was not on God's side but on the side of man. It resulted in abuse, exploitation, the wasting or spoiling of God's creation, and the harmonious relationship with God was broken. We may raise questions we but cannot escape sin by our own efforts. It is still a real, a big and a world-wide problem.

The bible does not mention kava anywhere but it warns about getting drunk and about loss of temper (eg Gen 9:20, 21; Eph 5:18). Drunkenness leads to debauchery, we are told. Kava is not really the same as many alcoholic drinks where drunkards really lose their temper, but concerning the weakness that results from the abuse of kava, the bible has a lot to say which can help God's church.

*Family life*

Marriage was instituted by God in the very beginning as a gift and needs to be lived in the way God intended it to be (Gen 2:18–25 especially v 24). In marriage a man leaves his father and mother to start a new family with his wife. Although two persons, a man and a woman become one in love sharing every part of their life, physical, social and spiritual. They should come to grow very close to each other and understand each other in love. One flesh also includes the physical or sexual part of their life. All these aspects of marriage are God's gift. However many families today, the abuse of kava is devaluing God-given marriage.

Genesis 2:24 speaks directly against some practices seen in kava bars; it speaks against polygamy. To be united is only possible between two persons not three or four (Matthew 19:5–6). This text also speaks against divorce. To be united means marriage should last forever till death separates (Matthew 19:6).

Children are God's gift to parents. God commanded the man and the woman to teach their children as part of their parental role (Deut 4:9;11:19; Eph 6:4). Parents should not expect their children to be good without teaching in the home, and parents are to teach not only with words but also through their actions; they are a model for their children.

The bible also speaks against prostitution. It says that being united with a prostitute is defiling for a member of the body of Christ. He who united with a prostitute is one with her (1 Cor 6:15f).

For many people today, the love for kava is growing stronger while the love for God grows weaker. Jesus (Matt 24:12) warns that, 'Because of the increase of wickedness, the love of most people will become cold'. This could be applied to kava drinking; giving too much time to kava leads to weakness, people not doing their work in the church properly. Jesus says, 'You cannot serve two maters because you will love one and hate the other' (Matt 6:24). Those who are addicted to kava serve kava as their god, and this leads to apostasy (Matt 2:24). The first commandment forbids us to make anything else apart from God to be our God (Ex 20:1, 2).

Most people say, 'Kava is just food like any other food', quoting Jesus' words in Matthew 15:11, 'What goes into a man's mouth does not make him unclean but what comes out of his mouth, that is what makes him unclean'. When we look in terms of our daily meal time and the amount consumed, you cannot eat four to five plates in a meal, as some have four to five coconut shells or even more at a kava bar. It is not the question of what is consumed, but how it is consumed. Having more than what you should have is already a sin, as eating too much (Phil 3:19; 1 Cor 6:13).

*Christian freedom*

We need to come to a better understanding of our freedom as Christians. John Calvin states, 'Christian freedom is something that needs to be discussed . . . Many Christians waver, hesitate and are afraid.'[4] The most important thing to note is that it is 'Christian' freedom, not political or any other sort of freedom, and it must be lived and practiced; it is the way God through Jesus intended us to be. We have a living example in Jesus himself and in the apostles. Many Christians have taken this freedom for granted even when they have acted in disobedience to God. But we cannot ignore the responsibilities of freedom which are part of the gospel.

---

4 John Bailie, editor, *et al* Calvin's Institution of Christian Religion, Vol XX (London: SCM Press), 833.

*Free from what?*

Vanuatu is an independent nation which achieved its political freedom from slavery under British and French governments. Freedom comes when there has been slavery and the apostle Paul has a lot to say about the nature of Christian freedom, especially in his letter to Galatians.

i) Freedom from law and sin

Says Paul, 'Before Christ came we were held prisoners by the law . . . (Gal 3:23) 'So also, when we were children, we were in slavery to the basic principles of the world' (Gal 4:3). The church in Galatia was made up of two peoples, Jews and Gentiles. The Jewish Christians who were Judaizers were insisting that the Gentile Christians must keep the law and the ceremonial practices of the Old Testament, especially the practice of circumcision (Gal 6:11f), in order to earn righteousness from God. According to the apostle Paul, to be a prisoners of sin (Gal 3:21) and a prisoner of law are the same because the law reveals sin. Most rules and requirements concerning such physical and external practices as circumcision, eating and drinking and observance of religious festivals, are added on by men and Paul continued to oppose them (see also in Col 2:6–23). These laws serve merely as a pointer to Christ who is the reality which was to come and is now here.

ii) Freedom and the PCV

Paul was writing to a totally different place culturally, educationally, spiritually, and geographically. However his message may be very relevant to even though it was written to people of different background. The fact of us all being in slavery under sin cannot be ignored as Paul rightly says, 'The whole world is a prisoner to sin' (Gal 3:22). For Paul this included slavery also to human regulations. There are no Jews in the PCV but there are many who are like Jews in some way. For example, many sessions and presbyteries have rules and regulations concerning the use of kava. I remember in the year 2000 in a presbytery meeting of southern islands at Sulphur Bay where a resolution was passed that pastors who are serving in parishes are not to use kava. It became a man-made rule or law. Any pastor found drinking kava was guilty of breaking that particular law. Without that resolution there was no stigma of sin in relation to the use of kava in a place where kava is highly valued. The PCV must be careful not to impose or insist on human laws and regulations but 'to teach the law of the spirit from within the heart of every Christians (Gal 3:1–5) that we acknowledge and confess Christ as the reality and fulfilment of everything' (Col 2:16–17). The more we make laws, the more disciplinary actions come; it even sometimes chases people out of the church. We cannot do anything of our own to add on to what God has done in Christ which is adequate and sufficient.

### iii) Free to obey God

Freedom here is not free to do anything one wishes to do, as Calvin states, 'Some in relation to this freedom withdraw from obedience to God and break out into unbridled license.'[5] Freedom from God in Christ is freedom for obedience to God. Still in his letter to the Galatians, Paul says that to be a law-keeper is to be enslaved by the law. As a slave, he has to do everything to please his master; if his master assigns him work, then that needs to be done. These poor servants do not really know whether they have fully done what their master requires. Since we are free, we are no longer slaves, 'but sons who are generously and candidly treated by their father, who do not hesitate to offer half-done and even defective works, trusting that their obedience and readiness of mind and will is accepted by their Father, even though they have not achieved what their father intended'.[6] So it is a joyous and not burdensome thing to obey God. This obedience is not because of the law, in this we can only pretend but our obedience is because we are saved by God in Christ and willingly obey from our hearts (Deut 6:5; Matt 22:37).

### iv) Use of freedom for the good of others (weak) for Christ sake.

The church is a group of people who can be categorized; some are weak in conscience and others are strong in faith. Therefore freedom needs to be lived and exercised by the strong keeping in mind those who are weak, the very people for whom Christ died.

Paul in his first letter to the Corinthians (chapter 8), deals with a situation of eating food sacrifice to idols and sold in the market place. The people say, 'These gods are nothing.' They considered themselves free to go into the Corinthian temple dedicated to Aphrodite, the goddess of love whose worshippers practiced prostitution and ate the meat sacrifice to idols. In response Paul draws attention to two dangers to be aware of. First, this practice causes weaker fellow Christians to fall; secondly Christians can also get caught up in such practices. Paul says that when you sin against a neighbour, you sin against Christ (1 Cor 8:12).

Kava bars especially in the two towns Port Vila and Luganville are similar to the Corinthian temple. Drinkers do not go there only to drink kava but also to find women, and buying their kava can result in prostitution. This is dangerous for Christians especially leaders. They are to be a good

---

5.   *Ibid*, 834.
6.   *Ibid*, 834.

example to others, and they themselves can also get caught in such evil practices. Many will say, 'It is all right to use your freedom and go to the kava bar'. The apostle Paul says, 'Be careful that the exercise of your freedom does not become a stumbling block to the weak' (1 Cor 8:9). He continues, 'If what I eat causes my brother to fall into sin, I will never eat meat (drink kava) again so that I will not cause him to fall' (v 13).

There are right times to use our freedom and right times for renunciation of it. For example, when Paul went on a journey with Timothy as his companion, 'he circumcised him because of the Jews who lived in that area, for they all knew that his father was a Greek' (Acts 16:3), but he did not do the same with the Greek, Titus (Gal 2:3). Paul did not want anybody to make him a slave to any law because freedom is through Christ, and he wanted the truth of this gospel to be upheld.

Diversity in practice or behaviour is seen here but there is no change of purpose and mind. If you know that what you are going to do will cause your weak brother to sin, then do not do it because he then will be encouraged to follow your example; but at the same time such renunciation is not to enslave you again to the law. Paul is a good example of this diversity (1 Cor 9:19–22) when he says (v 22), 'I have become all things to all men so that by all possible means, I might save some.' To be weak is not to be one with them in their sin but to identify with them, to come to their level. So 'Nobody should seek his own good but the good of others.'(1 Cor 10:24; Phil 2:4)

How can we love God who is invisible? Our love for God is to be demonstrated by our love for our visible friends and neighbours who are around us and especially those who are in the fellowship of the church (1 John 4:12)

## My theological perspective

All things were created by God in the very beginning, including kava. The creation of human beings is the climax of God's good creation. The question is, 'Does that mean that all things are good for humans to consume?' Certainly not, because God created some things that are not good for human to consume and others that are good for humans to consume. Nowhere in the bible can we find God commanding people to drink kava. Kava was discovered, used and traditionally handed down from generation to generation. The difference between the two (Kava + Man) is that human beings were given the authority to rule and the ability to distinguish between good and bad; this is not so with kava. As a result of sin, humans abused God's good creation for selfish gain and this has resulted in the problems of the world. For Christians, Christ has given a new heart by his Spirit and a new approach which leads us to know and relate to creation in a better way. Let Christians be sensitive to the way the Spirit is leading and be responsible for themselves and for the people around them, for the sake of God. As for me, I believe that kava in itself is not sinful but man may be sinful by abusing it. For example it is all right to drink in moderation but not excessively. It would be better rather to speak out against the sinful way a human being, as God's representative, is abusing kava.

## Conclusion

My personal observation is that the church (especially the PCV) is declining in her commitment and financial contribution, and has more and more vacant parishes in the presbyteries. There are a large number of pastors without charge and there are many members moving to other sects. To me one of the contributing factors is that the abuse of kava is causing the church to lose its holiness. My intention in this paper is not to encourage people to drink kava and not to forbid the drinking of kava, but to bring to light, in relation to what the bible says, some of the wrongful uses of kava and the consequences of abusive kava drinking. In this light, one must judge and make a decision for himself as to how he can live for God's glory maintaining the true value of God's redeemed church, and looking to a better land where sin is no more.

## Bibliography

Bailie John *et al*, editors *Calvin's Institute of Christians Religion*, Vol XX (London: SCM Press).

Prior R, *Gospel and Culture in Vanuatu 2: Contemporary Local Perspectives* (Melbourne: Gospel Vanuatu Books, 2001).

## Traditional Interviews

Nahao Nipio, Loukatai Village Tanna 2003

Iapan Saman, Loukatai Village Tanna 2003

Seake and Ialun, Louinio Village, Tanna 2003

## Health Interview

Dr Christopher J Tari, Northern District Hospital Santo 2003

# A Comparative Study of Heaven and Hell
## With Reference to Vanua-Lava
## in the Banks Islands

## By Keith Kalapitas

### Introduction

In this paper, I will compare Vanua-lava Cultural beliefs and Christian beliefs about God (the gods), heaven and hell. In the missionary period between the 1850s and 1930s, Christianity came to cover almost the whole island of Vanua Lava. Many people responded to what Christians were trying to teach them. Since that time, belief in God and understandings of heaven and hell have been important.

As part of this paper, there will also be a section on biblical understanding in which we will focus on the Bible as God's revelation to us. The Bible will clarify for us the concept of the true God whom we worship.

### Cultural belief about the gods

Before the arrival of Christianity to our islands, our ancestors were already worshippers. There is not one island around Vanuatu where the people did not worship and did not believe in something. This applied to the whole Pacific Islands. When you study the history of the South Pacific, you may find out what particular gods people believed in and worshipped. This ancient belief and worship is still practiced today in some parts of Vanuatu; there are mission 'bush workers' who are discovering this fact as they go to parts of our islands where Christians have not previously been.

The traditional gods are considered to be very powerful gods and are understood to solve the needs of the people. In 1909 one of our people, John Star told a mission worker not to waste his time worshipping the invisible God because it took more time for the invisible Christian God to answer our needs. This indicates that the people believed in gods and thought them to be powerful. In those days many gods were worshipped and many kinds of rituals were used in worship and were strongly observed and practiced.

In and around the year 1500 when there was no Christian belief as yet, the people of the island of Vanua-lava also had their own gods. Some of these gods were made out of wood and stones while others took the form of sharks and various other creatures. These were worshipped and recognised by the people as personal gods; the people believed that they saw them face to face. While Vanua-lava had many different kinds of gods who were worshipped in ancient times, they believed in a supreme god who was known to the islanders as 'Qet'. Vanua-lava was the most historical island with many stories about Qet, his many works and his creation of the environment. The people were known to say prayers to Qet. His creation stories are told from generation to generation and many believed he was the supreme god in Vanua-lava and also in the whole group of Banks Islands.

Qet is like a person but also a spirit; he has a mother and father but no one can describe him fully; no one can tell what he looks like or what colour he is; unlike a person there is no story about where he died and was buried. Qet is said to be living on Taplengleng but works around the Banks Islands; people around these and other islands ask for something in his name and he answers them. So Qet is present everywhere; people who worship him believe they are worshipping the living God. Also, they believe that after death there is resurrection to heaven which Qet prepared for obedient people, and hell for the disobedient.

Now let us compare the beliefs of our ancestors who worshipped the two kinds of gods described above, and the beliefs of Christians who confess the true and loving God. We should note that today some Christians have turned to worship the idols, and some people have not agreed to become Christians. We also have many churches in Vanuatu worshipping different kinds of prophets although their belief is centred on the one God. In some ways, it was similar in Vanua-lava in the 1500s when the people believed in many gods even though they worshipped what they called the one real God. People do not know where Qet has gone since Christianity has come. They know stories of his childhood but there are no stories of his death.

*Heaven*

Let us explore the meaning of the term *Bene* which is Vanua-lava language for heaven. There is a belief that there is a heaven but nobody knows who created it or exactly where its location is. Some people of Vanua-lava have thought that heaven is somewhere up in the sky and others have thought that heaven is on earth but unseen. *Bene* is described as everlastingly happy where there is no sadness and pain

In traditional culture, heaven is a place where righteous people live, those who follow Qet faithfully and do not commit sin. They believe that there is sin (Beng); it means to be disobedient. Let us take the example of one who commits adultery with another woman or another man. One has to do go through a reconciliation process to restore a right relationship again and to do away with the sin. This is done through a pig killing ceremony as a means of reconciliation. By doing so, a person is then prepared for their future destiny; their hope is for heaven. The ceremony of reconciliation must be done by the high chief (*Tovesmel*), the one who is the highest and most

234

holy person in the community. At the end of the ceremony the chief concludes with his message: 'Dig the ground and bury what both of you have done and stop talking about it'. This is done in order for Qet to forgive their sin and make it possible for them to enter into heaven rather than to go to hell.

Many people believe that heaven is real. Talking to an old man about 130 years old who could not walk any longer, he said to me,

'Before Christian teaching arrived, I had already learned everything about heaven and hell. I was 30 years old and I was baptised and the people taught me how to worship the God "Yahweh" and to live a righteous life because there is heaven for the faithful and hell for the wicked. The concept of heaven and hell was not new to me but was part of what I already believed. So heaven as you can see was real to me even though Christianity had not arrived yet in Vanua-lava. In those days, when someone died, the people cried, believing the dead person had departed from them to another world, the world of the dead. After they were buried, people stayed together for five days, believing that the person will then rise from death to life and go either to heaven or hell.'

In Tagoloa, Samoans described heaven not as a single place but as several places; the heavens are a 'holy habitation' of the deity. The ancient Samoans also believed in village gods and family gods. They worshipped images of stones, birds, fish, insects and beasts. A family would get together regularly to pray for forgiveness to their own gods. When one of the family members died they had to give an honourable burial. In the case of a death at sea, if the body was found the family would go to the beach and spread a mat (Tapa) on top of water and then pray. Then if a crab, snail or any insects crawled on the spread of the mat, they would fold it and give it an honourable burial in the family ground. It was believed that the spirit of the family member who died in the sea turned into a crab or into whatever form they buried. The feast for the whole village, honouring the death, was arranged by the family after the completion of the funeral.

It is interesting also to compare beliefs in other parts of Vanuatu. In South Pentecost they also had a traditional belief in a heaven similar to the people of Vanua-lava. They believed that when a person was dead they turned into a ghost or spirit and went to heaven.

## Hell

Before the arrival of Christianity, hell was not known in the same way as it is today. However, the people certainly knew about its existence. When the god of Vanua-lava created the islands in the Banks group, they believed that he also created hell. Hell in Vanua-lava language is called *Weresor*. People in those days believed that their destination after death was determined by their behaviour. Hell was a final destination for people of bad behaviour; it was a place of suffering.

When the people thought of hell they identified it as an island and they thought you could tell if someone was going there after their death by looking at their eyes. After the death of someone in the night you could hear people crying on the island.

In Samoa they also believed in hell, and that hell is located in a cave in the Southern part of Upolu.

Some people around the Banks islands have slightly different ideas about hell. Some Vanua-lava Qet worshippers believed that when a bad person died, immediately they went to hell. There was no waiting for any final judgment; after five days you would go to this place of suffering. Although the people knew about hell as a terrible place, some people still practiced murder and stealing. Others who were afraid of this place called hell, made their reconciliation by pig killing and paying fines to their opponents because they did not want to enter into this terrible place.

## Christian belief

### Belief in God

It is possible to know God but we are limited in our ability to describe God fully. The impression in Vanuatu is that a large majority of people believe in God or at least in some kind of Supreme Being or supernatural force. But the same people are not sure about the finer points of Christian belief. Far fewer people today are prepared to go along with what the church traditionally taught. For many people today it seems that believing in God has very little relevance, but with the organised religions and with smaller groups of committed believers there is a strong belief in the existence of God as if this is the only possible option.

For further discussion about these issues we may ask the question; 'What is God like?' or 'Does God exist?' These two questions are the most critical and important questions which many people ask. Scientists and theologians put the second question first; 'Does God exist?' This was also a struggle of the early Christians. The beginning of the twentieth century was a period of hope for the Christian church. During this time, the Western church grew effectively in all parts of the world without meeting serious opposition. As time has gone on, major changes have taken place. Some other old faiths are finding more popularity and there is a new power of resistance to the gospel.

As we look around Vanuatu, we can see that most people offer their prayers to God because they believe that God created all things; all livestock, fish, human beings, etc. The Christian God is the 'Alpha and Omega'. He formed the earth from chaos. He made man to glorify him forever and out of love for the world he sent His only Son Jesus Christ that whoever believes in him should not be drawn into hell but have everlasting life with him in heaven.

To be truly Christian is to believe that it is possible to know God. God has made himself known by revealing himself to us through Jesus Christ. His revelation began in the history of Israel and continued about two thousand years ago in Jesus Christ, being born as a man, and saving people from hell. The climax is the death and resurrection of Jesus. We know that the Christian God is a God of love; he loves the poor and the rich, the sinner and the righteous.

### Belief in heaven

What will heaven be like? Almost everyone in Vanuatu asks this question. Our concept about heaven should be clear so that it will be able to be communicated rightly to our children. We know about heaven through the divine revelation that has been given to us in scripture and we may be surprised at how much scripture has to say. Heaven is very important because the biblical teaching on life after the death is concerned about where we will be. Human beings are God's children. He is our Father and gave us a guarantee that we will dwell with God for eternity. God promised through Jesus that he will go and prepare a place for us. The life we will enjoy there is abundant life. Jesus tells his troubled disciples that he is going away not to build a house but to prepare a place for them. Jesus tells us heaven is rich and full of a living relationship between God and his created order.

Heaven therefore will be the enjoyment of a perfect relationship. It will be a situation in which one will never be alone, never lack company, never feel isolated but always be completely in God's presence. The relationship enjoyed in heaven, between Christ, others and ourselves will be perfect in every way.

### Belief in hell

The Christian teachings indicate that hell is an eternal separation and the final judgment. Scripture frequently affirms the fact that there will be a great final judgment of believers and unbelievers. They will all stand before the judgment seat of Christ in resurrected bodies and hear his proclamation of

237

their eternal destiny. Then the Lord will say to the unbelievers: 'Depart from me, you cursed into the eternal fire prepared for evil doers' They will go away into eternal punishment (see eg Matt 25:31–46).

It is unfortunate that many of the older versions of the English Bible use the one word 'hell' to translate several words in original languages. However, in the minds of English speaking people hell is a place of terrible torment where the wicked dead are sent for final punishment.

This idea of hell is true to Christian belief. All Christians believe in the existence of hell following the revelation of God through the Bible. However, Christian emphasis is strongly against this terrible place. God sent his Son Jesus Christ to save us from our sins, not wanting to see believers drawn into the lake of fire. Christians throughout the world now endorse this belief through the divine revelation of God, the Bible which is God's Word. The story of Lazarus and the rich man told by Jesus (Luke 16:19–31) illustrates that hell is eternal separation from God, and there is no chance to escape when you enter into this eternal punishment.

## Similarities and differences

### Similarities

As we consider the concepts and beliefs of the traditional culture and the Christian faith, there are many similarities.

Both groups of people see their gods (God) as Creator. Vanua-lava has their supreme god named Qet and this is similar to the Christian God. Furthermore, God had a Son and Qet had children. Christians worship of God and the worship of Qet by people of traditional culture are much the same; they are both holy occasions. 1500 years ago all the people from Vanua-lava and Vanuatu as a whole were cultural worshippers of their gods, just as today Christians worship God. Both gods are powerful and can answer prayers and give people what they need. Both gods are alive; the Christian God is in heaven as the bible says, and Qet existed on Vanua-lava. Also, both were present everywhere and both gods are invisible. The two groups of believers believed in the existence of heaven and hell, but with slightly different concepts. Both groups believed heaven is the happiest place and hell is the worst place. Furthermore in both cultural and Christian ideas every human being has a soul and after death our soul will go somewhere, either to heaven or to hell. When a human being dies he turns into spiritual flesh as the bible states, and traditional belief is that he turns into a spiritual ghost.

These in summary are the many similarities between the Christian belief and our traditional cultural belief.

*Differences*

Having outlined the similarities of both traditions, we will now look at the differences. First, in relation to the cultural belief in Qet as creator, he doesn't live in heaven as the Christian God lives, but he lives on the earth. It is believed that Qet has a gardening area, a house area and a place of fishing. The Christian God doesn't have anything such as this; he does not have a house which he built nor a garden area of his own. But Christian believers build church houses or temples as God's dwelling place.

Qet has a father and mother; he also got married and had children, and he needed to have food each morning. The Christian God did not marry and did not have a mother and a father and does not need food.

The Christian God is the creator and sustainer of life. He lives in heaven as his dwelling place, a place holy and separated from this sinful world. Qet lives in the visible world and God lives in an invisible world. Qet then can be said to be under the sovereignty of the Christian God.

People knew about heaven and hell in cultural belief but they could not fully interpret life after death. In traditional culture, believers had the idea that when people died, their spirits turned into a worldly ghost and wandered around the island (Vanua-lava). However, Christian believers understand about life after death that our spirits go to hell or to heaven.

**Biblical teaching**

In the biblical teaching, heaven is part of God's Creation above the earth. It serves as a home for God and his heavenly creatures. As human beings we think of heaven as above, earth as beneath, water as around and hell as beneath. Everything in heaven is created in God's order.

The Bible informs us that heaven is our eternal dwelling place; it is described as resting with God forever. It is a place of rejoicing and living together with God. As God's dwelling place heaven is not a place where God can isolate himself from earth but it is the divine workplace from where he sends blessings to his people. Only the faithful person can enter into heaven.

The Old Testament speaks of heaven as showing the sovereignty of the creator God and of the divine desire to communicate with and provide for human creatures. It tells us that the souls of humans who have left the earth are taken up to heaven (Gen 5:24; 2 Kgs 2:11). Christians believe that the primary location of heaven is above, following the Greek word translated 'heaven' as 'above the earth'.

In the four hundred years before the coming of Christ there were extensive discussions among Jewish theologians concerning the Old Testament doctrine of ever-lasting punishment. Generally speaking the

Pharisees taught that there is ever-lasting punishment, while some thought that punishment for the ungodly lasted only a year before they would be annihilated.

The New Testament states that Christians are citizens of heaven (Phil 3:20). In the parable about the rich man and Lazarus (Luke 16:19–31) Jesus taught us that there is heaven and hell as an eternal resting with God or eternal separation from God. Maybe the rich man did not even know about heaven and hell, or maybe he did not believe in the place; he thought it was a false message. But at the end he believed in the existence of these two places God had prepared for us. In Revelation 22:5 the author explains how beautiful heaven is, 'There will be no more night. They will not need the light of a lamp or the light of sun, for the Lord God will give them light. And they will reign with him forever and ever'.

While heaven is a happy place, there is also another existing place created by God called hell, the abode of the dead, especially as a place of eternal punishment for unbelievers. In Matthew 16:18 hell is not simply a place of the dead but represents the power of the under-world. Jesus said the gates of hell would not prevail against His Church.

The New Testament teaches about the concept of punishment for sin after death. There are many terms which the New Testament uses: lake of fire, second death, eternal separation. The Bible tells us that there is another life after this earthly life, both for those who are qualified for the blessing and for those qualified for punishment.

The New Testament, in the passage of teaching in Matthew 7:23, Jesus says: 'I will tell them plainly, "I never knew you, go away from me, you evil doers."' Jesus used these words in a parable to affirm everlasting punishment. Hell is separation from God's presence in heaven where God dwells with his people. 'Every tree that does not bear fruit is cut down and thrown into the fire.' Hell is a terrible place of suffering and pain caused by fire (Matt 13:18–23). Those who follow their own desire against the Word of God will all be punished and will be thrown into the lake of fire.

I want to conclude with the Word of God in the Ten Commandments, a warning against idol worshippers. In Exodus 20:3–5 it says 'You shall have no other gods before me, you shall not make for yourself an idol in the form of anything in heaven above or on the earth beneath or in the water below, you shall not bow down to them or worship them.'

## Conclusion

As soon as Christianity arrived in Vanua-lava, the missionaries spoke against the traditional belief in Qet. Christians sharing the good news stated that Qet is an idol. They illustrated from the teaching of the bible that the

Christian God is the only God of all creation. They emphasised that there is only one creator and one God; any god apart from the Christian God is an idol. This is why many cultural believers turned to the God of the Christians.

In conclusion I would like to emphasize that cultural belief of the people of Vanua-lava and the Christian belief of the church all tie up together in a belief in the Almighty God, and in their understanding of heaven and hell. There are similarities and differences in their beliefs. The central theme of this paper has been to describe and compare these beliefs.

## Bibliography

North B, *The Rich Man and Lazarus* (Edinburgh: The Banner of Truth, 1960).

Conyer, AJ, *The Eclipse of Heaven* (London: IVP 1992).

Oliphant, SK and Ferguson, SB, *Hoping for Heaven* (Leicester: Crossway Books, 1995).

Williams C, editor, *Four Interviews on Hell* (Grand Rapids: Zondervan, 1992).

Gruden W, *Systematic Theology* (Grand Rapids: IVP, 1994).

## Interviews

Father Gregory Manliwos, at Vitimboso, 6 April and 30 November 2002.

Father Henry Butu, at Sarakata 26 and 28 March 2003.

Mr Shem Ganileo, at Talua 29 March 2003.

# Conclusion to this volumes

Because this volume is a twin publication with Volume 4, both arising from the same project, it makes sense for the conclusion to be made up of two parts—first a repeat of some of the material which appeared in the conclusion to Volume 4, and secondly some additional comments in relation to Volume 5. I close with a word about the extension of the Gospel and Culture in Vanuatu project beyond the shores of Vanuatu.

*i) From the conclusion to Volume 4*
There is a lot of energy among the churches in Vanuatu for tackling the issues of the relationship between the Christian Gospel and the cultures of Vanuatu.

The fact that such a large quantity of material was submitted for this publication, leading to a requirement to produce two separate books, is an indication of this. More importantly, there seems to be an emerging confidence on the part of local church people to speak their mind on gospel and culture issues and to put their ideas into print. As noted in the conclusion to the previous volume: 'There are indications that the younger generation of leaders in particular are able to explore the issues of gospel and culture in an open way, neither accepting blindly the traditional approach of the early missionaries nor rejecting out of hand their approach. There is a readiness to respect their own cultures while exploring how the Christian gospel engages with these cultures.'

This series of volumes is also serving the purpose of gathering together unique historical and cultural material, and providing an avenue where new research can be documented and preserved. This will prove to be a valuable resource in the future.

This two-volume project is also considerably more ecumenical in its breadth than the previous three volumes, with contributions from the Church of Melanesia which is now a partner in the Talua Ministry Training Centre, the Evangelical Protestant Church and the Roman Catholic Church. It is hoped that this ecumenical involvement will grow, providing opportunity for varying perspectives on church history, varying local experiences of church life, and varying approaches to the way in which the gospel engages with local cultures, to be articulated. All church traditions in Vanuatu are confronted by the same challenges and it would be a real benefit if there can be more conversation across the churches about how to respond.

*ii) Additionally*
Volume 5 has featured a topic of significant interest and debate in the churches in Vanuatu, namely the role of women in leadership in both the

culture and the church. Even the two official partners at the local Talua Ministry Training Centre have reached opposing conclusions about whether or not to ordain women as Ministers and Priests. Having said that it is clear that there are quite opposing views within each of the traditions; to realise this, you need only read Sharyn Wobur's case for the ordination of women priests in her own tradition, the Church of Melanesia, and the telling comments of Mary Luan about the obstacles faced by ordained women Ministers in the Presbyterian Church. It is noteworthy too that the other articles on this topic, both from well educated Ministers of the Presbyterian Church who have been newly appointed to the teaching staff of Talua, take quite different approaches and reach opposing conclusions about the ordination of women. The points raised in the four separate articles in this volume will serve to promote further discussion on this sensitive and unresolved national issue. Each of the four contributors has taken a distinct approach

The remaining topics cover a range of contemporary issues challenging the life and mission of the churches in Vanuatu. Although some of them are familiar and favoured topics (for example kava, marriage, nakamal, land, peace, sacrifice) which have appeared in one form or another in previous volumes, the authors in this volume have approached the topics in quite distinctive ways, bringing the uniqueness of their own local village experience into their material. Other topics appear for the first time in this series. Morrison Marcel has tackled the prevalent and vexing issue of divisions in local communities, Simon Vani has taken up the theme of migration, identifying this as a part of his own cultural tradition from the beginning, and Keith Kalapitas has introduced the topic of heaven and hell.

The great majority of material in this volume comes from the students of the Ministry Training Centre. As part of the requirements of their final year as ordination candidates, they are required to do a serious peace of research. In almost all cases, this research takes the student into an engagement between the Gospel and their own culture, and it does so in such a way that the student is forced to put their own personal views. The result of this is that the research papers set down current views of the younger generation of would-be church leaders on the relationship between the Christian Gospel and the cultures of Vanuatu, the very topic which forms the overall theme of this whole publication series and a topic of urgent local and international significance for Christian mission.

One of the challenging elements for all those who are engaged with this topic in Vanuatu is the place of Scripture and the use of and authority of particular texts from both the Old and New Testaments. There is a common tendency, not surprising when the background of over one hundred and fifty years of Christian mission in the South Pacific is understood, to consider that any and all texts from the bible speak an authoritative word on a particular issue. In some cases a writer draws his reflections only from particular texts from the Old Testament without any consideration of the significance of the New Testament. This tends to produce a relatively arbitrary or selective approach (why some texts and not others?) not only to the bible but to the resources of the Christian faith in addressing any particular issue. The place of Scripture in Christian theology remains a fundamental matter for ongoing learning.

Where to now? The first thing to say is that there is no doubt in my mind that the challenges of the relationship between the Gospel and the cultures of Vanuatu, which first challenged the early missionaries and which became prominent in a new way with the national independence of Vanuatu in 1980, will not diminish. If what is happening within the community at Talua is any indication, the churches are becoming more seriously engaged with these challenges. The appointment of two of the new Presbyterian Church staff to Talua, Fiama Rakau as principal and Selerik Michel, is pertinent in this regard because both of them have had long experience in the issues of Gospel and Culture and both are well qualified to teach in this field. The commitment of Talua to develop its own Bachelor of Divinity programme over the next five years provides a further opportunity and challenge to shape something which will assist the local churches to train leaders who are increasingly able to guide and teach their people, in both urban and local village communities, about the significance of the Gospel in their own local cultural contexts.

As for this publication series, the local working group in Vanuatu has already set down particular projects to be pursued. Recognising the seriousness of land disputes as a national problem, a plan is under way for the working group to arrange a series of workshops and conferences across the churches and islands at which the topic of land will be tackled as a topic of Gospel and Culture. The material from this would be recorded and published. There is also an acceptance of the need for a thorough reference book on Gospel and Culture which would serve the students and staff of the Ministry Training Centre.

iii) An invitation was extended to Fiama Rakau and me by the Protestant Church of Timor Leste to lead a series of workshops on Gospel and Culture with a group of young pastors and lay leaders in Dili in November 2005. The church there had heard about the Gospel and Culture in Vanuatu project and it appealed to them as a valuable resource for their own context. Timor Leste achieved its political independence in May 2002 and like Vanuatu in 1980, the achievement of independence has prompted a resurgence of interest in and commitment to the local people's own tradition and culture.

244

In the wake of national independence, the Protestant Church has identified four main issues which need to be addressed by the churches, one of which is Gospel and Culture. (The remaining three are socio-political matters, ecumenism and other religions.) In order to begin the process of tackling this issue, they decided to learn from the generation of experience of the church in Vanuatu. Discussion is also under way to establish a formal partnership between the two churches. Who knows what the consequences may be for the evolution of the Gospel and Culture project in these fledgling nations of the world?

# About the contributors

Fiama Rakau, from the village of Iasoa on the island of Futuna and a pastor of the Presbyterian Church, is the newly elected Principal of the Talua Ministry Training Centre.

Selerik Michel, from the village of Eratap on the island of Efate and a pastor of the Presbyterian Church, is a newly appointed lecturer at the Talua Ministry Training Centre and teaches in Gospel and Culture

Sharyn Wobur from Gaua in the Banks islands wrote this paper as a final year ordination student of the Church of Melanesia

Mary Luan from the village of Lawa in South West Bay on the island of Malekula wrote this paper as a final year ordination student of the Presbyterian Church of Vanuatu

Winston Elton from the village of Toga in the Torres islands wrote this paper as a final year ordination student of the Church of Melanesia

Edward Meswia from the island of Hiu in the Torres wrote this paper as a final year ordination student of the Church of Melanesia

Simon Vani from the village of Samaria on the island of Tanna wrote this paper as a final year ordination student of the Presbyterian Church of Vanuatu

Morrison Marcel from the village of Puanangisu on the island of Efate wrote this paper as a final year ordination student of the Presbyterian Church of Vanuatu

Benjamin Tosiro from the village of Lamoru on the north of the island of Pentecost wrote this paper as a second year ordination student of the Church of Melanesia

Amanrantes John Fred from the village of Bonvor on the south coast of the island of Malekula wrote this paper as a final year ordination student of the Presbyterian Church of Vanuatu

Emmanuel Tanihi from the village of Amatbobo on the north of the island of Pentecost wrote this paper as a final year ordination student of the Church of Melanesia

Colin Steve Sosori from the village of Anmalabua on the north of the island of Pentecost wrote this paper as a final year ordination student of the Church of Melanesia

Gideon Paul from the village of Lorum on the island of Santo wrote this paper as a final year ordination student of the Presbyterian Church of Vanuatu

Christopher Iawak from the village of Lokotai on the island Tanna wrote this paper as a final year ordination student of the Presbyterian Church of Vanuatu

Keith Kalapitas from the island of Vanua-lava in the Banks wrote this paper as a final year ordination student of the Church of Melanesia

*Benjamin Tosiro*

*Collin Steve Sosov*

*Edward Meswia*

*Emmanuel Tanihi*

*Mary Luan*

*Morison Marcel*

*Sharyn Wobur*

*Simon Vani*

*Winston Elton*